Dreams Can Assist You in Loving and Being Loved. . . .

The mere telling of your dream to your lover will often make the experience more objective, so that you will comprehend dream messages that may have baffled you before. Be especially alert for your own and your partner's "Hidden Agendas." These are old, often outdated attitudes and belief systems formed in the dreamer's past, usually in early childhood.

Sometimes these Hidden Agendas account for sexual inhibitions or an inability to communicate one's true preferences in lovemaking. Our secret fantasies or wishes for various sorts of foreplay may be mirrored in our dreams. Discussing such dreams together eases the way toward making such wishes known to each other.

When you examine your dream notebook, look for clues to symbolically erotic dreams, noting in particular the emotions you experienced during the dreams and immediately upon awakening. Share these memories with your lover, using the ensuing discussion to lead to a frank and honest exchange of your sexual fantasies. Such confidences should enhance and deepen your intimacy and romance. . . .

PATRICIA MAYBRUCK, PH.D., is a psychologist and counselor who specializes in dream research. She is a faculty member at Napa Valley College and conducts workshops and seminars for corporations in the San Francisco Bay area. Dr. Maybruck is the author of *Pregnancy and Dreams*.

ROMANTIC DREAMS

How to Enhance Your Intimate Relationship by Understanding and Sharing Your Dreams

Patricia Maybruck, Ph.D.

Foreword by
Stanley Krippner, Ph.D.

POCKET BOOKS

New York   London   Toronto   Sydney   Tokyo   Singapore

An *Original* publication of POCKET BOOKS

POCKET BOOKS, a division of Simon & Schuster Inc.
1230 Avenue of the Americas, New York, NY 10020

ISBN: 978-1-4516-1415-2

First Pocket Books trade paperback printing January 1991

10 9 8 7 6 5 4 3 2 1

To
My Beloved
Husband and Family

Contents

Acknowledgments   xi

Foreword *by Stanley Krippner, Ph.D.*   xiii

Preface   xv

Part One:
The Basics of the Dream Language of Love   1

Chapter One: *Conversations in the Dream Language of Love*   3
Chapter Two: *Why We Dream*   16
Chapter Three: *Translating the Dream Language of Love*   33
Chapter Four: *Dream Clues for Finding Your Ideal Mate*   58

Contents

Part Two:
Interpreting the Dream Language of Love 121

Chapter Five: *A Brief History of the Dream Language of Love* 123
Chapter Six: *Learning from Modern Experts* 138
Chapter Seven: *Loving with Dreams* 156

Part Three:
Fluency in the Dream Language of Love 181

Chapter Eight: *Creating Your Own Dreams of Love* 183
Chapter Nine: *Making Your Fantasies Come True* 201
Chapter Ten: *Keeping Your Romance Alive* 221

Bibliography 245

Appendix: *Relaxation Techniques for Dream Control* 251

Index 259

Acknowledgments

Countless thanks and endless gratitude to my late dear friend Faith Clark Quinn, Ph.D. The memory of your unconditional love, creativity, wisdom, and infectious sense of humor continues to nourish and inspire me. Thanks are also due Cecil Clark, Ph.D., for patient advice about computers and psychological tests. Also to Robert Quinn, Ph.D., for your suggestions and guidance—we are bonded both by our friendship and our shared memories of Faith's eternal romance and beauty.

Special thanks are due to the couples and single dreamers whose confidences led to the writing of this book. Without your trust and willingness to share your intimate thoughts, *Romantic Dreams* might still be "only a dream."

Thanks also to the many students and participants in my workshops and seminars, with extra portions of gratitude to "The Dream Team" of St. Helena—especially Deborah Boisot, Hedi Desuyo, Phyllis Dunlavy, Virginia Hahn, Mary Joseph and Dream Baby Grace, Julie Pearce,

Nancy Stanley, and Katrina Von Male. Your faithful attendance at my study groups and public appearances, as well as your generous feedback, have been a continuous source of emotional growth and support.

These dreamers have also contributed much to my knowledge of loving relationships: Deki and Jon Fox, Linda Appleby and Kevin Loughran, Celia and Bob Dwyer, Heidi Fox and Andrew Keyser, Candice and Charles Fuhrman, and Marilyn and Greg Hunt. You are living proof that true love does exist and last.

This list of acknowledgments would be incomplete without Theo Gund and Candice Fuhrman, my tireless literary agents. Your encouragement and expert advice have been an invaluable part of the realization of my goal of helping others. Similar thanks to my editor at Pocket Books, Claire Zion. Your critiques have been insightful, yet never wounding, and your words of praise have heartened me at times when I feared the Muse had flown.

Special thanks to Angela Coppola. Your generous sharing of your dreams and inner thoughts contributed much to this book. Also to Ed Osgood and Allen Stanley, two friends who both told me their dreams and added much to my understanding of the male *persona*.

My appreciation to Stanley Krippner, Ph.D. Your continuing counsel and support as both mentor and friend are a source of both academic and emotional growth. Gratitude in great measure to Maria Watts of Saybrook Institute for your ever present reassurances and enthusiasm. Also to Patricia Garfield, Ph.D., and the many other members of the Association for the Study of Dreams who have so willingly shared their ideas and research.

Finally, heartfelt love and gratefulness to my family: Jon and Deki, Nyima and Dawa, darling little Wesley, Heidi and Andrew, my sister Mary Pendergraft Gibson, and my dear husband Milton, for the romance you have added to my life. May all your sweetest dreams come true!

Foreword
by
Stanley Krippner, Ph.D.

Love is not a simple phenomenon. Some Greek philosophers spoke of four types of love: *eros* (sexual love), *agape* (altruistic love), *philia* (love for family or comrades), and *storge* (love for neighbors and acquaintances). Contemporary psychology has identified three components of dyadic love or love between two people: passion, commitment, and intimacy.

The sharing of dreams can pervade all four types and all three components. Shared erotic dreams can enhance a sexual relationship. Shared spiritual dreams can empower a cause and illuminate a transcendent relationship. Dream sharing can enrich conversations with one's parents, children, siblings, friends, neighbors, and even with strangers. In what Patricia Maybruck has termed a "dream dyad," dream sharing can inflame passion, strengthen commitment, or provide a unique way in which intimacy can be deepened.

Dr. Maybruck's four-step method for dream interpretation is one that can be learned quickly and used easily. It is one of the quickest and most useful approaches that I have seen for decoding dream symbols and metaphors. And, as Dr. Maybruck points out, the simple act of telling a person one's dream will bring the two individuals closer together.

When dreamers record their dreams, they write a report that typically connects a series of action-oriented images (usually visual). Many dreamworkers (including Dr. Maybruck and myself) believe that these reports can help dreamers understand their behavior, their experiences, and their motives. Some psychotherapists are convinced that their clients will benefit from an understanding of their dreams because, on reflection, dream activities often appear to be metaphors for the dreamer's waking concerns. And several writers, artists, and other creative people who made deliberate use of their dream narratives and images, claim that their scientific, technological, athletic, or artistic breakthroughs resulted from dreams that were serendipitously recalled or deliberately incubated.

In 1985, a literary scholar claimed to have discovered a poem written by William Shakespeare that had eluded recognition for centuries. The controversy over this long-buried nine-stanza love poem, in which one lover asks another "Shall we dream?" is still unresolved, but it has exactly the same rhyming scheme as Puck's song in *A Midsummer Night's Dream*. And there is no controversy over the fact that this play is replete with dream dyads, one of whom remarks to the other, "And by the way let us recount our dreams."

Dr. Maybruck echoes this call. Her book should enhance the life of all dream dyads who read it and, to again cite *A Midsummer Night's Dream*, it will give them new pleasures as they "quickly dream away the time."

Preface

When a boy dreams of bedding a concubine, he is a man; when a girl dreams of the tree bearing dates, she is a woman.

—*a Turkish proverb*

Not only are men's and women's dreams distinctly different; recent psychological research indicates that many aspects of the thought processes of each sex are usually dissimilar. These differences are the result of a synthesis of physical, genetic, and environmental influences which are almost impossible to tease apart.

For example, females reach puberty and mature earlier than males, so that women usually reach the typical crisis points of adolescence, adulthood, and mid-life sooner than men do. Yet, the 1948 and 1964 Kinsey reports of sexual behavior established that males reach sexual peaks earlier. Decades of research comparing female and male dreams show that each sex has markedly different dreams, and that explicitly sexual dreams occur much sooner in males than they do in females.

Dr. John Nicholson, British psychologist and author of *Men and Women: How Different Are They?* points out that women tested for verbal fluency score higher on average than do men. On the other hand, males generally score higher on tests for spatial abilities—the ability to manipulate objects in space. Nicholson speculates that this spatial ability may account for the fact that, after age eleven, boys usually score higher in mathematics than do girls. Since males have been the hunters and gatherers of the human race for so many thousands of years, it can be argued that these spatial skills are genetic or learned. Certainly, it is only comparatively recently that women have been encouraged to develop such talents.

This is not to say that either sex is intellectually superior. The essential point here is that we are different both biologically and in the conditioning we receive from our society, and that these differences influence the way we perceive the world and each other. In *The ESO Ecstasy Program*, Dr. Alan Brauer cites numerous cases researched in his work as a sex therapist which indicate that most men express themselves with *thoughts*, whereas women express *feelings*. Although these differences lend an air of mystery and the challenge of the unknown to most romances, sometimes it seems miraculous that any couples are able to find a common meeting ground on which to build lasting relationships.

The idea for this book first occurred to me while I was helping new parents understand their dreams. These couples had participated in my doctoral research project, a study of dreams during pregnancy (which led to my first book, *Pregnancy and Dreams*). When these couples complained that the romance had faded from their marriages since they became busy parents, we began examining their dreams for clues to what had gone wrong. One new mother confided, "There's hardly any time nowadays for sex. And when we do get around to it, we're both too tired, or the baby cries and interrupts." This woman's dreams frequently portrayed her as vainly searching for an important, lost article. In one dream, the lost item was a pendant with a golden heart—clearly a symbol for the romance which was missing in her life.

Obviously, these new parents needed some commonsense guidance to arrange their schedules so they'd have at least one evening a week for privacy and intimacy. However, I soon discovered that many other couples who had baby-sitters or whose children were older (sleeping through the night, or even off to college or their own homes) had a common complaint: "The romance is gone from our life together. What happened?"

In my dream study groups, we soon learned that some couples continue to be romantically "in love," while others find themselves in conflict, or at best resigned, when the euphoric bloom of courtship and the honeymoon recedes. Further, their dreams reflect the state of their relationship, whether it is one of disillusionment or continuing enchantment.

When we discussed dreams, I was surprised to find that many couples had only vague ideas about each other's true feelings. One of the fundamental keys to a successful relationship is open and honest communication. Yet there can be no true communication when one or both partners holds unexpressed beliefs deep within the unconscious. Many of my students were honestly unaware in their waking lives that they had these "hidden agendas"—yet their dreams clearly revealed belief systems which were often totally at odds with those of their partners.

At the turn of the century, Freud called dreams "the royal road to the unconscious," and this observation is as true today as it was in the 1900s. By using their dreams to gain access to each other's unconscious thoughts and wishes, couples can achieve a type of communication which promotes deep and lasting bonds of empathy and love.

While psychologists and marriage counselors have long used clients' dreams as an avenue to the uncovering of innermost thoughts and feelings, the effectiveness of this therapeutic tool is not generally known to the lay public. Moreover, most couples are unaware that they can learn to use their dreams for this purpose without professional guidance.

For example, in one of my workshops on men's and women's dreams, two participants I'll call Bill and Diana related dreams which concerned their feelings about Diana's desire to continue her career after marriage. For several weeks, the central themes of Bill's dreams had been that he was abandoned. Diana's dreams reflected feelings of being trapped or suffocated. Once this couple saw each other's viewpoints, so clearly symbolized in their dreams, they were able to find a solution to their conflict.

Neither Bill nor Diana had realized the intensity or depths of the other's feelings before they learned to share their dreams. After the workshop, they continued this sharing on a daily basis, and eventually they married.

The same techniques for sharing and understanding dreams which this couple learned in my workshop are detailed in this book. These methods are simple and do not require your attendance at a workshop, or private sessions with a therapist. However, after studying this book you may wish to form your own "dream study group," in order to share your new dream interpretation skills with friends or relatives. Several of my former students have "dream parties," where all the guests share dreams. They report it's a fascinating, delightful way to spend an evening.

Although the names are changed to protect privacy, all quotes in this book are the actual words of students in my classes, workshops, and seminars, and from volunteers who participated in my research of the dreams of couples. Their stories will show you how to enhance the intimacy and romance of your own relationship, as well as how to use your dreams to resolve the inevitable conflicts which arise between most couples.

Of course, if your relationship is in serious danger of divorce or breaking up, you may need help from a counselor, psychologist, or your church pastor or rabbi. It is not my intention to belittle the valuable guidance such counselors can provide, or to discourage anyone from seeking help. Rather, it's my belief that any couple with the desire to recall and share their dreams can benefit from the techniques described in this book. It makes no difference whether you are dating, living together, married, or what your backgrounds or ages may be. Every human being has dreams every night, and all can learn how to understand these messages from the inner self, messages which can improve and enhance any relationship.

For instance, Rob was a man in his early fifties who worried about recurring dreams of his wife's death. He was afraid to tell his wife of twenty years about these nightmares, for fear she'd assume he was secretly wishing she were out of his life.

After we discussed Rob's recurring nightmares and his personal associations to his dream symbols, he became aware that both he and his wife were approaching a "mid-life crisis." Many of Rob's fears about aging were surfacing in his dreams. Frequently, a dream about a death or funeral reflects an unconscious awareness that some aspect of the dreamer's life is coming to an end, rather than any actual death. Thus, Rob's dreams symbolized the passing of a way of life (their youth), rather than being predictors of his wife's imminent demise.

By sharing their dreams, Rob and his wife learned to communicate their feelings more openly to one another, so that they were able to weather the transition to middle age with equanimity. Moreover, they were able to have their own "Dream Dyad" sessions at home, without the need of a counselor's intervention.

Incidents of this sort point up what is a little discussed yet quite valuable therapeutic use of dreams. When retelling a dream, most people think of it as something which "happened" to them, or as something they witnessed, much like a play or movie. We tend to forget that our dreams are actually creations of our own minds, and that these visions are composed of our own emotions, thoughts, experiences, and memories. This tendency to view a dream objectively has an advantage in that the dreamer, often unwittingly, reveals attitudes and feelings which he or she might never admit under other circumstances.

Another little known advantage of dream study between couples is that dreams can help increase sexual arousal and fulfillment. By learning the skills of dream incubation and lucid dreaming described in later chapters, you and your partner can actually dream about a topic of your choice (dream incubation). With practice, you can also learn to be aware you are dreaming during the dream (lucid dreaming), so that you can direct the action and dream characters. Thus, if you wish to dream about sexually explicit situations, you can program yourself for this type of dream. If you wish to meet your lover in your dreams, you can arrange that appearance during a lucid dream.

It's best to study this book one chapter at a time, sharing it with your partner if possible. Those who have not yet found the lover of their dreams will also find this book of tremendous help, since it teaches the ways every dreamer can learn to recognize the unexpressed emotions and attitudes which may be at the root of an inability to maintain lasting relationships.

After you learn how to understand the "Dream Language of Love" this book describes, a fascinating new world will open up. You'll read the actual experiences and dreams of the thirty couples whose dream notebooks form the basis of the text, as well as numerous dreams from unattached men and women who used my methods to better understand themselves and to find their own, special true love.

As a woman who has been married, had two children, divorced, and has now been happily remarried for twenty-five years, I have brought to this book my own experiences as well as my years of dream research with hundreds of couples. It is my hope that *Romantic Dreams* will help other couples rediscover the romance which may be missing from their lives, and will help them develop the close, bonded intimacy which makes life a meaningful, exciting adventure.

Patricia Maybruck, Ph.D.
St. Helena, California
January, 1991

The Basics of the Dream Language of Love

Dreams are almost synonymous with romance and love. Since the dawn of history, the dreams of lovers have been immortalized in poetry and song. Only the most cynical could brush aside those rapturous, ecstatic feelings so movingly expressed by Shelley:

> I arise from dreams of thee
> In the first sweet sleep of night
> When the winds are breathing low
> And the stars are shining bright.

Like the world's greatest lovers, you too can live the romance of your dreams—by using your own sleeping visions to deepen the bond between you and the one you choose as your dream companion. Let fluency in the Dream Language of Love be your goal. Let dreams be your vocabulary as you develop trust, sensitivity, communication, and the deep bonding which comes from unconditional, mutual love.

This section, Part I of *Romantic Dreams*, lays the foundation for you to learn the nuances of dream vocabulary, dream phrases, and "dream grammar" or dream structures. You'll learn the Dream Language of Love the way you learned English—by hearing it and then repeating what you heard. You didn't begin by first learning grammar; you first learned how to say things and how words are arranged. It was only after you knew conversational English fairly well that you began studying grammar.

In a like manner, *Romantic Dreams* starts you off in Chapter 1 with typical dreams from other couples, and a brief demonstration of the ways they use dreamwork conversations to learn their own, personal inner messages of the night. This chapter will also give you an overview of what to expect as you study this book. Then, the next three chapters will help you understand why you dream, what dream communications you may receive, and how to choose your dream partner. Come now, and begin this fascinating course in the Dream Language of Love.

Chapter
ONE

Conversations in the
Dream Language of Love

"When Peter and I were dating," Lisa told my dream study group, "we began telling each other our dreams. It really made me feel he was interested in my deepest thoughts—and it was fun, a different way to get to know each other." Peter added, "When she told me a sexy dream she had about me, I knew she was getting serious. Now, look what's happened—we've been living together three years!"

"Well, *our* dreams certainly aren't that idyllic," Rosemarie commented. "Jim and I have awful nightmares when there's the least little problem between us." Her husband Jim agreed. "That's one reason we're here," he said. "We'd like to know why it is we only have nightmares when we dream about each other. Does that mean our marriage is in trouble?"

"While we're on the subject of dreams and love," Sharon chimed in, "I keep dreaming about this wonderful man, a real Prince Charm-

3

ing, but the guys I meet never measure up. Is it possible to make my dreams come true?"

This chapter will show you how the couples I've worked with learned to use Dream Conversations to:

- Enhance feelings of intimacy
- Develop a climate of mutual trust
- Improve communication skills

Additionally, this opening chapter will give you a brief overview of the information and simple techniques you can expect to learn as you read *Romantic Dreams*.

PROMOTING INTIMACY. Lisa and Peter inadvertently discovered one of the most powerful qualities of dreams: the mere telling of your dream to another person makes you feel closer. If that person is the special one in your life, this sharing can enrich your relationship.

Moreover, when your partner tells you his or her dream, you can use this information in several ways. First, you can help your partner search for the meaning or interpretation of the dream. During this process, as you encourage the other person to tell you associations that the various elements of the dream bring to mind, you'll be gaining insights into your partner's attitudes—often in delightful and unexpected ways.

Next, the fact that the other person has revealed these inner truths will open the way for you to make similar revelations about yourself. In an almost magical manner, the sharing of dreams creates a safe climate, an atmosphere which encourages closeness.

BUILDING TRUST. By listening to your partner's dream, and then giving your enthusiastic interest, you will have strengthened the trust between you. This trust must be established before true communication can occur between any two people, be they friends or lovers.

Romantic Dreams will show you how to develop this climate of trust with another, as well as ways you can use dream sharing to improve your communication skills. For example, when Rosemarie related a recent nightmare, the group helped Jim change his responses. This is Rosemarie's frightening dream, with Jim's interruptions shown in parentheses:

> Jim and I were in a lovely restaurant, lit only by candlelight. I was nude except for my best jewelry, as were all the other diners— but Jim was wearing a suit and tie. (Jim laughs.) Jim gave the waiter our order without even consulting me and that made me mad. (Jim: "I'd never do that!") Then the waiter brought this ugly stew pot and plunked it down on the middle of the table. Hot oil spattered onto us as a monster head rose up out of the pot. I began to scream and the monster grew until it towered over us. It was a hideous bloodsucking vampire. (Jim: "You shouldn't watch so many horror movies on TV!") As the monster reached for my necklace I woke up, terrified.

After Rosemarie told us her nightmare, the other group members explained that Jim should allow her to finish her description before commenting, and that even then he should refrain from any criticism. "Let *her* tell *you* what she thinks it means," Peter advised.

Even if you do not yet know the art of dream interpretation, you've probably already guessed that Rosemarie perceived Jim as an overly controlling person, and that this both angered and frightened her. However, the fact that Jim had consented to attend a dream study group with his wife indicated his willingness to change.

IMPROVING COMMUNICATION SKILLS. To help Jim and Rosemarie learn the art of trusting communication, we had her retell her dream, while Jim listened attentively. Next, he asked what she thought the dream might mean. "The first thing I noticed," Rosemarie told him, "was that what you order for us—what you think is right—may turn out to be actually dangerous. Like the monster in the pot. The night I had that dream, you'd told me you decided to buy a new sports car. Not only wasn't that what we need or what I might choose, but it might also wreck our budget. Guess I see that as being dangerous right now."

Without defending himself, Jim next asked, "What do you think the other parts of the dream meant, like your being nude while I was fully dressed?"

"Oh, that's easy," Rosemarie said. "I 'show myself'—my feelings, my opinions—maybe too much. And you keep your feelings hidden· from me."

To our surprise, Jim's face and tone softened. "Guess I've been afraid I'd lose you if I didn't act like a 'take charge' guy," he admitted, putting his arm around Rosemarie. "And, if you knew what I'm really feeling, you'd think I'm not very strong, not man enough for you."

Rosemarie's eyes filled with tears as she snuggled against Jim. "This is what I want," she sighed. "Your real feelings are all the strength I need."

Dreamwork as Therapy for Couples

This brief exchange between Rosemarie and Jim demonstrates the effectiveness of dreamwork with couples. Although dreamwork is a tool used by some group psychotherapists and marriage counselors, little has been written about the topic.

In a textbook for marriage counselors, *Changing Families*, edited by J. Haley, several marriage counselors say that the use of dreams "may produce more spontaneous . . . interaction . . . on a safe level." In another text, *Family Therapy, Theory and Practice*, marriage counselor P. Papp advocates the sharing of dreams as a valuable tool in brief therapy with couples groups. In the *Journal of Sex and Marital Therapy*, Dr. M. Goldberg points out that the sharing of feelings as the dream is retold can improve closeness between partners. "The Use of Dreams in Couples Therapy," an article by Dr. Richard Perlmutter and Dr. Raymond Babineau, for the professional journal *Psychiatry* states that "A dream shared by a member of a couple is a way of tapping into their unconscious communication," and that by using dreams, the therapist can help the couple "translate the unconscious communication into the language of awareness and growth."

Little has been written for the general public about the almost magical ways couples can use dreams to enhance intimacy. *Romantic*

Dreams will give you tips in every chapter on the many ways you and your partner can use your dreams to resolve the inevitable conflicts which arise in any relationship. These include:

- The Dream Dyad
- Discovering each other's Hidden Agendas
- Conflict resolution
- Creating erotic fantasies and dreams

THE DREAM DYAD. When two people share their dreams for the purpose of understanding one another, this "duet" or "dyad" can become a special part of their lives, a time when they reveal their deepest thoughts and feelings. Lisa and Peter, whose remarks opened this chapter, spontaneously created their Dream Dyad when they shared their dreams during their first dates. Over the years, they developed the climate of trust which is a prerequisite to any lasting romance. *Romantic Dreams* provides simple directions for the creation of your own Dream Dyad with that particular person in your life.

HIDDEN AGENDAS. An example of a secret motivation or "hidden agenda" was Jim's attitude toward his wife. Because he assumed that Rosemarie wanted him to be the "strong silent type," Jim was playing an uncomfortable role which actually hurt and bewildered her. *Romantic Dreams* will show you how to understand your dreams to discover repressed feelings and attitudes you may not even be aware you have, those hidden agendas which may be erecting barriers between you. Once you've identified these unconscious feelings and motives, solutions to the conflicts they're causing are more easily found.

CONFLICT RESOLUTION. All relationship conflicts are not as easily resolved as were Rosemarie and Jim's. However, this couple's nightmares reflected miscommunication and the erosion of the trust they'd originally had in one another. These are probably the most common causes of broken marriages and failed relationships. *Romantic Dreams* can help you identify the specific areas where you and your partner are misinterpreting each other's behavior and attitudes, and will show you ways you can use dream sharing techniques to rebuild the trust these miscommunications may have damaged.

EROTIC DREAMS AND SEXUAL FANTASIES. Even if you're not having erotic or sexy dreams about your partner, *Romantic Dreams* will teach you how to create and share these ecstatic experiences. Using the fantastic powers of your imagination, you'll learn how to confide your secret sexual fantasies and even to indulge in them in the safety of your dreams.

Finding Your Ideal Mate

If, like Sharon (who complained that the people she met never measured up to the lover of her dreams), you haven't yet found your ideal mate, this book will teach you how to tap into the incredible storehouse of information contained in your own mind. This knowledge can help you evaluate others, identify the sources of stress and tension in your life, enhance your self-confidence, and keep your romance alive after you've found it. You'll learn that your dreams are the key which will open the gates of your inner world, so that you'll be able to recognize those personality types who have the potential qualities you need in a mate.

Learning the Dream Language of Love

Let *Romantic Dreams* be your guide as you master a new Language of Love. To begin this easy course, Part I will give you the preparation necessary for any study of a new language. First, you'll learn the basics of how and why we dream.

Although much about dreams remains a mystery, scientists have made great strides since the 1950s when researchers discovered that rapid eye movements (REMs) indicate that a sleeping person is dreaming. After a brief overview of the latest scientific studies of the brain activity which appears to cause us to dream, you'll discover the many functions of dreaming, from the resolution of conflicts and problems to the ways some dreamers are able to acquire new knowledge, and even to predict future events.

Next, you'll learn simple techniques for recalling and recording your dreams. Once you've mastered these easy procedures, you can expect to learn how to decode "dream hieroglyphics"—the mysterious images and symbols of dreams. You'll learn the language in which these signs are depicted, and will begin to recognize the meaning of the images in your own dreams. You'll discover the many different kinds of "dream stories," from those dreams which help solve problems and conflicts, to nightmares, as well as the many rare and unusual sleep adventures such as flying dreams, telepathic, and symbiotic dreams.

To help you find the ideal mate of your dreams, Chapter 4 provides profiles of many personality types, both male and female. After you find your own profile, you'll learn how to "match" yourself with the opposite sex, and how to recognize the patterns of your attitudes and behavior which may have prevented you from making healthy choices in the past. Chapter 4 will also explain the differences in the dreaming styles of various groups, so that you can better understand how your partner's dreams may be reflecting a background or a stage of life which may be different from your own. For instance, the dreams of women vary at different times during their reproductive cycles. During menstrual periods, women often dream of men as enemies or intruders; during the fertile part of their cycles, they usually dream of men as friends and lovers. You can use information of this type to make you more sensitive to your own emotional needs and to those of your partner.

Part II of *Romantic Dreams* gives you a brief history of the Dream Language of Love, from ancient times to the present. Next, you'll learn the various interpretation methods passed on to us by people who have already studied this fascinating idiom of dreams. As you become adept at interpreting your own dreams, you'll discover the delightful benefits of dream sharing and dreamwork with your partner.

By the time you reach Part III, you'll be prepared to attempt two marvelous skills of advanced dreaming: dream incubation and lucid dreaming.

DREAM INCUBATION. An "incubated" dream is one which you choose to have, rather than a spontaneous dream, which occurs without your consciously choosing to experience it. Yes, it is possible to actually decide what you'd like to dream about, and then to fall asleep and have a dream on the topic of your choice! Development of this skill will give you access to the creative powers of your mind so that you'll be able to find solutions to problems and conflicts, enhance your emotional and spiritual growth, and even meet your lover in your dreams.

LUCID DREAMING. A "lucid" dream is one in which you are aware you are dreaming *while you're having the dream*. Like many people, you may have thought, during a dream, "this can't really be happening—so I must be dreaming"—however, you probably awakened at that moment. Skilled lucid dreamers are able to remain asleep after having this realization, and with practice are even able to direct the action or plot of the dream, converse with dream characters, and change the setting and other elements of the dream. Using lucid dreaming skills, lovers are able to meet in their dreams. Some even resolve problems and conflicts they're unable to confront successfully in waking life.

A word of caution here: these advanced dreaming skills are not easily achieved. When some people hear about incubated and lucid dreams, they conclude that they can quickly learn these techniques and then can use them to resolve all their problems, and can "kill" or destroy nightmarish dream characters.

In the next chapter, you'll learn that dreams are one of the most important activities of our brains and minds. Many dream psychologists now believe that a primary function of dreaming is to help us resolve conflicts and problems which upset us in our waking lives; therefore it becomes important not to interrupt this function by severely altering dream content. The monsters of our nightmares may have a purpose. Rather than using incubation or lucid dreaming techniques to avoid these disturbing dream elements, it seems a wiser course to use these skills to aid you in understanding them.

For example, after Rosemarie became adept at dream recall, she attempted to incubate her "monster in the pot" nightmare again so that she could discover more about its purpose. After becoming deeply relaxed, just as she was drifting off to sleep, Rosemarie silently repeated, "Tonight I will dream about the monster in the pot, and I'll ask it what it wants from me." The next morning, Rosemarie recorded the following:

This time I'm in our backyard hot tub, soaking in the nude. It's night and the stars are out, really beautiful, and I'm wishing I could share this with Jim. I can see him in the house and am trying to get his attention but he doesn't hear me. Then the water gets almost unbearably hot and begins to gurgle and boil. Out of the middle of the tub, the same hideous monster rises up. It does look like a creature from a horror movie, almost like a dragon, with a scaly skin and an enormous mouth with bloody fangs. This time I'm just as scared as before and I climb out of the tub. But instead of running, which I want to do, I stay and ask the monster, "What do you want from me?" It smiles with this gruesome grin and roars, "I'm here to make you angry! Stand up and defend yourself!" Then it reaches out a huge claw. As I jump back in terror it scratches my neck and grabs a handful of my hair, yanking me back into the tub. I scream for Jim. "He can't help you now!" the monster bellows. Over my shoulder I see that the house is dark, and realize Jim has probably gone to bed. I start pounding on the monster with my fists and stick my fingers into its fiery eyes. "Ouch! Don't do that!" it whines in a wimpy voice. But I keep hitting it and as I do, it deflates like a rubber toy. I feel relieved and jeer at it, "You're not so terrible! You're just full of hot air!" and then I wake up, laughing.

When we discussed her incubated dream in class, Rosemarie admitted that she had great difficulty expressing anger. "My mother was a very angry woman," she told us, "but she never let us kids show our tempers. She was always yelling and punishing us for the least little thing. My way to escape was to be as quiet and good as I could be.

I guess I still do that. Arguments really scare me. I guess my dream monster was trying to show me that anger really isn't so awful."

By using dream incubation methods to clarify the meaning of her nightmare, Rosemarie learned much more about herself than she might have if she'd attempted to vanquish her personal boogeyman. Her husband Jim commented, "This explanation makes me feel a lot better, because it hints that I am not the only one in the family who doesn't reveal feelings! Guess we both have a lot to learn about expressing our emotions."

Paradise Found

By the time you've reached Chapters 9 and 10 of *Romantic Dreams*, you'll probably be enjoying a new closeness and intimacy with your partner. These final chapters will teach you:

- Lovemaking with visualizations
- Making sexual fantasies come true
- Creating erotic dreams

VISUALIZATIONS OF INTIMACY. By learning to relax deeply and to let your imagination roam, you and your partner can visualize lovemaking in ways that might never occur in the normal course of events, or even in your spontaneous fantasies. You'll learn how to combine the favorite positions and caresses which you both have into one "creative daydream," and then to integrate this creation into your deeper consciousness through visualization techniques.

SEXUAL FANTASIES AND EROTIC DREAMS. Contrary to what you may have heard or read, daydreams and fantasies are not usually of the sexual variety. Dr. Jerome Singer and Dr. John Antrobus, psychologists who have spent more than twenty years investigating daydreaming, tell us that this fascinating mental activity most often occurs when we're involved in some boring, humdrum activity. Moreover, the topics of these flights of fantasy are rarely sexual; when they are, they're usually rather tame compared to pornography or X-rated films.

Erotic and "wet" dreams are equally disappointing in content and diversity.

However, you can learn how to deliberately invoke erotic dreams which can carry both you and your lover to new heights of ecstasy. *Romantic Dreams* will show you how to develop these creations and to mold them to your individual needs and tastes. You'll learn how to enjoy these visions in the safety of your dreams, without the fear of consequences which may normally inhibit you in waking life.

When your erotic dreams suggest different sexual activities than you're currently enjoying, future chapters will show you and your mate how to rid yourselves of the inhibitions which may have been preventing you from enjoying the intense pleasures which are possible when two people are bonded with the communication and trust their shared dreams can inspire.

A FEW WORDS OF CAUTION. Concerning sexuality and any erotic exchange between couples: nothing in this book is intended as an indication of what is moral or immoral, "right" or "wrong." Rather, I have sought to provide the most current information as well as the opinions of counselors and sex therapists. What you may think is ordinary or "normal" may be outrageous or unthinkable to someone else. It's up to you to consider the materials offered in these pages and to choose those suggestions which you and your partner feel are acceptable to your own values and standards of behavior.

Since each person has specific states of health, it's also important to consult your own physician or therapist should you have any sexual dysfunctions or unusual sexual reactions which may suggest abnormalcy. However, by approaching these pages with an open, inquiring mind, most readers can find safe, easy techniques in *Romantic Dreams* for the enhancement of sexual pleasure and intimacy.

Keeping Your Romance Alive

This final chapter will teach you how to continue to use your newfound dream interpretive and sharing techniques to make your romantic union last a lifetime. We'll explore the latest research from sex and marriage counselors, such as Masters and Johnson (*On Sex and Human Loving*), and Pearsall (*Super Marital Sex: Loving for Life*). By adding dream sharing to the suggestions of these noted sex therapists, you can release your deepest, most intimate feelings to one another without fear that your romance will fade or die.

You'll discover that your dreams can kindle and reaffirm your passion and love, as well as defuse any anger or hostility which may be hampering total communication and trust.

Summary

This chapter introduces you to the notion of "conversational dream language," which simply means the sharing of your dreams with others. If you haven't done so already, begin now by telling your most recent dream to your mate (or a close friend, if you haven't yet found a romantic partner). Urge him or her to respond in kind, and listen attentively, without interrupting. Then encourage each other to "decode" the dreams, mentioning whatever associations you may have to the various dream elements.

Unless you're already experienced at dream interpretation, when you try dream sharing you'll probably find that your dreams make little sense. This book will show you how to understand the messages your inner self is sending, and will explain all these aspects of the Dream Language of Love:

- Why we dream
- Dream recall; understanding dream symbols; types of dreams
- Profiles of different types of dreamers
- Dream history
- Methods of dream interpretation
- Loving with dreams: the Dream Dyad; conflict resolution; discovering Hidden Agendas; erotic dreams and fantasies
- Creating your own dreams: dream incubation and lucid dreaming
- Advanced lovemaking with dreams and visualizations
- Keeping your romance alive

If you're among the many who, like Sharon, have not yet found your ideal mate, this book can help you better understand which prospective partners may best fit the unique personality your dreams can reveal. You'll learn how to avoid the unhealthy choices you may have made in the past, and how to use your dreams to build the self-esteem you'll need to find and keep alive the romance of your dreams.

After you have learned and practiced a few elementary steps to help you recall and interpret your dreams, we'll briefly review the history of dream psychology and research. You can use this information to deepen your understanding of the latest techniques for working with dreams.

By studying *Romantic Dreams* with your partner, you can expect to discover new insights about yourself and each other, clearing away the residue of past misunderstandings and resolving new problems and conflicts as they arise. Further, you'll be able to use your dreams, your enhanced communication skills, and the hitherto untapped powers of your imagination to add excitement to sexual activities and to ignite the pleasures of deeper intimacy and closeness.

Then, as you become more proficient with dreamwork, you will discover the endless possibilities which open to those who are able to control or deliberately create dreams about a topic of their choice. With all these techniques at your disposal, you and your partner can explore other powers of your minds and imaginations, increasing the pleasures of your erotic hours together.

Finally, we will look at the ways other couples have used their dreams and the resulting close communication and trust to keep romance alive in their relationships. You'll find out what men and women truly want from each other, and how to use this knowledge to keep the fires of passion burning in your own partnership. Let *Romantic Dreams* guide you and your mate to the inner growth which gives added meaning and wisdom to your lives together.

Chapter
TWO

Why We Dream

"The reason I had a weird dream last night was that I overate at our favorite pasta restaurant," said Frank. "I think most dreams are caused by eating spicy foods, or sometimes a need to go to the bathroom." "Oh no," his wife Sarah objected. "It's not that simple. Our brains have two hemispheres. The one on the left is for daytime thinking. That part shuts off when we sleep, and the right side takes over. Dreams are really our sleeping thoughts."

Frank and Sarah were new students in my dream study course for couples. Others commented that they'd read about recent research which found that dreams are like some sort of "garbage" or "trash" which our brains discard while we're asleep.

The Anatomy of Dreaming

All these ideas have some basis in truth or fact. Dr. Patricia Garfield, author of *Women's Bodies, Women's Dreams*, presents evidence that

16

body states—including indigestion and a full bladder—*do* have a measurable effect on our dreams. While Sarah's notions of the hemispheric theory of brain activity are somewhat distorted, until recently scientists did believe that dreams arise from the brain's right hemisphere. Further, it is true that the renowned codiscoverer of DNA, Sir Francis Crick, has put forth the supposition that dreams are the computer-like brain's way of "erasing" noncomputable data.

However, none of these theories adequately explain the cause of dreaming. Since the 1950s, when researchers in sleep laboratories discovered that every normal person's eyes move rapidly from side to side (REMs) when a dream is taking place, scientists have made great strides toward our understanding of dreams. Yet much about their physiological origins remains a mystery.

Lower Brain, Upper Brain

The lower brain, or brain stem, is actually a continuation of the spinal cord. As this stemlike "stalk" emerges from the spine, it thickens and spreads into the upper brain areas. Dr. Robert W. McCarley and Dr. Allan J. Hobson, neuroscientists at Harvard Medical School, tell us that this part of the brain sends out impulses at the end of a deep stage of sleep, impulses which cause certain neurons to fire off, somewhat like microscopic fireworks. In turn, this activity causes the brain to be flooded with the chemical *acetylcholine*, a neurotransmitter which signals other brain cells and also stimulates visual images. These visual stimuli probably cause a sleeping person's eyelids to twitch with the REMs which researchers associate with the onset of dreaming. Meanwhile, the upper brain is receiving information which tells it that body movement is occurring—even though our bodies usually remain inert while we're dreaming. This inertia is another effect of the upsurge of acetylcholine, which shuts off the nerve links that would set our bodies in motion if we were awake.

The frontal part of the brain, which examines and programs incoming data, attempts to explain these internal signals by composing a plot or story—a dream—which incorporates the images, sights, sounds, body activity, and emotions it is receiving.

A simple analogy might be the game children sometimes play, of imagining that cloud formations are people, animals, or landscapes. In a similar fashion, the frontal brain, and especially its right side, may assign meanings to the flashes and patterns it receives from the lower brain during sleep.

Right Brain, Left Brain

Sarah's idea that dreams arise from the right side of the brain has some merit. In fact, until recently dream researchers thought this might be the case. Sarah had probably heard or read about the hemispheric model of brain research which has received so much attention by the media in recent years.

BOTH SIDES WORK TOGETHER. One misconception the public often has about the relationship between these two halves of the brain is that they work independently of one another, almost as if we had two brains with different tasks assigned to each half. This is not true. On the contrary, most researchers now agree that both hemispheres are continually active. In *Symposium on Consciousness*, Dr. David Galin suggests that each side has a different style of thinking, although it can and does organize and interpret the same types of data.

In *Consciousness: Brain, States of Awareness, and Mysticism*, Galin points out that the brain's two hemispheres are connected by a strong bridge of tissues, the *corpus collosum*, which is composed of 200 million nerve fibers. This connecting bridge is constantly sending information back and forth between the two sides. When the corpus collosum has been surgically disconnected for medical reasons, patients are able to think and function in one style or the other.

In fact, it was observations of such patients which led scientists to the discovery of the two cerebral hemispheres, as well as to the realization that information received on the right side of the body is processed by the opposite, *left* side of the brain, while incoming data on the body's left side is processed by the *right* hemisphere. Also, it was discovered that some strongly left-handed people's brains functioned the opposite of right-handed ones.

LEFT AND RIGHT BRAIN TRAITS. The left hemisphere is analytical in nature, and better able to break down a topic into its component parts. For this reason, it excels at language and certain mathematical tasks. The right side, on the other hand, quickly grasps the *gestalt* or the whole, the overall picture and meaning. Thus, the right hemisphere is more likely to be involved in the brain's efforts to make sense of the images and pictures it receives when we begin to dream.

However, this does not mean that the left hemisphere is inactive. Rather, it appears to be inhibited or resting when the right hemisphere is busy computing incoming data.

In a similar fashion, the reverse usually occurs when we're awake, with the left side making a complex array of logical choices and judgments. People whose left hemisphere is highly developed tend to be logical, rational, well organized, and analytical. Those whose right hemisphere prevails in waking life tend to be more intuitive, creative, and to perceive overall patterns rather than specific parts of a puzzle, problem, or idea.

Your understanding of this hemispheric brain activity can help you better understand yourself as well as assist you in your choice of a romantic partner, and is discussed in more detail in Chapter 4.

HEMISPHERIC ACTIVITY IN DREAMS. Dr. John Antrobus, a psychologist at City University of New York, tells us that both the right and left hemispheres of our brains are active during sleep. Since both hemispheres of the frontal brain are bombarded with signals emitted by the brain stem, both are likely to attempt to process the information.

However, since the signals being received are mainly visual, the right hemisphere probably provides most of the explanation by running through its immense memory, a veritable library of stored images and sensations—all we have experienced in a lifetime—and choosing those which appear to match the incoming data.

OUTSIDE INFLUENCES ON DREAMS. Frank's belief that dreams are "caused" by indigestion, a need to go to the bathroom, or other outside influences, bears consideration. You may have noticed that a ringing telephone or alarm clock may appear in your dreams as a church bell or fire truck or some other related idea. Or, perhaps you've dreamed of bathing or swimming when your bladder was full.

Recent investigations by Maeva Ennis and Dr. Peter Fonagy at the University College, London, England's sleep lab shed light on the way events or stimuli which occur while we're asleep may change the content of our dreams. These researchers played tapes while their sleeping subjects were having REM sleep. Half the volunteers were given a name, while the others had blank tapes. More than 60 percent of those whose tapes presented names "incorporated" these into their dreams. Some of these were subtle, such as the name "Robert" which emerged as a rabbit in one dream and as a burglar or robber in another.

Ennis and Fonagy also found that more dreams were influenced by outside sounds when these were presented to the left ears of the sleeping subjects. This seems to support the idea that the right hemisphere, which processes information received on the left side of the body, is the primary processor of dreams.

Same Lifestyle, Different Dreams

The ways in which the same words were processed and incorporated differently by different individuals in the British studies also emphasizes another important aspect of dreams: the meaning of any dream *depends upon the individual dreamer*. Dream researchers have established that dreams almost invariably reflect the concerns and events of our waking life. Since everyone's personal life is different, it makes sense that the meanings a dreamer assigns to a dream will depend upon that individual's specific lifestyle and personality.

For this reason, it's important to be able to interpret your own dreams rather than to rely on "dream dictionaries" or the meanings others may assign to the images of your dreams. While people who have similar lifestyles, ages, and backgrounds may have similar dreams, there will always be individual differences even within groups of people who share many of the same concerns.

For example, Marcia and Herb were a couple remarkably like Rosemarie and Jim, whose dreams were described in Chapter 1. Like Jim, Herb needed to be in control, making all domestic decisions despite his wife's desires and competence. Rosemarie, whose dream of the "Monster in the Pot" vividly portrayed her feelings about Jim, even had a background much like Marcia's. Both women were natives of a suburb near Washington, D.C. They were the same age, had been married almost two years, and were college graduates. Notice the apparent similarities between Rosemarie's "Monster in the Pot" dream and the following dream from Marcia:

> Herb and I were at a concert in this dream. All the other people in the audience except me were men, dressed formally in tuxedoes. I looked down and to my horror I was naked! I felt trapped, because if I got up and ran out I'd have to crawl over the laps of the men in our row. I put the program over my crotch and covered my breasts with my hands. The lights dimmed and I was grateful for that, at least. Then Herb looked at me and said, "You're looking nice tonight, Honey. Is that a new dress?" The curtains rose and a man and woman came on stage to sing. He was in a tuxedo and she was nude, too. Herb whispered, "That's a stunning costume she's wearing!" The woman didn't seem to know she was nude, and began to sing some operatic thing I'd never heard. I felt ashamed and confused and woke up feeling the same way.

As we discussed Marcia's dream, it developed that her associations to her public nudity were quite different from those of Rosemarie, who believed this symbolized the way she openly expressed her feelings (unlike her husband Jim, who hid his emotions out of fear of not being manly enough). Marcia explained, "Being exposed like that stands for the way I feel a lot of the time, vulnerable and, well, sort of helpless compared to men. In fact, sometimes I think Women's Lib is just a joke, because when you get right down to it, *all* women still take a back seat to men."

Future chapters will describe in more detail the ways Marcia and Herb learned to use their dreams to resolve the conflicts which were destroying their romance. For now, the important point is that each person usually has her or his unique interpretation of any dream element. A dream element that symbolized open expression of emotions to Rosemarie represented vulnerability and helplessness to Marcia. Once you learn to recognize the ways your own mind selects specific images to depict issues in your own distinctly individual waking life, you'll be well on the way toward becoming an advanced dreamworker.

The Functions of Dreaming

Since the publication of Dr. Sigmund Freud's classic *The Interpretation of Dreams* in the 1900s, psychologists have pondered the reasons all normal people have for dreaming. Although modern scientists are now discovering the biological origins of dreams, we still are not sure of their purpose.

Psychologists' Theories

Most dream researchers agree that nearly all dreams reflect the concerns of our waking life. In early stages of REM sleep, this connection to waking life is more obvious: a homemaker who scorched the breakfast toast may have a dream which begins with a fire, or an office worker who had a disagreement with an employer may dream initially of being a soldier on a battlefield. Dream psychologists call this early part of a dream the "day residue." However, we can only guess at the purpose of this type of imagery.

We do know that, when subjects in sleep laboratories are awakened at the onset of REM sleep and thus deprived of dreaming, they become mentally disoriented to the point that their health begins to suffer. Dr. Montague Ullman, coauthor of *Working With Dreams* and founder of one of the earliest sleep laboratories (Maimonides Medical Center in Brooklyn, New York), tells us that every normal person dreams at least three to five times per night, with the dreams becoming longer each time. The last dream you have just before awakening is usually the longest—sometimes lasting almost an hour—and the one usually most easily remembered.

However, even when you do not recall your dreams, they seem to have a purpose. Most dream psychologists agree with Ullman that the principal functions of dreaming are

- To make us aware of the emotions surrounding recent experiences
- To awaken us when these emotions are unusually intense
- To heal us emotionally

Some psychologists also believe, as did Freud, that another purpose of dreaming is to help us discharge repressed or unexpressed emotions. Additionally, Jungian psychologists (therapists trained in the teachings of Dr. Carl Jung) believe that dreams function as both guiding influences on our waking lives and as a means to better understanding those aspects of ourselves which we have not acknowledged prior to the dream.

EMOTIONS IN DREAMS. Notice that all the schools of thought about dream functions listed above emphasize the importance of emotions in dreams. In fact, Ullman sees the understanding of our emotions as the primary purpose of dreams.

Following are excerpts which demonstrate the variety of emotions dreams may express:

- *Kirk, 38-year-old photographer*: I was chasing this blond woman through tall grass . . . She disappeared . . . I began to panic, as if my life depended on catching her.
- *Gina, 40-year-old nurse, Kirk's partner*: Dreamed I had a penis . . . felt very powerful and pleased with myself.
- *Carl, 45-year-old mechanic*: At my mother's grave, crying . . . Maureen was there . . . Felt great sorrow and pain, thinking, "She may be next to die."
- *Maureen, 42-year-old homemaker, Carl's wife*: Got into my station wagon and found it all ripped up inside . . . even the steering wheel was bent . . . Started yelling, it made me so mad.

ROMANTIC DREAMS

- *Sean, 25-year-old Air Force lieutenant*: Dreamed we crashed on a desert island . . . felt depressed until we discovered some friendly natives . . . One was my wife and I was overjoyed.
- *Margo, 24-year-old secretary, Sean's wife*: A message came over the teletype that Sean's plane had crashed . . . began to cry and woke up feeling scared.

Although a couple's dreams may occur on the same night, and appear to reflect the dreamers' concerns about the same issues, their emotions are usually different. Kirk's nightmare about chasing an unfamiliar blonde reflected his anxiety over his competitive feelings about Gina, his live-in lover. This couple had recently entered therapy, and Kirk admitted to feeling inferior about his progress toward self-understanding. Gina, on the other hand, was losing her feelings of low self-esteem to the point that she dreamed she was as confident and powerful as Kirk, and even had a body to show it!

Carl's worry and emotional pain about his wife Maureen's serious illness were mirrored in his dream of his mother's grave, while Maureen's dream reflected her anger about her health and the surgery she had to undergo.

Sean and Margo, the Air Force couple, lived in a constant state of tension while he was stationed in a potentially dangerous area abroad. Naturally optimistic, Sean's dreams tended to have upbeat, happy endings as in the one above in which he found his beloved wife even though he'd crashed on a desert island. Margo's nightmare showed her to be less resilient, depicting her fears of the worst case scenario. Yet she told me she'd learned to welcome such fearful dreams. "For some reason, after I have one of these nightmares, I actually feel better and less worried about Sean," she commented.

In her scary dreams, Margo may have released some of the stress she felt about the constant dangers her husband was facing, so that her fears were lighter after such dreams. Sometimes, simply becoming aware of your emotions about recent events or an intimate relationship may be all you need to assist you in making a decision or accepting some difficult circumstance.

24

UNCONSCIOUS HELP FROM YOUR DREAMS. You may have noticed this function of your own dreams on some occasion when, unable to make a decision, you decided to "sleep on it." Next day, even though you may not have recalled any dreams about the topic, you knew exactly what to do. In all probability, you dreamed about the problem, your dreams suggested the solution which best acknowledged your feelings, and your mind integrated the decision so that you knew what action to take when you awoke—even though you may not have recalled the dream.

At other times, the conflict may remain a dilemma, and the dreams we have may appear incomprehensible. Or, you may not even be aware that any conflict or problem exists—yet you find you're awakening frequently from disturbing or nightmarish dreams. These are the times when your dreams are probably alerting you to the fact that you're repressing some potentially explosive emotions, or that your inner self can show you ways to heal yourself from some psychological wound.

THE PURPOSES OF NIGHTMARES. Frightening or nightmarish dreams may be attempts by your sleeping mind to get your attention focused on a circumstance or problem you've been avoiding. Although sweet dreams are delightful, the fact is that most of us don't recall them nearly as well as we do those from which we awaken with fear and a sometimes pounding heart.

Further, there may be something happening in your waking life which reminds you of a fearful period or even frightening moments in your childhood. Marcia's feelings of vulnerability and helplessness, of being trapped by formally attired men while she herself was naked, suggest a helpless child more than they do an adult, married woman. In *The Nightmare*, Dr. Ernest Hartmann points out that children, who usually feel much more vulnerable and at the mercy of outside influences, have more nightmares than adults. When adults are under stress or experience a traumatic event, the resulting feelings may remind them of childhood fears and so they may have childlike, nightmarish dreams.

It's also worth noting that some medications, as well as street drugs, may cause nightmares. Marcia had been taking medication for hypertension. Effects of this prescriptive drug, combined with her anxiety about her marriage, may have precipitated Marcia's frightening dreams. As she and Herb began to resolve their conflicts, Marcia's blood pressure became normal, she was able to discontinue medication, and her dreams also became less fearful.

Hartmann also notes that certain personality types tend to have nightmares more than others. Such people have what he describes as "thin boundaries," and are frequently more sensitive than those with "thick" boundaries. Such sensitive people usually experience every event more intensely; as a consequence their dreams tend to be more nightmarish, almost as if what others might see as merely annoying becomes to them a trauma. Kirk, the photographer who dreamed of a frantic chase, and Marcia, Herb's wife, were both sensitive types who seemed to feel much more pain about small events than did their mates.

If you or your partner suffer from frequent nightmares, this may simply mean that you have similar thin boundaries and need to insulate yourself more than others do from life's routine pains and stresses.

Dreamers' Theories

The very nature of dreams makes it impossible for scientists to observe them directly. Since all we know about dreams is secondhand, the result of whatever the dreamer is able to tell us, I decided to find out from dreamers what they observed about themselves after intense dream study, in order to compare their theories with those of the researchers.

At the end of a six-week seminar of dreamwork with twelve couples, I asked them to tell me what they thought were the functions of their dreams. In addition to their agreement with the psychologists that dreams helped them identify repressed emotions, thus enabling them to target sources of stress in their daily lives, they listed the following:

- Conflict and problem resolution
- Creativity, inspiration

- Warnings of physical dysfunction
- Development of psychic powers
- Information about "past lives"
- New knowledge
- Forecasts of future events

RESOLUTIONS OF CONFLICTS AND PROBLEMS. The overwhelming response to "Why do we dream?" was "to resolve conflicts and find the answers to problems." For example, Bill and Diana were an engaged couple who used dreams to resolve what appeared to be an impasse in their relationship.

For several weeks, Bill had objected to Diana's insistence that she wanted to continue her career as a buyer in a large department store chain. Bill, a successful advertising executive, protested that, if they had children, Diana should do everything possible to make their babies feel nurtured and loved—including breastfeeding, which he claimed would be impossible if Diana returned to work after childbirth. Meanwhile, Diana felt that Bill's views belittled her rights as a woman and her hard-won independence. During this period, Bill had this dream:

I'm at an enormous, outdoor bazaar. It's arranged like a men's clothing store, with very expensive items on display under colorful canopies. There are thousands of people shopping and these outdoor pavilions seem to stretch to the horizon. I'm shopping for a new wardrobe and go from stall to stall, loading up with many clothes to try on. There are these cabana-like booths for fitting rooms. I'm feeling excited and happy. It's like being at a fair or fiesta. There's music and free refreshments. I take my armload into a fitting room tent, and there's a little boy in there, crying. He's lost. I pick him up and go out to find a salesperson. I tell a white-haired woman who seems to be a manager about the boy and she just shrugs and says, "That's not *my* problem!" and walks away. I start yelling at her (and then I woke up feeling angry and frustrated).

When Bill talked about his associations to this dream, he realized that "shopping for a new wardrobe" symbolized his plans to marry Diana—a situation that would change his lifestyle. Bill also thought the lost child in his dream might be himself, both as a child and in his current predicament. It developed that Bill's parents had died in an accident when he was small, and he'd been raised by rather strict grandparents. Like the elderly woman in his dream, Bill's grandmother had shrugged off his childish problems.

When Diana heard Bill's dream, she immediately understood that his seeming overreaction to her desire to work after marriage stemmed from his fear and anger about his own feelings of abandonment as a child.

During this same phase of their struggle to resolve their conflicts, Diana reported this dream:

(This is a recurring nightmare for the past several weeks. Each time it's almost the same.) In this dream I wake up (actually, I was still asleep, dreaming), sensing someone is in my bedroom. Straining to hear and see, I can just make out the shadowy figure of a man coming closer to my bed. Then I realize it's someone familiar—for a moment it seems to be my Dad. I lie back down and relax but then, all of a sudden, the man looms over me and presses a pillow onto my face. I'm smothering! Can't breathe. I begin trying to push away the pillow and start screaming for help. Then I wake up with my heart pounding and in a cold sweat.

Encouraged to discuss her father (who seemed to be the central figure in this recurring nightmare), Diana insisted she loved and trusted him. Then she added, "At twenty-one, I had to create a big scene and finally left home in order to have my own way about any-thing—what I wore, what I ate, what I thought, the career I wanted." As Diana talked, Bill was able to see that his insistence on her quitting her job cast him into her Dad's mold, in Diana's eyes.

These rather obvious interpretations of Bill's and Diana's dreams barely tap the reservoir of insights to be found in these imaginative creations of their sleeping minds. In later chapters, you'll learn how to understand every nuance of such dreams, and how to apply those decoding techniques to your own dreams. The important point here is that my students unanimously agree that their dreams are primarily helpful in the resolution of problems and conflicts—as Bill's and Diana's dreams so dramatically illustrate.

EARLY DIAGNOSIS OF PHYSICAL COMPLICATIONS. The next most frequent response was that dreams alerted the dreamers to physical symptoms of illness, usually before they had any idea of any such complications. Following are excerpts from dreams which gave such warnings to the dreamers:

- *Frank, 39-year-old appliance store manager*: Dreamed the store's walls collapsed . . . a refrigerator fell on top of me . . . couldn't get my breath . . . but I got out okay. The next day I developed a real cough and a chest cold.
- *Sarah, 30-year-old homemaker, Frank's wife*: The same night Frank dreamed about the store caving in, I dreamed I was in a meadow full of beautiful wildflowers . . . started sneezing uncontrollably. (In real life I've never had allergies to flowers.) A day later I came down with this awful head cold.
- *Tammy, 27-year-old actress*: (Worried I might be pregnant again, because my period was late.) Dreamed I was at the health club . . . started to dive into the pool . . . saw it was empty . . . stopped just in time. Couldn't figure out why my bikini bottom was wet when I hadn't gotten into the pool after all. Two days later, my period started.
- *Ward, 51-year-old winemaker*: I see what looks like an X-ray of my stomach . . . It's full of grapes and there are tiny little Italian peasant women stomping on them. One huge grape bursts. (Woke up with bad stomach pains and later found out I have an incipient ulcer.)

When we remember that the latest theory of the biology of dreaming says that our forebrains search from recent memories to find explanations for the impulses being sent from the lower brain, it seems logical that the most conveniently handy memories may be information about our bodies, which the brain is constantly monitoring. Thus, it is possible that our unconscious may know quite well the state of our health before we are aware of any dysfunctions or symptoms.

Frank's and Sarah's dreams gave them both warnings that respiratory infections were imminent. Several months later, Sarah called to tell me that another dream had warned her of a cold coming on. She'd taken large doses of vitamin C right away, and was convinced that this prevented her from becoming ill, although her husband Frank suffered again from a chest cold.

Tammy was one of the volunteers for my research of the dreams of pregnancy. After her baby was born, Tammy stayed in touch, giving reports of her progress and her dreams. "I don't want to have another child yet," she told me on the occasion of her dream of the empty swimming pool. "I think that dream was telling me that my womb, symbolized by the pool, is empty," she explained, "and the damp panties probably stood for my period, which started soon after I had that dream."

Ward, the winemaker, told our dream study group that he dreams frequently about grapes and bottles, as well as other accoutrements of his business. "So, at first I didn't understand the significance of the X-rays of grapes in my stomach," he said. "Then when my doctor ran tests and told me I was getting an ulcer, I immediately thought of that dream." Ward added that the "peasant grape stompers" in his dream may have symbolized the approach of the crushing season, when he usually experienced unhealthy stress. To break this cycle, he hired extra help and took a vacation during the crush. To his relief, Ward's next tests showed that his stomach was healed.

While the majority of the dreamers I questioned about the functions of dreaming believed that these are to help solve conflicts or problems and to warn them about impending illness, other responses included the gaining of new knowledge, revelations about past lives, development of psychic powers, and forecasts of future events. All these fascinating ways dreams may help us will be discussed in future chapters. After you learn how to decode the symbols of your own dreams, you'll learn how to use this information to enrich your emotional life and your romance.

Summary

This chapter has explained the latest thinking about the anatomy of dreaming and the functions of dreams. Although neuroscientists, psychobiologists, and dream psychologists have made considerable progress in their research, much about the causes and functions of dreaming remains a mystery.

Researchers now believe that dreams originate in the brain stem, located at the base of the skull just above the spinal cord. As we enter deep phases of sleep, the brain stem emits impulses which stimulate visual centers so that we "see" a veritable light show of shapes and colors. At the same time, the brain chemical acetylcholine inhibits body movement (with the exception of tiny actions beneath the eyelids, causing the Rapid Eye Movement or REM sleep which signifies that dreaming has begun).

Confronted with signals that we are seeing and feeling this activity, the upper brain "explains" these perceptions by creating a story or dream, based upon data drawn from its immense storehouse of memories. Since everyone's memories are different, each dreamer's images usually represent that person's individual lifestyle and experiences.

Other circumstances also affect dream content, including body state and outside stimuli occurring while the dreamer sleeps. Thus the dreamer's health (such as indigestion, menses, pregnancy, or even the onset of a bad cold) may be reflected in the dream narrative, as well as sounds such as ringing telephones, alarm clocks, or nearby voices.

Psychologists theorize that the functions of dreams are to make us aware of unexpressed emotions. My poll of dreamers reveals that they believe their dreams serve to resolve conflicts and problems, inspire creativity, warn them of impending illness, and provide new knowledge.

Before proceeding to the next chapter, take a few moments now to consider your own dreams in the light of this information. Then, read on to discover how you can recall more dreams and learn to relate them to your waking life.

Chapter
THREE

Translating the
Dream Language of Love

The best method for translating or interpreting your personal Dream Language of Love is "hands on" experience. No amount of attendance at seminars or study groups on dreaming, or even reading about dreams, can substitute for actually recording your own dreams and then examining them for the messages your unconscious is sending you.

This chapter will teach you:

- An easy way to remember your dreams
- Decoding dream hieroglyphics (symbols)
- Types of dreams you may have

Dream Recall

To fully comprehend the almost magical nature of your dreams, you must first be able to remember them. Even though most people accept the scientifically established evidence that every normal person dreams three to five times each night, many still insist that they never dream. In reality, these people are probably simply unable to recall dreams, and are missing both one of life's greatest pleasures as well as an easy way to achieve emotional growth and to enrich romantic communication skills.

There are a number of methods of dream recall recommended by psychologists. These include: having an observer awaken the sleeper after Rapid Eye Movement (REM) commences—the typical sleep laboratory technique; posthypnotic suggestion, either self-administered or provided by a professional hypnotist; audio taping of dream memories immediately upon awakening; and keeping a handwritten dream notebook, journal, or diary.

THE DREAM NOTEBOOK. By far the easiest and most effective method of dream recall is simply to *write it down* when you awaken. Although you can do this without any special instructions, you'll find it even easier if you follow the method I have developed with many clients and students. The easy directions we have found most effective are:

1. Purchase a loose-leaf notebook with ruled pages, and place it next to your bed with a pen or freshly sharpened pencil. Some people like to keep extra pages and pens in the bathroom or kitchen, for use at any moment they might spontaneously remember a dream.
2. Before retiring, write the date at the top of a page, and jot down any "unfinished business" from the day's events, or the residue of any unexpressed emotions you may have had. Dr. Gayle Delaney, author of *Living Your Dreams*, explains that this clears the mind and helps you focus on the dreams you anticipate. Also, tomorrow a review of your notes about yesterday's unresolved issues may help you interpret that night's dreams.
3. Now, write, "When I wake up, I will remember my dreams." Put aside your Dream Notebook and settle down for sleep.
4. If you're alone, repeat this sentence silently to yourself, over

and over: "When I wake up, I will remember my dreams." If your partner is beside you, and is sharing this adventure, you can whisper this sentence together as you drift off. Many people find that this is an effective way to put themselves to sleep. The repetitive sentence becomes a kind of "mantra" or hypnotic suggestion which quiets the waking mind and allows the unconscious to take over.

5. When you awaken, *try not to move*. Lie still, eyes closed, and review the memories and dreams uppermost in your mind. In *Creative Dreaming*, Dr. Patricia Garfield explains that the mere act of getting up quickly may place your mind in its alert, awake mode so that the night's messages may sink deeply and irretrievably into your unconscious.

6. Once you've fully reviewed your dreams in your mind, sit up slowly, open your eyes, and write down whatever you recall. If you remember more than one dream, number each one and describe each. Try to include as many details as possible about the setting, characters, and action. Pay special attention to any feelings you recall having during the dream, as well as the way you felt upon awakening.

7. If any element of a dream reminds you of something else in your life, jot that down in parentheses. For example: "a cat leaped through the window in my dream (it looked like a cat we had when I was a child)" or "the man in my dream looked like Johnny Carson (we were watching the Carson Show on TV just before bedtime).

8. Don't worry if time seemed distorted, or if any part of a dream seems absurd. This is the nature of dreams, which have little to do with the way we perceive things when we're awake.

9. Now, briefly note what you think the dream might mean. If your dreams seem totally incomprehensible, don't be discouraged. As you become more comfortable with this new language, and as you learn more about dream symbols, your inner self's messages will become easier to decode. Put your Dream Notebook aside, and come back to it later in the day for a fresh perspective.

If you've followed the above directions faithfully, and still remember nothing, don't give up. Give yourself a mental pat on the back for the effort, and try again tonight. It may take your unconscious several days to become convinced that you truly want to recall your dreams.

CONTACTING YOUR PERSONAL DREAM POWER. If you've attempted dream recall for a week and still have no memories, it's time to contact your "Dream Power." Even if you have no difficulties remembering dreams, this "mental imagery" may help you recall details more vividly.

Developed by British dream psychologist Ann Faraday, author of *Dream Power* and *The Dream Game*, this technique consists of: closing your eyes, relaxing by taking several deep, cleansing breaths, and then imagining that the part of your mind which dreams is a being or person. Accept whatever image may pop into your mind, no matter how unusual it may be. Some people "see" a godlike being. Others envision an elderly, wise counselor, an ordinary human, or sometimes even a talking animal. Whatever image comes to mind, name it your Dream Power and then ask it, "Why won't you allow me to remember my dreams?" If for any reason no image comes to mind, simply let your imagination roam until you think of what for you might be an ideal personification of a wise and powerful being.

At a time when my own dream recall was blocked, I tried this method and my Dream Power (a beautiful Grecian goddess) replied, "You do not give serious attention to my dream creations, so why should I let you recall them?" Next, I humbly asked my Dream Power to allow me to remember, and promised to respect and cherish my dreams. Since then, I've had no problem with dream recall.

After you envision your own Dream Power, accept whatever answer you imagine receiving. If your Dream Power does not give you an answer, proceed to tell it your resolve to give more serious attention to the dreams you're permitted to recall. You'll probably be amazed at the results.

For example, Frank had difficulties with dream recall until he tried this technique. (You may remember that it was Frank who thought initially that dreams arise from indigestion, and whose later dream of his store's walls caving in warned him of an oncoming chest cold.) When Frank rather reluctantly envisioned his Dream Power, he reported:

> I immediately got a flash of Uncle Jeremiah. He wasn't really my uncle. He was the janitor at my junior high school. I used to sneak down to his basement room whenever I felt scared or depressed. He seemed very wise and after being there awhile I went away feeling comforted. Today, I'd probably see him as an old bum, but then I really looked up to him. Anyhow, in my imagination I asked Uncle Jeremiah, "Why can't I remember my dreams?" and he said, "Become a child again, Frankie. Believe in magic and magical things will happen." I felt pretty silly, but that night instead of telling myself I'd remember my dreams, I said over and over as I fell asleep, "I believe in the magic of dreams." Next day, I woke up with a very clear memory of two very long, complicated dreams!

Once you've begun to remember your dreams, you'll be ready to begin translating them into the language of your waking style of thinking. Always bear in mind that your dreams appear as images and feelings, somewhat akin to a three-dimensional movie. Since your waking mind is constantly operating with a more logical, linear style, memories of the night's visions may at first appear illogical or as if they're filled with unintelligible hieroglyphics.

Translating Dream "Hieroglyphics"

When you translate the images of your dreams into words, you have created a *dream symbol*, and have found the "Rosetta Stone" which is the key to the language of your dreams. It's as simple as that. The difficult part is permitting your imagination to roam freely when you're awake, alert, and operating in a mode of thinking which tends to be unimaginative. To help you do this, I have devised the following easy, four-step procedure:

1. Parse your dream record
2. Note your associations to each dream element
3. Note your emotions during and after the dreams
4. Determine how these associations and feelings relate to your waking life

STEP 1: PARSING A DREAM. When you learn a new language, typically you converse in it, imitating someone who speaks it well; then, you learn the way sentences in the new language are structured—what your grammar teacher probably called "parsing." In a similar, yet much easier fashion, you can break down the structure of your dream records. This will help you highlight the important elements, avoiding the distraction of those descriptive words which may prevent you from grasping the essential meaning of the dream.

Please don't be put off by the school days sound of parsing. My method is much easier than what you may have experienced when trying to learn a foreign language such as Latin, Spanish, or French. All you need do is to circle all the important nouns in your dream report, and then underline all the action words (verbs). Later, as an additional refinement, you may wish to note words which modify these highlighted nouns and verbs, by marking them with arrows. For now, all you need do is to circle and underline your dream's main elements and action. For example, let's take Bill's dream of the little lost boy in the outdoor shopping pavilion, and parse it by circling its nouns and underlining its verbs:

I'm at an enormous, outdoor bazaar. It's arranged like a men's

clothing store, with very expensive items on display under colorful

canopies. There are thousands of people shopping and these

outdoor pavilions seem to stretch to the horizon. I'm shopping

for a new wardrobe and go from stall to stall, loading up with

many clothes to try on. There are these cabana-like booths for fitting rooms. I'm feeling excited and happy. It's like being at a fair or fiesta. There's music and free refreshments. I take my armload into a fitting room tent, and there's a little boy in there, crying. He's lost. I pick him up and go out to find a salesperson. I tell a white-haired woman who seems to be a manager about the boy and she just shrugs and says, "That's not *my* problem!" and walks away. I start yelling at her (and then I woke up feeling angry and frustrated).

Already you can see the bare bones of a story or plot for Bill's dream, simply by listing the circled and underlined words: I'm at a bazaar, with thousands of people, it stretches to the horizon, I'm happy and excited, shopping (for) a (new) wardrobe, loading up with clothes, feeling excited and happy. In a fitting room, there's a little boy, lost, crying. When I try to get help, a white-haired woman shrugs me off, saying it's not her problem. I yell at her, and awake feeling angry and frustrated.

STEP 2: ASSOCIATIONS TO EACH DREAM ELEMENT. After you've parsed your own dream record, let your imagination roam freely, and write down a "definition" or very brief description of each of the circled words. For example, here are Bill's associations to the nouns in his dream:

- *Bazaar*—a splashy display of all kinds of goods for sale; lots of people, bargaining for the best prices; or, maybe "bizarre" meaning strange or weird.
- *New wardrobe, clothes*—suits, shirts, shoes, socks, underwear,

everything I might wear; what's on the outside; maybe the way others see me; my lifestyle.

- *Fitting room*—a place to try on clothes, to see if they look and feel right, if they fit.
- *Little boy, lost, crying*—a helpless young male human; a male child who is scared, vulnerable, and lonely.
- *White-haired woman*—an elderly female whose age makes her get respect which she may not deserve; she may be a grandmother.

Notice that Bill had several associations to almost every dream element. As he proceeded to consider each of these possible meanings to find his personal dream symbols, Bill learned to eliminate the ones which did not seem to have any relevance to his waking life or his inner thoughts. In another dream, at another time, the same dream elements might suggest entirely different symbols. In other words, a symbol does not always mean the same thing, even to the same person.

STEP 3: EMOTIONS EVOKED BY THE DREAM. If you neglected to write down how you felt while the dream was in progress, look for clues in words you used to describe the nouns or verbs. Obviously, Bill was pleased with his dream surroundings, which were colorful and festive, until he found the lost little boy. When help was refused by the older woman, he felt angry and frustrated. Bill did not understand how important his dream emotions were, until he related the other dream elements to his conflict with Diana. After he'd done Step 4 of my interpretation process, he realized that his dream emotions were a direct parallel with those he felt both as a child and now, as he prepared for marriage with Diana.

STEP 4: HOW DREAM ASSOCIATIONS RELATE TO WAKING LIFE. At this point you'll need to stretch your imagination a bit further. Concentrate on the definitions or associations you've made to your dream elements and ask yourself if there is anything at all in your waking life which could also fit these descriptions.

For instance, when Bill tried this with his descriptions of the word *bazaar*, he told us, "It might fit our engagement, which has been sort of splashy with an old-fashioned announcement party. Most of our friends just live together and if they do get married, they skip the engagement part and just have a wedding—usually something simple. Diana and I have sort of put ourselves on display, being engaged. And, now we're both 'bargaining' about how the marriage will be. The new wardrobe is obvious—it symbolizes the new life I'm about to begin as a newlywed. As for the fitting room, I guess I'm 'trying on' my ideas with Diana right now, about the way I want things to be, such as her stopping work."

Bill had a bit more trouble relating the little lost boy of his dream to his current life, until Diana reminded him that he himself had felt lonely and vulnerable as a child, after his parents' deaths. "That's it!" Bill exclaimed. "And the white-haired lady who couldn't be bothered with the boy's problems symbolized my Grandmother, who had that exact attitude towards me!"

When you've discovered the true messages of your dreams, you're likely to react as Bill did, with a "Eureka! That's it!" type of response. Respect your dreams as creations of your personal, individual inner self, rather than relying on dream dictionaries or the interpretations others may try to impose. Once you've puzzled out the meanings of your own dream elements, those hieroglyphics should become intelligible. When you have assigned meanings to these elements, you have, in effect, created a *dream symbol*, and are well on the way toward becoming a skilled dreamworker.

By choosing the important parts of your dream and then determining the thought, feeling, or event your unconscious intended it to represent, you have not merely interpreted; you have, in fact, created a dream symbol unique to your personal, deeper consciousness.

For more practice in parsing and interpreting dreams, let's look again at the dream Diana reported around the same time Bill dreamed of the lost little boy:

(This is a recurring nightmare for the past several weeks. Each

time it's almost the same.) In this dream **I** wake up (actually, I was still asleep, dreaming), sensing someone is in my bedroom. Straining to hear and see, I can just make out the shadowy figure of a man coming closer to my bed. Then I realize it's someone familiar—for a moment it seems to be my Dad. I lie back down and relax but then, all of a sudden, the man looms over me and presses a pillow onto my face. I'm smothering! Can't breathe. I begin trying to push away the pillow and start screaming for help.

Then I wake up with my heart pounding and in a cold sweat.

You may recall that Diana told us she loved and trusted her Dad—yet she had to leave home at twenty-one in order to escape his control. "We're on speaking terms again," she told us, "now that I'm engaged. Dad has already let me know he thinks marriage will 'put a damper' on some of my ideas which he thinks are 'too pushy' for a woman."

Here are Diana's associations to the circled words in her nightmare:

- *My bedroom*: a private place where I can be myself without fears of disapproval.
- *Shadowy man's figure*: a male I can't see or make out too well.
- *Bed*: a soft yet firm place to rest and sleep; another private place.
- *My Dad*: my father, who gave me everything I needed and wanted as a child, but has never really accepted me as an adult.
- *Pillow*: a soft cushion meant for comfort, to rest your head upon—not to be used to smother you!

Diana summed up the plot of her dream this way: A man I can't make out too well comes into my bedroom and tries to smother me with a pillow. Screaming for help, I wake up. "If the man was my Dad," Diana told us, "this dream might be reflecting my fear that I can never get his approval unless I let him smother me."

When another group member asked Diana if the man could also stand for someone else in her life, some male she "cannot quite make out," she replied, "Well, it could be Bill, because sometimes I can't figure out his motives at all." Then she exclaimed, "That's it! This dream just shows that I'm really worried that Bill will turn out to be like my Dad, and will try to control me that same way."

By working together to understand their dreams, Bill and Diana were able to discover each other's "hidden agendas." Bill wanted Diana to be the mother he lost; she feared Bill would dominate her just as her Dad had done.

Once they understood that these opposite forces were working to destroy their relationship, this couple was able to resolve the conflict. Diana continued working for several years after their marriage, being careful to allow plenty of time in her busy schedule for "play," doing with Bill the fun activities he'd missed out on as a child. When she became pregnant, they both joined my dream study group for expectant parents. Then, Diana discovered that being pregnant changed her needs.

"Right now, I *want* Bill to 'smother' me, to pamper me," she told us. "The bigger my belly gets, the more helpless and vulnerable I feel, so it's really wonderful to lean on him." Bill agreed. "Up till now," he explained, "Diana has always noticed when the 'little boy' in me needed nurturing. Now, it's her turn and I love her depending on me." After their healthy baby boy was born, Diana decided to stay at home for a year. Then she resumed work part-time, and both she and Bill continue to share their dreams as a way of preventing misunderstandings.

Now, try your hand at my easy four-step process for translating your own dreams. After you've parsed a dream, circling the important nouns and underlining the verbs, list your descriptions of each of the elements. This process usually works best if you talk it out with someone else, especially with your mate. Another person can often lead you to a more imaginative association—and if the listener is your romantic partner, he or she may gain some valuable insights about both your feelings.

Types of Dreams

A general knowledge of the many types of dreams you may have can help you understand the messages your inner self is sending. Most dreams fall into these groups or categories:

- Daily reviews
- Problem and conflict solvers
- Affirmations and inspirations
- Negative issues, recurring dreams
- The nightmare
- Erotic dreams
- Paranormal dreams

THE DAILY REVIEW. Sometimes, dreams are merely a review of the day's events. For example, one evening after being annoyed by smoke from her next-door neighbor's barbecue, Diana dreamed her apartment was on fire. She dismissed this dream as inconsequential, merely a reflection of her irritation with her neighbor. (However, upon closer inspection, even these seemingly unexciting dreams may have hidden messages. Her apartment catching fire may have been a metaphor for Diana's fear that marriage to Bill would destroy her hard-won independence—a definite threat of destruction to the "place where she lived," or her strong identification with her single lifestyle.)

It's also advisable to remember that nearly all dreams begin with some reflection of "day residue," not only what we were thinking about as we fell asleep, but also any of the day's unexpressed feelings or uncompleted tasks or events. In *Dreamworking*, Dr. Stanley Krippner and Dr. Joseph Dillard point out that all dreams do not approach problems. Just as many of our waking thoughts are trivial, our dreams may reflect no more than an insignificant daily routine or casual idea. However, while most dreams seem to begin with reflections of this often banal day residue, be alert for shifts which may imply deeper, more important meanings.

Following are some excerpts from dream beginnings which indicate a daily review:

- *Monique, 28-year-old homemaker*: I was coming out of a su-permarket and found myself in the zoo instead of the parking lot. (Today I just barely got my grocery shopping done in time to take my Brownie Troop for a promised trip to the zoo.)
- *Claude, 30-year-old accountant, Monique's husband, the same night*: Dreamed our house had been burglarized, everything was a mess. (When I got home last night, found a lot of melted frozen foods on the kitchen counter where Monique had forgotten to put them away.)
- *Betsy, 23-year-old secretary*: Dreamt I was rushing, getting ready for a date . . . showering, discovered my whole body was covered with black ink that wouldn't wash off. (Had a really awful time at work today changing an old typewriter ribbon, got the ink all over myself.)
- *Hugh, 35-year-old construction crew boss*: Dreamed I was trying to fasten a sign outside the office but it kept falling down. (There was a minor earthquake yesterday afternoon while I was on a building site. No harm done except some loose boards and a sign rattled around in my truck.)

PROBLEM AND CONFLICT SOLVERS. This type of dream, rated by both psychologists and by my clients as one of the most important functions of dreaming, is not always easily recognized by the dreamer. Remember that dream researchers tell us our dreams are attempting to clarify unresolved emotions. Bearing this in mind, pay particular attention to the feelings your dreams reflect which may relate to some problem or conflict in your waking life.

Here are excerpts from several dreams which proved to be problem and conflict solvers:

- *Betsy (who dreamed of having an inky body, above)*: When I couldn't wash the ink off myself, I tried covering it with makeup . . . Nothing worked so when the doorbell rang I just opened the door and told my date, "What you see is what you get!" and he smiled.
- *Alan, 43-year-old journalist*: Driving on a steep, winding mountain road, feeling tense . . . Suddenly a huge semi was tailgating me and a slow minivan was just ahead . . . felt trapped.
- *Patty, 44-year-old social worker, Alan's lover*: A recurring dream about walking down a hallway and coming to a closed door . . . I'm afraid to go in there and I wake up.

Betsy, a Caucasian, thought her "inky" dream reflected her concern about an upcoming date with Richard, a black man. "He's very attractive and I really like him," she said. "I've been worried he won't find *me* as attractive as the black women he's used to dating. So I think this dream was telling me to stop worrying about such things as skin color." On their first date, Betsy told Richard about this dream and it served as an opening gambit for a lighthearted discussion about the issue of "mixed" couples. At this writing, Betsy and Richard are still going steady and plan to get married.

Sometimes a relationship conflict may be so unpleasant or uncomfortable that the dreamer is reluctant to face the issue. At such times, it may be difficult for the dreamer to make the necessary associations to the dream images which are offering a resolution or alternative course of action. If you find yourself in this type of impasse, it will usually be helpful if you can share your dream with a sympathetic person. If you're in the midst of a conflict with your partner, sometimes it helps to discuss your dreams with a third party, ideally a close friend who has a more objective view of your situation.

This was the case with Alan and Patty, who found themselves in conflict when Alan was offered a promotion involving transfer to another city. Patty had agreed to make the move, yet had not cooperated in the packing and planning. As the moving deadline approached, tempers flared and they talked of breaking up. When Patty described her recurring dream to her best friend Mary, at first she couldn't fathom what might be behind the dream's "closed door." With gentle prodding from Mary, Patty admitted, "I pretend to be adventurous, but really I hate doing anything new. Once I get comfortable in a routine, it actually scares me to make changes. And, whenever I have to do something new, I have this same dream." After this talk with Mary, Patty was able to explain to Alan her reluctance to move. It was then that Alan told her of his dream of being trapped on a mountain road.

"The semi truck, tailgating me, is probably my publisher, who's really pushing to get me to transfer to the paper's new out-of-town headquarters," Alan decided. "And, I guess the slow minivan is you, Patty, blocking me from moving ahead." Patty laughed. "That's me, all right—inching along in the same old rut!" Once this couple understood each other's Hidden Agendas, they were able to make the move they both really wanted. When anxieties loomed in Patty's mind, Alan was alert to her needs. After their move, Alan wrote me, "Now, when she gets a certain look on her face, sort of withdrawn and rigid, I know I'd better slow down, take time out to let her adjust."

AFFIRMATIVE AND INSPIRATIONAL DREAMS. Dreams can often help us find guidance, inspiration, and new confidence when we've chosen a difficult path of action. For instance, when Richard's parents voiced strong objections to his budding romance with Betsy because she was white, Richard had this dream:

The dream starts with me mowing the lawn at my Aunt Grace's estate. (Just today I was thinking I should trim the grass in front of our house, but I haven't been to Aunt Grace's big country place since I was a little kid.) Then across the fence that divides us from the neighbors I can see this beautiful garden, so I climb the fence and take some clippers out of my pocket. I want to cut one perfect rose, and start looking for it. Just as I'm about to cut this gorgeous pure white rosebud, Aunt Grace comes out and yells at me to get out of there. Her shouting startles me and I prick my thumb on a thorn. But I cut the rose anyhow, and climb back over the fence. "See," Aunt Grace scolds me, "you're bleeding. I told you never to cross that fence!" But I suck on my thumb and the bleeding stops. Then I take my beautiful rose in the house. As I'm smelling its wonderful fragrance, I wake up— feeling great.

It's obvious that Richard's dream of stealing a white rosebud symbolized his dating a white girl for the first time. Our dream study group helped Richard discover some other metaphors and puns in the dream: he leaves the "(es)state of Grace" and crosses the dividing line (fence) which has separated him and his family from whites (neighbors); and when hurt, he must comfort himself (sucks his thumb). Richard told us this dream reinforced his determination to continue his relationship with Betsy, despite his family's objections. He explained, "I'm sure this dream was my inner self telling me that, even though I may get 'pricked' a little, loving Betsy is worth it."

Carolyn and John, a couple in their early forties, also had dreams which affirmed their relationship. After they had just begun marital counseling, Carolyn described a dream in which she was outside her own body, peering down her esophagus.

"What amazed me, even as I was having this dream," Carolyn told us, "was the perfect ease with which I could do this. I could see right down inside myself without any effort or pain." She explained that, for years, she'd tried to persuade John to go with her for counseling. "Finally I just gave up," she said. "And now, after all this time, to my surprise, he suggested that we go. So, like in my dream, I'm now getting a look inside without any effort or pain." Carolyn thought this "out of body" dream experience was healing and affirmative.

During the same period, Carolyn's husband John dreamed about a local tomcat they'd nicknamed "Tuffy." John explained, "That cat is the terror of the neighborhood. Other cats avoid him, and he scratches or bites any people that get near. But in the dream, Tuffy jumped into my arms, let me stroke him, and even purred." Carolyn and John were highly amused by his dream of Tuffy, and thought it symbolized the way they were finally confronting issues in their relationship which had been "too tough to handle" before.

Sometimes dreamers who are experiencing stress in their waking lives receive helpful guidance from what they describe as religious or spiritual sources. These may be objects which take on a special significance, voices and music, or beings which may be humans, gods, or animals. Shortly after John's dream of Tuffy the tomcat, Carolyn dreamed of much larger cats:

It began on a busy street in Barcelona. The traffic was typically crazy, with double-decker buses, all kinds of cars and trucks racing by, much honking and shouting. But I was riding in the midst of all this on a little tricycle! Then I turned off onto a quiet side street and stopped at an empty courtyard which had a cyclone fence around it. I needed to get to the other side of the courtyard but it was filled with large, snarling cats of all kinds—panthers, cheetahs, lionesses (all the cats were females). I went into the area and began making gestures at the cats, telling myself I was "shamanizing" them. As I did this they became very docile and would lie down as I approached them. Then I came to a huge cat which refused to be tamed. She was unlike any feline I've ever seen—gray like a wolf, with a sleek pantherlike body. Long fangs. Hissing, very threatening. I was frightened until an old woman appeared and showed me how to tame the beast. The woman was very kind and wise and I woke up feeling as if I'd just had a deeply moving, spiritual experience.

When we discussed Carolyn's dream, she told us she thought it validated the emotional growth she'd been experiencing in recent months. The dream began by demonstrating her former, childlike self, trying to navigate through grown-up situations (in heavy traffic, on a tricycle). Next it depicted the second stage of Carolyn's life, as a young adult attempting to manage life with her wits (taming the ferocious cats). Finally, when she realized she didn't know how to cope, she discovered her inner strength (the wise old woman).

Maureen, the seriously ill woman mentioned in Chapter 2, had this inspirational dream in the hospital, the night before undergoing successful surgery:

At the start of this dream, I was at the body shop where Carl works. My wrecked car was there (the same one I dreamed about last week!). The whole place was full of cars that were broken and battered. I thought, well at least I have a lot of company. A really good technician was working on my car's engine and I watched for a while. Then I went to the cashier and asked her how long it would take to fix my car. She pointed to a door and told me to go in there to find out. Inside, it was like a little chapel with a stained glass window at one end. The window showed the Virgin Mary. I asked her, "Can they fix my car soon?" and suddenly she came to life and stepped down from the window! It was incredible! She came so close I could smell her scent (like roses) and I touched her long blue robes which felt like velvet. Then she stroked my face and said, "Be of good cheer. By this time tomorrow, your life will be in order." And I woke up, still feeling amazed and sort of prayerful.

Once again, Maureen dreams of wrecked cars, which represented to her the state of her health. This time, the setting is a "body shop"— an apt metaphor for the hospital. Maureen believed that her dream vision of the compassionate Virgin Mary helped her through the ordeal of surgery and her remarkably speedy recovery.

However, all dreams are not so positive or inspiring. This is logical when we remember that our dreams usually reflect the unresolved concerns and unexpressed emotions of our waking lives.

NEGATIVE ISSUES, NIGHTMARES, AND RECURRING DREAMS. When you and your partner ignore unpleasant or seemingly trivial matters, these are likely to be reflected in your dreams. If these negative issues seriously threaten the harmony of your lives, they may appear as nightmares which almost always demand your waking attention. If you have a recurring emotional problem, such as Diana's fear that all men would try to control her as her father had done, you may have a recurring dream every time this personality trait becomes active.

Following are excerpts which demonstrate these types of dreams:

- *Christine, 38-year-old recovering alcoholic*: The party we gave was a disaster . . . I sneaked into the bedroom and took a stiff drink of vodka. Woke up very scared.
- *Jason, 39 years old, Christine's husband*: Dreamt I was in a crowd on the street . . . a woman fell from a balcony twenty-one stories up.
- *Suzanne, 34-year-old artist*: Camping out in the wilds with Jerry and some others . . . Some strange dingo-like dogs are there . . . I befriend one . . . it projects a sense of trust to me (I feel love and warmth) and at the same time, a fierce "insane" quality (I feel terror).
- *Jerry, 42-year-old business consultant, Suzanne's lover*: People who are "friends" come out of our house. I know they are the "danger" we are fleeing, so I play friendly so they don't kill us.
- *Frank, the 39-year-old appliance store manager whose "Dream Power" was "Uncle Jeremiah"*: (A recurring dream that I'm in an earthquake, again after eating spicy foods.) I am shaken up but not hurt . . . See a woman close to the edge of a large crack in the street . . . Force myself to pull her to safety. Wake up feeling glad I did it and ashamed that I hesitated so long.

Christine, the recovering alcoholic, had been "dry" and just released from a twenty-one-day treatment program when she dreamed of sneaking a drink after trying to give a party which was a "disaster." The same night, her husband Jason dreamed of watching a woman fall from twenty-one stories above the street. (Note that Christine had been sober twenty-one days.) Both these dreams dramatically depict this couple's fears that Christine might relapse or "fall" back into her former addictive patterns.

Until they came to my group, neither had spoken about their anxieties. "I was afraid she'd think I don't trust her," Jason admitted when we discussed their negative dreams. On her part, Christine told us she'd been reluctant to confide her fears about a relapse, because Jason might think "all that money he spent on treatment was wasted." Once their anxieties were out in the open, this couple were able to give each other the loving support they both needed as Christine continued her recovery. Jason joined an Al Anon group where he met other spouses of alcoholics who shared his concerns. At this writing, Christine has been sober for nearly three years and their marriage is stable. "It's like falling in love all over again," Jason says. "Now she's like the girl I married, except she's become a woman."

Suzanne thought her dream of the wild, dingo-like dog symbolized her unconscious fear which she said "comes up around my doing things that a woman does to please a man. Like, I'm going to feed and nurture and love this friendly little ('male') dog and I fear (subconsciously) I'm about to be attacked (by the 'dark' side)." Suzanne's lover Jerry, on the other hand, had nightmares about possible, fatal danger from people pretending to be friends, as he tried to protect the woman he loved.

Both Suzanne and Jerry had histories of broken marriages and unhappy, painful love affairs. Very much in love, and determined to stay together, this couple took their dreams and nightmares quite seriously, using them as opportunities to confront the fears they'd come to expect because of previous failed relationships. Despite numerous tearful and argumentative episodes, they clung together and are now experiencing the joyous intimacy which can result from total communication and trust.

Frank and Sarah were another couple whose dreams served as an avenue to more open communication. Even though he now fully understood the most recent theories of researchers about the biological origins of dreaming, Frank still insisted his most vivid dreams occurred after he'd overeaten spicy foods. Moreover, these dreams could nearly always be classified as "recurring," because they usually began with an earthquake.

Frank is a Californian who lives near one of the more active faults, the site of frequent tremors, where "the big one" actually occurred in 1989. However, the other members of his dream study group, who lived in the same vicinity, rarely dreamed of earthquakes. Further, Frank claimed that he seldom if ever worried about the possibility of another such disaster.

When the group got Frank to parse his earthquake dreams and to tell us his associations, he said, "Earthquakes are when strong forces inside erupt. This causes everything on the surface to be shaken up—yeah, that's it! When I'm holding in some strong stuff, some feelings, then I try to stuff it down with spicy foods. Then, it all bursts out, into my dreams! No wonder I keep dreaming about earthquakes!" Even though some of the other group members didn't quite follow Frank's line of reasoning, this made perfect sense to him.

He next explained his latest earthquake nightmare, a portion of which is quoted above, by telling us, "Our marriage was about to be ruined, like that woman who was on the verge of falling into the crack when the quake opened up the ground behind her. And I just stood there, scared and resisting doing anything to save her, just like I acted so stubborn about coming to this group, or doing anything Sarah wanted that might help us get closer." Sarah interrupted, "And now, just the way you did in your dream, you've leaped to the rescue."

With his tendency to play devil's advocate and his initial skepticism, Frank injected a sense of balance into our group by constantly challenging all of us to be precise in our descriptions and theories. Then, when he began to recall and attempt interpretation of his own dream adventures, Frank's enthusiasm was all the more contagious. Beneath his blustering, Frank was essentially a shy, modest person, so that when he reported one of his "wet" dreams, the group felt that he had finally begun to trust us.

EROTIC DREAMS. When the topic of sexual dreams is mentioned, most people immediately think of the male, especially as an adolescent, having what is popularly called a "wet" dream. However, recent research indicates that women as well as men have sexual dreams from which they may awaken feeling aroused and sometimes orgasmic.

For instance, Lisa and Peter, whom we met at the beginning of Chapter 1, took special pleasure in telling each other their erotic dreams, and sometimes acting them out together. As our group got to know each other quite well over a period of months, Lisa told us about the first sexual dream she had after she met Peter:

Dreamed I was lying in my bed, masturbating. Then I realized Peter was in the living room and could see me through the open door, because I was reflected in the mirror opposite my bed. But I pretended I didn't know he was watching, and kept on caressing myself. When I was about to come, he came and got into bed with me, and I woke up still feeling really turned on.

You may recall that Peter told us that, when Lisa confided this dream to him, he "knew she was really serious." After they began living together, this couple frequently acted out Lisa's dream as a way of initiating their most passionate lovemaking.

After Lisa "broke the ice" by reporting her first erotic dream, Frank surprised us with this one:

Dreamed I was stretched out naked as a jaybird on some kind of padded table. I was in a hotel lobby and could see people coming and going in the distance, but they didn't notice me. Meanwhile four or five gorgeous dames were circling around me, flirting and looking me over. I had a big erection and they were admiring it! I didn't feel ashamed or anything like that, just very pleased with myself. Then they started getting closer, touching and trying to kiss me but I pushed them away. I said, "You can look all you want—but hands off! I wanta save this for Sarah." They laughed, saying I didn't say "tongues off" so they could kiss me, which they started to do. And then I woke up and remembered Sarah was away visiting her sister and I can tell you, I was darned disappointed!

When he told this dream, Frank got a big laugh from the group, and plenty of blushes from Sarah. Several weeks later, she told me what was already obvious—that she and Frank were experiencing a renewed vitality in their sex life. "Sometimes we even have dreams that are almost the same," she added.

These similar dreams between couples, which I call symbiotic dreams, seem to indicate a meeting of minds on a deep, unconscious level. Such dreams may fall into another, more thoroughly researched category, that of paranormal dreams.

PARANORMAL DREAMS. Webster's *Collegiate Dictionary* defines *paranormal* as "not scientifically explainable." Krippner and Dillard use the term "anomalous" to describe such dreams, which contain information not easily explained by scientific concepts.

Such dreams include those which seem to prophesy the future, "read" another person's mind, or deliver messages from the spirit world. Here are excerpts from apparently paranormal dreams from some of my clients:

- *Maureen, 42-year-old homemaker (who dreamed of the Virgin Mary before surgery)*: Dreamed I saw Mother . . . She was on crutches. (Next day we got word she'd broken her hip.)
- *Barry, 34-year-old homosexual hairdresser*: Dreamed I met this wonderful man named Edgar, dressed in black leather. (Soon after, I met Eddie, wearing the same outfit. Later he told me he'd been named Edgar and had changed it to Edward.)
- *Sean, 25-year-old Air Force pilot (who dreamed of finding his wife on a desert island, Chapter 2)*: When I was stationed in [the Middle East] dreamed I was part of a mission supposed to drop a rescue team to save the hostages in Beirut. We had to turn back because of engine trouble. (Next day, news of Lt. Col. Higgins' hanging came out. And I heard rumors about a failed rescue mission the day before.)

Most dream psychologists urge us to view such dreams with skepticism. In *Dreamworking*, Krippner and Dillard say there are five types of dreams which seem to predict the future: coincidental, inferential, self-fulfilling, pseudo-anomalous, and true anomalous dreams.

Using these criteria, Maureen's dream of her mother's broken hip may have been inferential. Maureen probably knew that women her mother's age often suffer from osteoporosis, a condition which makes them more prone to broken bones than younger women.

Barry's dream of meeting a man in black named Edgar may have been coincidental or self-fulfilling. The name is not unusual, and many men in the circles Barry frequents often wear black leather. When a prophecy is self-fulfilling, the dreamer may be unconsciously behaving in ways that make the dream appear to come true, so that Barry may have been unconsciously on the lookout for a man who fit his dream character.

Sean's dream of the airborne rescue mission may have been inferential. Certainly the service men at his overseas base were aware that such a mission might be attempted and that as pilots they might be involved. Sean may even have intuitively or unconsciously put together information which his mind somehow received without his awareness.

Unfortunately, some people exaggerate or lie about having paranormal dreams. This confuses the issue and is not easily discovered by researchers. Their motives may be simply to get more attention, to convince others they have "psychic" powers—or they may not even be consciously aware they are straying from the truth. Such fabricated dreams fall into the "pseudo-anomalous" category.

On the other hand, prophetic and telepathic dreams may very well be actual instances of truly anomalous phenomena. Only the dreamer can truly determine this. If you believe you've had a paranormal dream, after examining it with all the above criteria, you may be one of those rare individuals who are able to tap into a special source of creativity and knowledge.

Summary

In this chapter, you learned simple ways to recall and record your dreams. The easiest method is to keep a dream notebook. After jotting down any "unfinished business" of the day, place your notebook nearby, turn out the lights and settle down for sleep. As you drift off, repeat to yourself, "I will remember my dreams." Upon awakening, lie still, eyes closed, as you mentally review any memories. Then sit up slowly and write down all the details you can recall. If this method brings no results after a week or so, try visualizing your "Dream Power," asking for help in remembering your nightly visions. Once your unconscious is convinced that you're serious about studying your dreams, the memories will usually begin to flow.

Next, you learned how to begin translating the Dream Language of Love by organizing the structure of a dream report ("parsing") and then using your powers of imagination to assign meaning to dream elements, thus creating dream symbols which are unique to you as the dreamer.

To parse your dream reports, all you need do is highlight its principal nouns and verbs (circle the main characters and objects, underline the action words). It's also important to note the emotions expressed or implied in the dream. An easy way to discover the meaning of the highlighted words in your dream is to define each one, allowing your imagination to freely associate to any ideas which may arise as you try to define the words. Finally, connect these associations to events, ideas or people in your waking life. For instance, the word *bazaar* suggested to Bill a display as well as a place to bargain. In his waking life, Bill thought his engagement was a "display" or public announcement. Further, he and his fiancée were "bargaining" about the lifestyle they planned to have after marriage.

As you began to practice these simple translation methods, you also learned that your dreams may be of infinite variety, although they can generally be classified into several groups. These include daily reviews, problem and conflict solvers, affirmations and inspirations, negative issues and recurring dreams, nightmares, erotic dreams, and paranormal or anomalous dreams. Frequently, one dream may qualify for two or more types, such as Diana's dream of being smothered by a male or father figure, which was both recurring and nightmarish.

To further understand your own and your partner's dreams, it also helps to realize that each dreamer's unique personality traits are reflected in her or his sleeping visions. In future chapters, you'll learn more about the ways dreams can be as individual as fingerprints or snowflakes.

Chapter
FOUR

Dream Clues for Finding Your Ideal Mate

"He was the man I'd always dreamed of meeting."
"The first time I saw her, it was like a dream come true."
"On our very first date, I knew we were meant for each other."

All of us have heard or even made such statements. Yet all too often the intimate connection everyone needs and wants is elusive—or the cost of achieving it seems too risky or emotionally painful.

How do we know whether the person who "makes the juices flow" will in fact be someone we'll love forever, "till death do us part"? Just what is "true love"? How can we avoid choosing the same kind of partner who betrayed or hurt us in the past?

After exploring the meaning of "true love," this chapter provides some answers to these age-old questions, and shows you how to use your dreams to understand:

58

- Gender differences
- Differences caused by transitions, background, and value systems
- Extraversion-introversion
- Right- or left-brain types

After you've learned the many ways an infinite variety of traits, characteristics, moods, and emotions are portrayed in dreams, we will discuss the influence our parents' personality types may have on our choice of lovers. Then, there will be a brief overview of the tests and measurements psychologists use to determine categories of temperaments.

Additionally, you can try my Quiz for Identifying Personality Types—an easy, amusing way to discover your tendencies toward the numerous modes of thinking and relating. Even though most people discover they have the traits of more than one category, simply becoming aware of the ways we develop so many qualities can help you and your lover understand and accept each other's differences.

What Is "True Love"?

The word *romance* originated when brave knights aspired to "courtly" love, the love of a fair damsel—who was typically married to a nobleman, the knight's superior. In medieval France, when bards sang ballads of these courtly love affairs in which the knights aspired to noble deeds for the love of an unattainable lady, these songs were called *romans*. Hence, in olden times, the idea that romance does not include sex was held in favor.

However, modern lovers, especially in America, cling to an almost sentimental belief that romance, true love, and sex are one package which will magically happen and will last forever. Sadly, when the sparkle and tingle of the unknown are replaced by familiarity, when that "being in love" passion subsides, we often find ourselves committed to another person with whom we have little in common.

Dr. Paul Pearsall, author of *Super Marital Sex*, describes "falling in love" or "being in love" as an unstable, rarely meaningful, intense mood change caused by another person. Dorothy Tennov, author of *Love and Limerence—The Experience of Being In Love*, describes "limerence" as vacillating between elation and melancholy because of another person. Dr. Pearsall goes on to say that being "in love" or limerence is usually more lust than love and is a one-dimensional state which rarely lasts more than a few months.

Yet true, lasting love between a man and woman (and frequently, nowadays, between homosexuals) does not exclude lust and sex. Pearsall uses the analogy of clouds and sky—the two are different, yet one could not exist without the other; they are part of the same system just as are love and sex.

In *A Conscious Person's Guide to Relationships*, Ken Keyes, Jr., and his wife Penny Keyes say, "Although romantic love is a great feeling, building a relationship on it is like building a house on quicksand—the foundation is not stable." These counselors hold that unconditional love is what gives a relationship its stable foundation, its lasting quality. They define unconditional love as the ability to continue loving your partner no matter what happens, no matter what the conditions may be.

On the other hand, Alexandra Penney, author of *How to Make Love to Each Other*, claims that "the physical/emotional part of a relationship is one of the strongest foundations of true and lasting intimacy." Dr. Pearsall agrees, saying that love, the feeling and behavior of bonding, is ideally expressed between adult partners in sexuality, the physical, merging part of love.

In "How Do You Build Intimacy in an Age of Divorce?" an article for *Psychology Today*, journalist Carol S. Avery contrasts study after study of divorced couples and stable marriages. She concludes that "love flourishes in a mutual universe of shared secrets, deep understanding, complete acceptance."

From all these sources, we can conclude that true love depends upon (1) trust that arises from deep, honest communication between partners, (2) a commitment to stay together and make it work, and (3) the ability of both partners to keep the fires of passion and sexuality alive between them. You can use your new dream interpretation skills to reinforce all these goals. Further, as you and your partner become adept at advanced methods of dream control, you can use your dreams to keep romance and passion alive.

At this point, you may be wondering how you can begin, when you may not yet have found a partner or even a prospective one. Perhaps you're like Sharon, described in Chapter 1 as never meeting the man of her dreams. Or like Bruce, another of my clients, who complained that he continually chose women who betrayed his trust or turned out to be types who always wanted to change him. "Every time," he complained, "it starts out with her adoring me, almost to the point of worship. And I usually begin with the same feelings. Then, after a few weeks (once, it was actually three whole months!) she starts being critical and finally ends up nagging me until I break it off." When Sharon and Bruce learned to recognize their own needs and those of others by understanding how dreams could help them identify personality types, they discovered new tools which helped them find compatible partners.

Vive La Difference!

If all women and all men had the same temperaments, what a dull world this would be! So, instead of complaining that we cannot find a lover who agrees with us, a better course may be to enjoy the fact that humankind offers so much variety. Then, finding our true lover becomes a joyous adventure, one of discovering the many ways another person totally unlike ourselves can introduce us to experiences we might never have had otherwise. And on our part, we can have the thrill of sharing our own favorite things with one who may never have been aware these activities could be so enticing.

Since dreams mirror almost every aspect of the dreamer, it's possible to discover many of these delightful differences in temperament and tastes by examining dreams. For instance, dreams may reveal a person's sex, whether they're extraverts or introverts, right- or left-brain-dominant types, even moral values and sexual preferences. Understanding all these aspects of your own and a partner's personality can help you choose a mate who meets your needs as well as accept another's traits which may be different from your own.

Gender Differences

At a symposium on women's dreams, psychologist Dr. Patricia Garfield commented, "The Chinese have a saying: same bed, different dreams." Garfield's *Women's Bodies, Women's Dreams* adds new information to the data dream researchers have already amassed regarding the differences between male and female dreams.

RESEARCH INDICATES DIFFERENCES. Decades of investigations have consistently shown that women's and men's dreams are dissimilar. For instance, Garfield says that men's dreams often contain more unfamiliar characters, take place outdoors more often, and have more themes of aggression, competition, and violence than do women's dreams. Women's sexual dreams are more often with familiar men, whereas men are more likely to dream of sex with strangers, or sometimes even "faceless" women.

In 1971, Dr. Robert Van de Castle reported that women are more likely to dream about cats, and men about birds—while both sexes dream equally about horses and dogs. In 1984, Garfield's investigations for *Your Child's Dreams* revealed that, by the age of six, girls dream about both men and women, whereas boys dream of fewer people, with most of these being women. Young children of both sexes are more often victimized in their dreams, which are shorter and less complex than the dreams of teenagers or adults.

Van de Castle also reported the distinct qualities of women's dreams during menstruation, while Garfield's 1988 book provided more examples of the ways women's dreams change during their reproductive cycles. My own 1986 research of dreams during pregnancy revealed that expectant mothers' dreams are different from any other maturational phase. Thus, experts can usually tell from the content and general feelings expressed in a dream whether it comes from a male or female, and often can even make a well-educated guess as to the stage of life the dreamer was experiencing at the time of the dream.

When we realize that dreams reflect the personality and lifestyle of the dreamer, it's not surprising that gender differences are apparent. However, these differences are only partly explained by cultural attitudes. For instance, the dreams of "liberated," successful career women often differ markedly from those of successful businessmen. Garfield theorizes that basic dream characteristics occur because of specific physiological characteristics, especially those caused by hormonal changes.

DIFFERENCES DO NOT IMPLY SUPERIORITY. As I have already described in some detail in this book's Preface, research by neuropsychiatrists and psychologists reveals that the thought processes of each sex are different. This should in no way distress feminists or proponents of sexual equality, because it does not imply gender-based superiority. Rather, it simply means that, because of an intricate interweaving of many factors—hereditary, genetic, biological, environmental or cultural, as well as the influences of family, parental, and societal conditioning—each sex appears to use different approaches to problem solving and different thinking processes in most situations.

As a matter of fact, it has been my observation that these distinctions are somewhat less marked today than they were even three years ago, during the time of Garfield's research. As the traditional limits or boundaries of so-called male and female roles are becoming blurred by the advent of women into jobs formerly held only by men, and as men accept and attempt to adapt to these changes, our dreams are reflecting these expanded boundaries. However, the biological forces which influence much of our thinking and our dreams are not likely to change, regardless of the tasks each sex may learn to perform.

DIFFERENCES CAN HELP YOUR RELATIONSHIP. Considering that the thought processes of each sex are different, that our bodies are so unalike, and that many of us are still taught from childhood onward that "feminine" and "masculine" behaviors are so different, it's not surprising that our nation's divorce rate is so high. Yet these very differences invoke mystery and fear of the unknown, which may be the cause of those weak knees and palpitating hearts which often typify a budding romance. Moreover, the very qualities which make us different can contribute to a sense of balance in our lives, a feeling of wholeness rarely possible in any other way.

For example, Frank, our dream group's "cynic," had a stability and a tough, somewhat macho strength which his wife Sarah lacked. This reassured her, providing a kind of security she'd never experienced before they met. Sarah explained, "Whenever there's a crisis or any practical problem, I can depend on Frank to keep his head and see us through." On his part, Frank was uncomfortably aware that he needed to develop his more tender, sensitive side—traits he felt Sarah had in abundance. He commented, "She brings beauty and poetry into my life, and makes me take time to 'stop and smell the roses.'"

However, Frank and Sarah hadn't always seen their differences as providers of balance for their relationship. When they first came to my group, Sarah told me, "When we were dating, and for a while after we got married, I looked up to Frank and had that adoring, in-love feeling about him. Then I found out he just didn't like many of the things I enjoy. That turned me off, and I started to feel more inferior than ever. I was about ready to leave him, when he agreed to make an effort to understand where I'm coming from." Frank added, "Guess I couldn't stand the thought of losing her, so I was willing to try anything. Now, we go to the opera and ballet—and I actually like it."

USING GENDER DIFFERENCES TO PROMOTE UNDERSTANDING. Just as this couple courageously confronted their differences, you can achieve a better understanding of your partner's feelings and needs— as well as your own—by paying closer attention to your physical state when you dream.

In *The Psychology of Dreaming*, Dr. Robert Van de Castle describes his studies of the dreams of a group of women with the same educational background and in the same age group. During menstruation, these women's dreams depicted men as unfriendly or even hostile. At other times, male characters were attractive and friendly.

Garfield notes that during the ovulation phase, women's dreams often have images of babies, eggs, jewels, and round or fragile things.

During my research for *Pregnancy and Dreams*, some of the most beautiful dream reports appeared to indicate conception.

For instance, a couple who owned a vineyard had been trying to conceive for several months. Then the wife dreamed they were in the vineyard, noting with disappointment that the harvest was poor. The dreamer looked down to see large bunches of grapes growing from her belly. She called to her husband, "Honey, our vines may not have grapes, but I do!" She believed she had conceived just prior to this dream, and in fact her doctor told her the next month that she was pregnant at last.

Following are excerpts from dreams reported by other women during various phases of their cycles:

- *Marcia, Herb's wife, on the 2nd day of menstruation*: Dreamed Herb and his poker buddies locked me in the bedroom . . . I was crying and had a lot of bruises. (Herb has never hit me, in real life.)
- *Rosemarie, Jim's wife, 2 days postmenstrual*: We were at a wonderful ball . . . I was so popular, many men danced with me . . . next scene, Jim and I were making love and I had several incredible orgasms . . . Jim was so gentle and sweet.
- *Margo, the Air Force pilot's wife, 14 days after her period (probably ovulating)*: Opened my jewelry box and saw . . . all kinds of expensive, rare gems and jewels . . . one was a large pink pearl as big as a marble.
- *Ingrid, in her 5th month of pregnancy*: Trying to convince my husband our dog was hurt . . . it's head had been cut off . . . I gave the head to Curtis (my husband).

Marcia's menstrual nightmare of being attacked by her husband and his buddies may have been influenced by her physical state, since many women dream of unfriendly or hostile males during their periods. However, when she had this dream, Marcia was also quite troubled by her belief that "all men feel they're superior to women, and treat us accordingly."

Rosemarie, on the other hand—who also complained about her

"controlling" husband—dreamed that he'd become a sensitive, gentle lover. Further, the men in her wonderful party scene were also gratifyingly attentive. When this dream occurred, Rosemarie and Jim were still trying to resolve their conflicts. "This dream turned us both on when I told him about it," she confided, "and discussing it as a dream made it easier for me to tell Jim what I really like in bed."

Margo's dream of the huge pink pearl is an excellent example of Garfield's description of typical ovulation dreams. This may have been her dreaming mind's way of reflecting the fact that an egg or ovum (the pearl) was ready and awaiting fertilization.

Ingrid's dream of the decapitated dog (probably a symbol of her unborn child) may have been a reflection of her quite normal fear that the baby might not be healthy—a typical concern of expectant parents. She also thought this dream reflected her resentment of her husband's refusal to take seriously her worries and her discomfort as her abdomen grew larger. "In my dream," she said, "I finally got his attention by showing him that our beloved pet dog had really been injured. I just want him to show an equal concern about my pregnancy."

With our group's encouragement, Ingrid began telling her husband about her dreams. "When he heard the one about our dog being hurt, he really got upset," she told us. "Somehow, after that, his attitude changed and he started being really supportive. He's even started telling me his dreams, and now I realize he's just as scared about having a baby as I am."

HOW GENDER DIFFERENCES CAN HELP MEN UNDERSTAND. When a woman's dreams reveal that she's feeling aggressive or hostile toward men in general, or perhaps her mate in particular, he can feel reassured by knowing that her dream's antagonism may be a reflection of her physical state rather than indicative of actual rejection. Does her dream notebook from this time last month contain similar emotions? Do her dreams about two weeks later (during ovulation) portray more loving feelings? If so, these negative dreams may be responses to physical states.

If her hostile dreams appear to have little relationship to her cycle, they may very well be mirrors of unexpressed anger and should be discussed. In this case, she should be encouraged to voice whatever resentments are surfacing in her dreams. Even then, it's possible that the unloved male characters in her dreams may be depicting some troubling aspect of herself, rather than her partner. In any event, these are occasions where listening attentively and nonjudgmentally can help you both resolve differences which otherwise may become insurmountable barriers to trust and intimacy.

WOMEN CAN USE GENDER DIFFERENCES, TOO. In a like manner, when a man's dreams cast him as an aggressor, his partner should be aware that most men's dreams contain elements of belligerence or competition, and that these feelings are not necessarily directed at her. Further, if his dreams portray him making love to another woman, remember that this is also typical of most men, who frequently dream about unfamiliar sexual partners. Only by listening with an uncritical attitude can you hope to discover his associations to these seeming infidelities or promiscuities.

Such dreams may hint that he's longing for some type of sexual activity you haven't experienced together. Or, they may symbolically represent some type of "union," fusion, or cooperation which has nothing to do with sex. Perhaps some aspect of his personality which has been distressing in the past is now becoming resolved so that his dreams reflect feelings of unity and oneness, represented by the mating or union of himself and another person. For example, Frank had this dream after Sarah had persuaded him to attend a ballet:

Walking along a crowded city street, I saw a woman in a ballet costume. She was all in pink, with shiny tights and satin toe shoes. As I got closer, I saw little blond curls falling down onto her neck from her pinned up hair and I started feeling turned on. The sight of her neck and shoulders was so beautiful it made me dizzy! Felt this strong urge to touch her and I remember thinking I shouldn't be doing this, but I went right up behind her and put my arm around her waist. I could see this made her tremble and even though her back was to me, I could see she was crying. I told her I didn't mean to hurt her and began kissing the nape of her neck, which smelled wonderful, warm and flowery. We moved into a doorway and began kissing. It was real passionate! Couldn't see her face as it was dark but I felt I knew her very well. Then we both got so worked up we went on into the lobby of this apartment building, lay down on a sofa, and [had intercourse]. I came and just before I woke up I was whispering to her that I loved her so much, she was like a part of me. Then I woke up and felt pretty darn guilty, like I had actually cheated on Sarah, which I'd never ever do. What bothers me is that I never even saw her face!

As our group discussed his dream, encouraging Frank to make associations to its major elements, he realized that the ballerina symbolized his own feelings of sensitivity. "She was so delicate," he told us, "the slightest touch seemed to hurt her until she got used to me. And I guess I felt like that when we left the ballet that night. Like I'd cry when Sarah just held my hand, even though I felt real happy."

His wife Sarah agreed that Frank was beginning to acknowledge a more gentle side of himself—which he pictured as being feminine. "So the dancer in his dream was maybe that side of him," she said, "and now I think I'm really hearing Frank for the first time. This makes a lot of things click into place. Like the way he used to make such a fuss about trying out these things I like. Maybe he was afraid they'd make him cry! And, when he was so concerned about hurting the woman in the dream, I felt really moved, touched—not at all jealous." At this point, Frank told her, "We're not so far apart, after all. Guess we just have different styles."

Differences Caused by Transitions, Background, and Value Systems

Some of the impulses or drives which seem to compel us to be attracted to specific types are the result of stress. Sometimes, unconsciously seeking relief from tension or emotional pain, we may rush pell-mell into a relationship we might otherwise avoid. Such influences become especially noticeable whenever we make changes, and can affect the way we feel toward others and ourselves.

It's possible to find clues to your own and your partner's emotions and moods in your dreams, and then to postpone important decisions until you've regained equilibrium. When unexpected reactions cause conflicts, dreams can provide insights into both your own and your partner's attitudes.

Fatigue, stress, and aging often have marked effects on the dreams of both sexes. Some transitions may appear unimportant, temporary, or even beneficial, such as moving or renovating a home, losing a job, getting a promotion or new job—yet these changes frequently cause anxiety and will be mirrored in our dreams.

The dreams of stressed, divorcing people usually reflect the underlying causes of both timid and hostile behavior during these often traumatic changes. These fears and resentments may linger in the unconscious even when we believe we've resolved these concerns.

Further, when two people grew up in different subcultures such as different religious or racial backgrounds, the resulting ethical and moral positions may put them at odds until they learn to respect each other's value systems. By examining your own and your partner's dreams, you can discover clues to behavior and attitudes which may have nothing to do with your love for each other. Once this is understood, it should be easier to help each other accept the inevitable—and you'll often become closer in the process.

THE EFFECTS OF STRESS ON DREAMS. Both men and women have dreams reflecting anxiety, tension, and stress. Although anxiety is of a psychological nature, its effects often result in physical dysfunctions, including headaches, nausea, and rises in blood pressure. Sometimes these states appear in our dreams even when we're not consciously aware that we're experiencing anxiety. These may be instances of denial or repression, a fear of admitting that some circumstance or problem bothers us, or we may simply be preoccupied with other matters and not taking the time to monitor our bodies for signs of stress.

Such was the case with Peter after he and Lisa moved from San

Francisco to New York. Peter wrote, "Everything went so smoothly. We found a loft that's perfect for my studio and our living quarters. Even plenty of room for a nursery when the baby comes. Met some terrific new friends, tenants in the same building; they're expecting too. My assignment, an enormous mural, is going well. So I was surprised when I started having nightmares." Here's an example from Peter's notebook:

> Working on my mural, installing the first panels in the building, which was still under construction (in real life, it's finished and they've already moved in). Our next-door neighbor was the foreman and he told me I'd have to wear a hard hat and a gas mask. This made it tough for me to line up the panels correctly. I was on a high scaffold and had to yell to the crew below, directing them to move the panels, and they couldn't hear me through the mask. I took it off and Johnny blew a whistle, motioning me to put it back on. I yelled that we needed a walkie-talkie. Then I was on the ground, still arguing with Johnny. His wife Laurie was standing there, holding a baby. I said, "But your baby isn't due for months," and then I knew I was dreaming. Johnny then told me I'd better obey the rules. He showed me his hand, which only had four fingers, no thumb. Then Laurie held up their baby's hand and it had no thumb, either. I kept thinking this was only a dream but I couldn't seem to change it or understand what it meant. Also, my head was throbbing because of the hard hat. The headache got worse. Tried to take off the hat and it was stuck. Could feel my head swelling and woke up panting, in a sweat, with a splitting headache.

Peter thought this scary dream revealed that he'd been experiencing tension about all the important changes in his life. The move, new job, and the prospect of being a father were taking their toll on both his emotional equilibrium and his health. He thought the dream also revealed his unexpressed worry that the baby might not be healthy (symbolized by the missing thumbs on Johnny and his baby). After discussing his nightmares with Lisa, Peter commented, "I'm usually the one who's 'laid back,' not letting anything bother me, so I had a hard time accepting the fact that I, of all people, was getting strung out. So, we took a few days off and went to the country. Came back feeling rested, and—no more headaches, or nightmares either."

By paying close attention to each other's dreams, Lisa and Peter had learned special nuances of sensitivity to one another's needs. Following are excerpts from other couples' dreams which indicate symptoms of stress:

- *Carl, the 45-year-old mechanic, Maureen's husband*: Dreamed I was in a mental ward as a patient . . . I struggled but they put me in a straitjacket. (Woke up with my stiff neck really hurting.)
- *Maureen, during recovery from surgery*: Walking through a shopping mall, looked down and saw the seams of my dress had come apart and people were laughing. (Woke up to see my sutures had opened and I was bleeding.)
- *Betsy, engaged to Richard*: Lost control of my car and couldn't steer out of the way . . . A big truck was coming right at us. (Woke up feeling sick, nauseous.)
- *Richard, the same night*: Dreamed I was falling . . . could see a pit of hissing, poisonous snakes at the bottom. (Awakened with heart pounding, hyperventilating, a really bad anxiety attack.)

Carl explained that he'd gotten a glimpse of the hospital's mental ward while visiting his wife Maureen the day before he had his nightmare of the straitjacket. He admitted that his tight neck muscles had been bothering him for several weeks. However, between working and trying to run the household in Maureen's absence, he didn't take care of this annoyance. The result was that, once Maureen recovered, their doctor prescribed a neck brace so that Carl had to take time off from work. "Guess if you don't pay attention when you need a rest, your body will *make* you do it," he told us.

However, Maureen's nightmare served a better purpose by awakening her to the fact that her wounds needed immediate attention.

"Evidently I'd been so worried about what the biopsy might show, my blood pressure went up and somehow I strained so much the sutures broke," she said. "If I hadn't waked up and called for the nurse when I did, I might have lost a dangerous amount of blood. As it was, no great harm was done."

Betsy's and Richard's nightmares occurred the day before they planned to visit her parents, who strongly objected to their romance. "We'd both been pretending this prospective visit didn't bother us," Betsy said. "Then these awful dreams made it clear we were both secretly tense, to put it mildly!" Richard added, "So we postponed the trip. Decided not to go at all unless they become more friendly. It just wasn't worth putting ourselves through all that stress."

DREAMS OF AGING. Both sexes have dreams which depict the physical onset of aging. However, these may not be as nightmarish in quality as one might expect. Hartmann comments that, in healthy elderly people who do not have a history of frequent frightening dreams, nightmares may actually decrease with age. However, he notes two exceptions: cases where medications may stimulate nightmares, and cases of severe depression such as that associated with certain infirmities or with the isolation which unfortunately overtakes many elderly people.

Garfield notes that the older woman probably has more changes to face than at any other time in her life. These may include declining health, grief over loss of a spouse, deterioration of housing conditions, and worry about her grown children's problems.

Elderly men also face many of the same issues, which can give rise to a bewildering array of choices and transitions. Additionally, after age sixty-five, most men must confront retirement and the possibility that withdrawal from the business world may cause them to feel useless, isolated, or depressed.

On the other hand, men and women who developed strong self-esteem, good health habits, and coping skills in their earlier years frequently welcome the new freedom that comes with fewer responsibilities and more time to spend on leisure activities.

Whether they are troubled or happy in their later years, the new lifestyle is reflected in their dreams. For example, Georgia and Alec, a couple in their late seventies, joined one of my dream study groups in their search for a better understanding of their inner life. "Georgia always wanted to explore the meaning of dreams," Alec told us, "but we never had time, before. Now, we're beginning to realize how much we've missed by not doing more such things together." Alec reported this dream while they were planning a trip to France:

I was on the beach at the French Riviera (saw a poster of that scene recently when I was at the travel agent's office). Looked down at my body and saw it was like I used to be, trim and muscular, wearing a very brief bathing suit. All around me were these gorgeous dames. Many were nude, and others wore only those little string bikini bottoms. Began getting aroused and was embarrassed, so turned over on my stomach to hide the bulge! Only then did I notice Georgia was there on the towel next to me. She was also topless and also looked younger. What a sight! Beautiful! She smiled and told me maybe we're getting too old for such things. I grabbed her hand and ran with her into the sea, which was pleasantly warm. We were romping around in the surf when I saw we were both our real age again. And I was covered with dirt and mud. Tried to wash it off and thought I needed some soap. Then I woke up.

Alec, who bikes and jogs on a daily basis, thought his dream portrayed his frustration with his aging body. "It takes double the effort to keep in shape after forty-five or fifty," he said. "And the funny part is, inside, I feel the same—just as young and just as in love with Georgia as ever." As we discussed his dream, Alec realized it also revealed his continuing need for sexual intimacy. "When I was younger," he said, "I thought no one over fifty had sex, and any guy who did was 'a dirty old man.' So there I was, in my dream, old, dirty and muddy—and horny!"

During her husband's recital, Georgia was smiling and blushing. However, her modesty hadn't prevented her from doing her homework on the topic of sexuality in the elderly. "Masters and Johnson say that both men and women should have sex until they're just too feeble to do it," she told us. "It keeps us happy and fit," she went on, "but I read that men may lose their libido, and may need a doctor's help, especially if they're on medication. Thank the Lord, my Alec is okay in that department!"

Charlotte, a widow in her sixties, had dreams of a different nature, which mirrored her concern with declining health. The following dream occurred several days before Charlotte fell and broke her hip:

> Had a long dream about being in church. At first it was the usual service, hymns, sermon, and so on. Then the preacher asked us all to come down front to pay our respects to the deceased, and I saw there were about a dozen or more coffins behind him. I thought, oh no, I simply cannot go look. Maybe somebody I know is in those caskets. Maybe even me! So I sneaked out. As I was going down the front steps, suddenly the banister gave way. It fell off. I went to the other side to hold on and that banister fell off, too. Then I fell. Could see the ground a long way off and was trying to hang onto something, anything, to stop falling. Woke up terrified.

Charlotte feared that this dream was a prophecy of death—either of some friend or herself. Dreams of funerals or coffins rarely predict the death of the dreamer or a loved one; it's more likely they may be warnings of declining health, or perhaps the end of a lifestyle. A few days later, when Charlotte actually fell and suffered a fractured pelvis, physicians told her she was in the early stages of osteoporosis, a disease which affects elderly women whose levels of the hormone estrogen are not high enough for them to absorb enough calcium, so that their bones break easily. Tests also showed that Charlotte's fall may have been an early warning of an impending stroke. Thus, her accident may have been a blessing in disguise, since it alerted Charlotte's doctor that she needed a change in diet and medication.

All these examples of the ways dreams show the effects of physiological states also demonstrate how closely the physical and psychological are intertwined. Charlotte's dream may have been a warning of an impending stroke; at the same time, it mirrored her fears about death. While Alec's dream of the French Riviera may have been caused by his being aroused sexually during sleep, it also indicated his emotional attitudes about sexuality in elderly men.

Unexpressed emotions are the most obvious ways psychological influences are apparent in our dreams. Once you're able to identify the dream elements which reflect the individual dreamer's emotions, attitudes, and behavior patterns, your understanding of yourself and your partner should increase. Like Diana in Chapter 2, who was distressed about Bill's attitude regarding her working after marriage, you may discover dream clues which explain heretofore incomprehensible behavior. Once Diana realized that Bill feared abandonment (like the lost little boy of his dream), she was better able to see his viewpoint and to reassure him so that he stopped objecting to her career.

DREAMS OF DIVORCE AND FORMER SPOUSES. If you or your partner were recently divorced, evidence of these dramatic changes may be evident in your dreams. Dr. Rosalind Cartwright, in an article for *The Journal of Mind and Behavior*, reported her findings after carefully monitoring the sleep patterns and dreams of groups of married and divorced women. Those divorcing women who were depressed had marked changes in their sleep cycles, and their dreams mirrored their emotional trauma. Cartwright found that those women who had traditional rather than more liberated attitudes had more sleep disturbances, less self-esteem, and more frightening dreams.

It's been my observation that men's dreams during and for some time after divorce also often show strong evidence of emotional stress. For instance, Ben had been divorced two years and had what seemed a harmonious second marriage to Tammy. When this second wife became pregnant, Ben's dreams were more about his first wife than they were about his new relationship. This is a dream Ben reported when Tammy was nearing the end of her pregnancy:

In this dream it seemed I was reliving the awful experience of my first wife's stillbirth, except it was Tammy in the delivery room, with the doctor telling us the fetal monitors showed the baby's heartbeat had stopped. They did a fast C-section and I was there, seeing our poor, dead baby. Then the scene changed and I was on a river raft with Tammy. I said, "Oh, thank God you still have the baby!" because I could see she was still pregnant. Then we hit some rapids and she fell overboard. I was thinking, "This is all my fault, I should never have brought her out here in these dangerous waters," and I woke up feeling badly frightened.

As we discussed his dream, Ben realized for the first time that he felt guilty about the loss of his first wife's baby, and worried that, somehow, his own genes might have caused the defects which resulted in the tragedy. When Tammy objected that their physician had assured them the new baby was healthy, he said, "Yeah, that's what they said before, too. What's worse is that the whole experience wrecked my first marriage. Guess I'm afraid history is about to repeat itself." (As it happened, Tammy's delivery was quite normal, and she gave birth to a healthy baby girl.) As a result of this discussion, Tammy was better able to understand the reasons Bill had resisted attending Lamaze classes with her, and had said he'd prefer not to be present during her labor. Once Ben admitted his fears, he was able to overcome them and to participate in the delivery.

Garfield notes that women also dream of their former spouses, and speculates that these may be dream warnings, alerting the dreamers to similar behavior in their new mates. Penny had such an experience in her second marriage, with this dream of her first husband:

Back in my old house where I lived with Ron, my first husband. I was putting a special meal on the table when he telephoned to say he'd be very late, had to work overtime on a new account. (Ron was in advertising.) I was so mad when I hung up that I gave the whole meal to our two German shepherds. Then I sat down and cried, wondering why I hadn't at least kept some food aside for myself. Then I went outdoors where it was snowing. Kept thinking how stupid I was, didn't even wear a coat. Couldn't get back inside, had locked myself out. Woke up actually shivering even though it's summer and my bedroom was warm.

Penny thought her dream of Ron symbolized the way she was beginning to feel about Ward, her present husband. "He's a workaholic too, and I can't help wondering if it's me he's trying to escape by working late," she told us. "And all those feelings of being stupid, in my dream, are coming up for me now. I wonder if I've made the same mistake all over again, and I don't know how to change whatever it is I'm doing wrong."

Fortunately, Ward was also a member of our group. It was then that he told Penny about his dream of the X-rays showing grapes in his stomach—described in Chapter 2—and how this alerted him to an incipient ulcer. "It's not your fault that I've been a workaholic," he explained to Penny. "And it probably wasn't anything to do with you when Ron acted that way, either. But this time, I hope it's not going to end in divorce." Ward said he hadn't told Penny about his physical problems, for fear she'd be too worried.

This couple had just learned a valuable lesson in communication: it's nearly always best to be honest with your partner, even at the risk of causing undue worry. Ward and Penny also learned that sharing their dreams could help them understand each other's emotions around issues they'd been afraid to discuss openly before.

BACKGROUND AND VALUE SYSTEMS IN DREAMS. Just as Diana learned about Bill's background in his dream of the lost little boy, and as Sarah began to better understand Frank's opinions by sharing his dreams, you too can glean valuable insights about your partner by paying particular attention to dream elements and themes which indicate the source of specific attitudes.

Sometimes these traits will be at odds with your own convictions, and you may find yourself constantly clashing with your partner over seemingly trivial matters. While some other, more serious, conflict may be at the root of your disagreements, frequently these irritating clashes can be resolved once each partner understands how the other became emotionally attached to his or her position.

For instance, Georgia had a habit of leaving kitchen cabinet doors open so that Alec often bumped his head on them. Rather than provoke an argument, Alec went around closing cabinets for forty years of their generally harmonious marriage. Then, one night Georgia shared this dream:

I was in the old Victorian house where I was born, in San Francisco. Mother and I were preparing for a big party. I was setting the table and she called me from the kitchen to answer the front door. Outside I could see the man from the florist, with a large bunch of roses for our decorations. The door was stuck and I couldn't get it open. The man started to leave. I went to the open window to tell him to hand me the flowers but he didn't hear me calling and I woke up.

Georgia told us, "Everything 'stuck' in that old house. In those days, we actually hardly ever locked the doors because we might not be able to get in or out if we did." She smiled at Alec. "Maybe that's why I still go around leaving things open. And I know it bothers you. I guess it's hard to break old habits!" Alec said, "I'm absolutely amazed! For years, I haven't had any idea why you had that compulsion. Now, even if you still do it, at least I'll know why."

Herb and Marcia had a more serious problem, which had to do with Marcia's conviction that all men, and especially Herb, felt superior to women. The origin of her attitude became evident in this dream:

Dreamed I was in the supermarket and saw a boy about ten years old with his mother and little sister. Every time the mother turned away, the boy would pinch his sister. When she cried, the mother would tell her angrily to hush, to behave, while the boy stood and grinned behind their backs. Then in the check-out line they were right behind me when a guard came up and said we all had to be searched for shoplifting. The guard opened my purse and pulled out an expensive can of caviar. He put handcuffs on me and all the time I was trying to tell him that nasty boy had framed me. It was awful and I woke up trembling.

Marcia said this dream brought back memories of her own older brother. "He wasn't really that mean, though," she insisted. "Probably all boys pick on their younger sisters like he did to me." After some of the men in the group assured Marcia that her brother's treatment was not fair or typical, she finally confronted her denial system. "For years I've made excuses for him," she admitted as her eyes filled with tears. "He even molested me sexually when he was in his teens. Then when he died in 'Nam, I guess I just buried all those resentments. I really wanted to remember only the nice things about him, because I loved him so much."

Murmuring, "Oh, Hon, I never knew," Herb held Marcia as she sobbed. Looking over her shaking shoulders at us, he said, "No wonder she thinks all men are against her! Well, I'm going to do my best to change all that, from now on."

Many couples in my workshops have learned to use their dreams to help them understand the underlying causes of behavior and attitudes which, on the surface, seem irrational. Marcia and Herb are an excellent example of this process. Once Herb realized how deeply hurt his wife had been in childhood, when her older brother teased and tormented her, he became more sensitive and gentle when her fears of male dominance arose.

Pauline was another of my group members whose dreams revealed a conflict because of her beliefs and values. A widow at age fifty-four, Pauline fell in love with Matthew, a widower of sixty-five. As their courtship progressed, Pauline began having a recurring dream which she said upset her so much she was at first unable to speak of it or even to write it in her diary. As she began to trust the group and to understand that she need not take her dreams literally, Pauline finally was able to record the following:

Alone with a man . . . at a lakeside cabin, becoming quickly involved in a torrid love scene . . . begins with a welcoming hug . . . but quickly progresses . . . into deeply passionate kissing, extensive touching of each other, mutually exploring for bounds and limits which don't seem to exist for either of us. Finally pulling back, both apprehensive as we realized the depth of desire that

79

each had for the other . . . decide to go across the nearby Nevada border to get married so that we could legally claim and love each other with the depth of passion and desire that we acknowledged to each other—was very difficult to call a break at this time, but I knew that I couldn't live with premarital sex relations—my guilt complex would have a field day! So off we set, located an open wedding chapel, had the ceremony performed. The lake was beautiful, calm in the full moonlight, almost ethereal in quality. We hurried back to begin a full exploration of each. other and the full expression of our love and desire . . . we seemed to blend into each other, open, welcoming, embracing, and almost drowning in the passion, each reluctant to withdraw or separate, finally falling asleep locked in each other's arms . . . we awoke with the feeling of complete fulfillment, as if each had finally found the long-sought missing portion of each other, feeling complete at last. Once again we began mutually exploring, deeply, passionately kissing, touching, and losing ourselves within each other as again we became one . . . moving from one level of satisfaction and fulfillment to another and then another, climaxing as with thundering explosive fireworks—knowing again that each was complete at last within the passion and body of the other— reluctant again to separate but knowing that we could reexperience this fulfillment again and again and again as we would never really be separated from each other—a glance, a touch would recall our experience for us. (I awoke then, feeling tired, exhilarated, fulfilled, and complete at long last.)

Pauline seemed relieved to be able to share this exciting, recurring dream. She said, "It almost became a nightmare, as I could recall it vividly even during the daytime. It seemed as though my mind was almost totally focused on this dream whenever I had no other immediate activity to occupy my attention." Pauline added that she couldn't make any sense of the dream for a long time. At first, it frightened her. "I'm not emotionally ready, this soon, to deal with such activities," she protested.

This is a fine example of the way the individual's beliefs and values may influence dreams. Although many women might have welcomed such ecstatic sensuality, Pauline was shocked that her mind could summon up such visions. When other group members pointed out that her dreaming mind took care of this conflict quite neatly, by arranging a quick marriage ceremony, she still insisted that she wasn't "ready" for any such commitment. However, Pauline did accept the suggestion that her recurring dream might be her inner self's way of alerting her to the idea that two heretofore warring parts of herself had found and made peace with each other.

Personally, I would like to believe that Pauline's long dormant needs for sexual fulfillment were demanding her attention, and that her wonderfully passionate dreams were telling her that, in Matthew, she may have found the love she'd been lacking for so long.

Most people's beliefs and value systems are portrayed in their dreams. These can be additional clues which can help you understand your lover. Discussing your dreams together is an easy way to move gently into a frank and honest chat about touchy subjects such as sex, religion, politics, and ethics. Examine your own and your partner's dreams for clues to the emotions, moods, and behavior which may have baffled you, using this information to enhance your most intimate moments.

YOUR PARTNER MAY RESEMBLE YOUR PARENTS. In addition to the beliefs and value systems most people learn in their early years, other childhood influences can have a strong effect on your preferences for certain types.

In *Getting the Love You Want*, Dr. Harville Hendrix reminds us that we usually feel a strong attraction to a person and circumstances which evoke intense emotions about our parents. Hendrix says that we unconsciously attempt in our adult lives to resolve or change memories of feeling unloved or unacceptable to either parent.

Thus, a woman whose mother was stern and controlling may choose a man with these qualities, and then may set about trying to change him or getting him to treat her more fairly. On his part, the man may have had either a mother or father to whom he is reacting by his dominating manner toward the woman of his choice. When the unconscious confuses someone in your adult life with one of your parents in this manner, this distortion is likely to show up in your dreams.

For instance, Claude had a nightmare about finding his home burglarized, with his kitchen left in squalid chaos. In discussing this disturbing dream, Claude thought the messy kitchen reflected his having come home that day to find melted frozen foods all over the countertops, which his wife Monique had forgotten to put away. This rationalization clearly shows the way Claude was projecting his parental conflicts onto his relationship with Monique. Both his parents were alcoholics, so that Claude grew up in a slovenly household and was frequently unfairly punished by his drunken mother.

When Claude learned to identify Monique's personality traits, he realized she has many of his mother's best qualities, and even has the same build and coloring. However, Monique is not an alcoholic and would never abuse their children. It was then that Claude became aware that, when Monique acted in ways that reminded him of his mother, he was unconsciously assuming she would also reject or ignore him as his mother had done. Once this couple understood such influences, Claude began telling Monique about his negative reactions, and eventually saw her as the accepting and loving companion she really is.

By increasing your knowledge of the reasons you may be attracted to certain types, you can further refine your ability to choose more compatible partners or to resolve conflicts you may be having with your lover. Take a few moments now to notice the ways in which your choices in the opposite sex may have been influenced by your parents' personality traits, or even by their appearance. If you're aware that you or your partner is being affected by such programming, this knowledge can lead to better understanding and acceptance of behavior and attitudes you might otherwise deem undesirable.

Extraversion-Introversion and Right- or Left-Brain Personalities

Frank, whose strong emotions after the ballet were described earlier, was correct in noticing that he and his wife Sarah had different styles or approaches to the same situations. His tendency was to think and act in the logical, practical manner of a predominantly left-brain personality, while Sarah, more in touch with her right brain's thinking style, tended to value the artistic and creative more than she did what her husband called "life's realities." At the same time, Frank exuded self-confidence and seemed quite comfortable with strangers, while Sarah usually appeared shy and quiet, waiting until she knew our group well before she revealed her inner feelings. In psychological terms, Frank could be described as an extraverted, left-brain type, and Sarah as an introverted, right-brain type.

Although Frank and Sarah are typical of many couples, they are by no means the rule. All people who tend to be either right- or left-brain dominant may not be correspondingly extraverted or introverted. This section will describe research about personality types and will explore the following combinations of thinking styles many people exhibit:

1. Extraverted, left-brain or right-brain
2. Extraverted, bilateral
3. Introverted, left-brain or right-brain
4. Introverted, bilateral

As you read about these different personalities, it's very important to keep in mind that *most people exhibit some of the traits of each type*. Except for those rare individuals who have undergone brain damage or surgery which separates the two sides of the brain, nearly everyone uses both hemispheres.

Moreover, people who lack certain characteristics can learn to consciously access the potential skills of either the right or the left brain. Just as Frank was discovering the pleasures of the right-brain activities Sarah enjoyed, so can anyone. In a similar manner, those who are extraverted can develop more introspective thinking habits, and introverts can learn to relate more easily to the outside world.

Since Freud's earliest observations, psychologists have been investigating the ways different people react to similar situations. An understanding of some of this research can help you in all relationships with others, and especially with your Dream Dyad partner.

EXTRAVERSION-INTROVERSION. As long ago as 1921, Dr. Carl Jung was formulating a theory designed to distinguish various psychological types. Jung believed that people in general are either extraverts or introverts, that they either turn outward or inward in their relationship to their environment.

Although Jung's concepts have been so thoroughly accepted by the public that today almost everyone uses the terms "extravert" and "introvert," there is usually some confusion about the original meanings. Jung's extravert was outward-absorbed, more interested in life outside her or himself, tending to agree with the majority. On the other hand, Jung described the introvert as being self-absorbed, one who "tends to retire too much from outer life." Today, the general public considers the extravert as someone who is social and the introvert as one who is shy. However, Jung intended broader meanings for these terms.

For instance, Jung further categorized the two types as to whether they functioned intellectually or emotionally. Thus, an extrovert might "*think* himself into an object" or might "*feel* himself into an object." In other words, when a naturally outgoing, extraverted person is an intellectual type, he or she will relate to others and to courses of action in ways thought to be in conformity with "laws" and "rules" of conduct. When the extravert is a feeling type, he or she will act toward others and to the environment with emotionally motivated behavior. In a similar fashion, introverts may tend toward intellectual choices or toward those based on subjective feelings.

JUNGIAN VS. HEMISPHERIC BRAIN THEORIES. In many ways, the theory of hemispheric dominance parallels Jung's concepts of extraversion-introversion. If the science of neuropsychology had been as advanced in his time as it is today, he might have used our knowledge of right- and left-brain traits to further refine his concepts of psychological types. Instead of subdividing his extravert and introvert types into those who relate by feeling or thinking, Jung might have used the terms right- or left-brain dominant.

You may recall the descriptions in Chapter 2 of the ways the two hemispheres or sides of the brain affect our waking thinking processes as well as our dreams. In general, people with a well-developed left side will be more linear, excelling at the kind of one-step-at-a-time logical sequences which are the basis of language and, in a slightly different way, mathematics. Right-brain types generally see the entire picture rather than parts of it, and are usually more creative in such fields as art and music. (However, since music—especially in the classical tradition—has a basic mathematical structure, many left-brain types become successful conductors and composers.)

Using this knowledge of extraversion-introversion and the two kinds of hemispheric thinking, we can group many people into "personality types" which exhibit typical traits. (Again, please remember the admonition that *nearly all people have some of the traits of each type*. In other words, as you read these descriptions and look for your own or your partner's identifying traits, you'll probably discover that you seem to fit into more than one category.)

EXTRAVERTED, LEFT-BRAIN MEN. It's been my experience that people like Frank, our group's skeptic, are examples of the type of macho, extraverted man who has been programmed since early childhood (by parents, other children, teachers, or society in general) to believe creative or right-brain activities are "sissy," feminine goings-on, to be shunned whenever possible.

Such men usually got approval for "masculine" behavior, so that, if they had the talent, they became athletes or learned to excel in other so-called "manly" roles such as mechanics or carpentry. These activities may have required so much time and energy that they never developed other potential gifts which might have required more solitude and a type of thinking which limited them physically.

Frequently, such males became extraverts, enjoying the camaraderie and admiration of others like themselves as well as that of both men and women whom they could make feel protected and secure. Yet many men who present a macho exterior carry a deep, often unexpressed longing for what Jung called the *anima*—the very side of themselves which being successful in their manly roles may have stunted.

This and other Jungian terms are explained more fully in Chapter 5. For now, you can understand the conflict many men in this typology often experience simply by realizing that the concept of *anima* in a man refers to an unconscious picture of an ideal woman, with qualities generally considered "feminine" by society at large—such as emotional expression, sensitivity to others, or attention to "right-brain" characteristics such as intuition and creativity. When a man who is extraverted or macho resists developing these traits, he may find himself unable to form satisfactory relationships, or may feel stirrings of self-doubt or pangs of conscience.

My friend Bert typifies such a dilemma. An accomplished amateur athlete, a successful entrepreneur with a thriving freight and import-export business, highly regarded in political and social circles, Bert nevertheless felt an emptiness in his life and, at age sixty-five, was suffering from undue stress and inexplicable depression symptoms. Under the guidance of a Jungian therapist, he learned to record and interpret his dreams. This one eloquently portrays Bert's inner turmoil:

> I was driving in the country and would meet this young man from town to town, but off the road in the country. I asked how he could meet me like this without a car. He said he traveled in the forest and was able to make the same time without any vehicle (by some conjured-up miracle?). Next scene I am in his room. He has just received a present of various encyclopedias and dictionaries, which he has put on shelves in his bedroom. He is fussing with pictures for his wall. Has some old Mickey Mouse ones that I thought incongruous for a man with such psychic powers.

After Bert recorded this dream, he allowed his mind to freely associate to the images it depicted, and wrote the following: "This may be my guide. In searching for a name I came up with ALBERT, a name I have not liked in the past (sissy, pristine, too intellectual). But ALBERT has access to knowledge through books and has psychic powers of transportation. I must try to communicate with him further, spend time with him. He could perhaps guide me in my spiritual search and identify MYSELF, as I have assumed names and personas that I am not." Bert told me he thought his dream was giving him this message: "Find yourself, let ALBERT (your more sensitive, intuitive, intellectual self) be your guide, take time for SPACE, learn ALBERT's magic way of transportation from point to point, use reference books."

Bert went on to describe his male side, in Jungian terms his *animus*, which seems "savage, inconsiderate . . . [such men] kill for power, lust for sex, destroy animals for food, greedily accumulate money for security and power . . . Animus can be the instrument of terror, of Hitler." And yet, Bert also told me that "without this male *elan vital* there is no inspired life, no cultural explosion. As it's said in *Clockwork Orange*: we cannot remove the evil in the male and not touch the greatness of man. And God, do I admire the greatness in men and their achievements in the world to date!"

Without being completely aware of it, Bert was well on the way to integrating the sensitivity and spiritual values he so admired. We'll continue his story and meet his wife in future chapters. For now, it's important to notice that Bert's dream and his waking reactions to it were providing clues indicative of his personality type. Sociable and outgoing, adept at business negotiations, Bert is seen as a success by his peers—yet he is troubled that he has spent most of his life involved in these outward, extraverted pursuits.

In the dream, a young man who clearly represents the undeveloped, more intellectual side of himself, amazes and attracts Bert with a magical way of dealing with many of the pursuits which concern Bert in his waking life. The man, whose very name of Albert evokes images of femininity in Bert, seems to know more about transportation, Bert's area of business expertise, as well as the spiritual issues Bert is struggling to understand. By coming to terms with his need for the intellectual nourishment he had once thought of as "sissy," Bert was moving toward a more balanced personality. Although he will probably always be extraverted and predominantly left-brain, he was learning to develop the skills and intuitive thinking processes of his right brain.

EXTRAVERTED, RIGHT-BRAIN MEN. Another type of extraverted man may become a right-brain thinker. As parents learn more about allowing their children honest emotional expression, more males are growing up to become right-brain personalities. Those with innate talents may become painters, sculptors, musicians, and writers, who are better able to think in terms of the *gestalt* or whole, in images rather than parts of a problem or puzzle.

Such men are often more likely to express their feelings, remember their dreams, and be interested in other people's emotions than are those with predominantly left-brain thinking styles. They may wholeheartedly embrace "New Age" concepts such as daily meditation, attempts to enhance psychic powers, and adherence to astrological predictions. Politically, these men are often liberals and deeply concerned about civil rights, minorities, the homeless, famine, ecology, and the state of the world.

However, sometimes males in this typology may be unusually preoccupied with personal emotional expressions (especially the development of their professions, if they're artists, writers, poets, or musicians) and hence may show little or no sensitivity to a partner's needs. Their liabilities may also include an inability to manage financially, tendencies to experiment with recreational drugs, and a general hedonistic, the-world-owes-me-a-living attitude. These traits may be the result of overly permissive parenting or even a rigid, overly disciplined background against which they rebelled in order to express themselves.

Peter, whose dream-sharing relationship with Lisa is described in previous chapters, is a typical right-brain thinker with many of this type's faults and assets. Naturally outgoing and emotionally open, twenty-eight-year-old Peter is a moderately successful artist. After he and Lisa had a disagreement about money, he told our group this dream:

Standing on our front lawn, I'm admiring the evening sky when it suddenly becomes filled with a bright, fiery red cloud. Just above my head, in the middle of the red cloud, a yellow star appears, with beams of bright yellow light radiating out from its points. Then the whole sky seems to spin and the yellow becomes liquid. It swirls out into the red, creating splashes of orange. It looks like someone dropped a huge blob of yellow onto a red canvas and then spun it around, making the colors merge. I feel myself being pulled up into the whirling liquid colors. At first I'm afraid and start yelling for help. Then as my whole body enters the colors I feel hot, but not burned. I try to catch some of the orange and it goes through my fingers like air. I can see now it's more colored lights than liquid. Then my head comes out into the dark, ordinary night sky. Looking down I can see my body, still in the reddish orange lights. I feel a bit scared again and stretch my toes down but cannot quite touch the earth. (Then I woke up.)

Peter told us he got up immediately and began to put his dream on canvas. "I thought it was simply another inspiration for a painting," he explained, "but Lisa thinks it has some other meaning, something about our argument the night before." Lisa nodded, saying, "I'm not denying this is probably one of Peter's inspirational visions. But at the same time, I think it may have another message for him."

As we questioned Peter about his associations to this vivid dream, he suddenly grinned and told us, "The night before, Lisa was telling me my 'head is always in the clouds.' And that made me mad. Sounded just like my parents. Well, there it is in my dream—me with my head in the clouds, can't get my feet on the ground!" It developed that Lisa's paycheck as a legal secretary was covering most of their expenses while Peter waited for commissions on his last gallery exhibit. "She wants me to get a temporary job," Peter said, "and if I do that I'm afraid I won't have time to paint." Despite Lisa's worries, Peter did eventually get his fees. When he received a substantial grant for a mural in a large corporation's new offices, Peter and Lisa moved to

New York. After this move, they wrote that they'd gotten married, and had their first child.

Although her thinking style was more left-brain than Peter's, Lisa usually welcomed Peter's insights and his sensitivity to her needs. She commented, "Sometimes I get the blues, really sad or feeling sorry for myself. At those times, he drops everything—even a big art project—and listens. That's usually all I need to get back to my normal self. If not, he nearly always says or does something so outrageous I can't help laughing."

EXTRAVERTED, BILATERAL MEN. When men are able to access both hemispheres with equal ease, and are also inclined to relate to the world around them as though they belong and are a vital part of it, they are what I term extraverted, bilateral types. Such men often grew up in families where their interests in so-called masculine activities received no more praise than did their development of skills in more imaginative pastimes. Often they had sisters and brothers and engaged in good-natured competition in both sports and the arts. The Kennedy family might be an example of the kind of environment which would encourage bilateral, extraverted personalities.

Other men of this type may have arrived at their bilateral abilities through conscious, determined efforts to strengthen their less dominant side. For instance, many male psychologists have confided to me that they chose their professions in efforts to understand their own right-brain experiences. The examples given earlier of Frank and Bert indicate similar efforts to achieve this balance. Although, at this writing, Frank and Bert have not yet reached their goals, their willingness to study their dreams and to explore creative expressions such as the ballet and literature has already brought them into closer harmony with their more right-brain partners.

Extraverted, bilateral men are usually comfortable with other men and also quite sensitive to women's emotional needs. Lou, a forty-year-old attorney who fell in love with Florence, a thirty-two-year-old C.P.A., provides an example of the way such a man can use his bilateral skills to improve his love relationship. After one of my lectures, this couple approached me to describe their recent discovery of the fascinating world of dreams.

"When Lou started telling me about his dreams, I thought it was nonsense," Florence said. "Then Lou gave me some articles in *Newsweek* and *Time* about the latest science of dream research, and I agreed to find out more." The next week, Florence mailed me this dream record:

> Dreamt I was in my office, reading some tax law books, trying to figure out a way to help a client save on a very high tax bill. The phone rang and it was Lou, telling me he got a promotion because of my advice. I told him I wished I could do the same for this client and he laughed and started singing "Seventy-Six Trombones" from our favorite musical. I thought he was just too pleased about his promotion to listen to my troubles. This made me sad and I woke up.

Florence wrote that when she awoke from this dream, she suddenly realized she had the solution to her client's problem. "The song, 'Seventy-Six Trombones,' reminded me of something important. I vaguely recalled that my client's company had made some rather expensive improvements in a building they owned at 76 West Main Street," she explained. "I could hardly wait to get to the office to check it out—and sure enough, I found a deduction they hadn't claimed, and was able to save them thousands of dollars in taxes. Dreams are amazing!"

An especially relevant aspect of Florence and Lou's relationship was that, both in her dreams and in their waking interactions, Lou successfully appealed to Florence's left-brain thinking style. By being aware of Florence's tendency to trust more left-brain-oriented information, such as the "scientific, factual" reports in news magazines, he was able to effectively motivate Florence to explore dream study, a topic she might normally distrust. Even in Florence's dream, Lou appealed to her left-brain tendencies by humming a tune related to numbers, Florence's field of expertise.

After this couple joined my dream study group, Lou told us the following dream, which clearly depicts his extraverted, bilateral personality:

My law partners and I are competing in a relay race with another law firm. Two of us have to run along a path through a dark forest where we are to exchange our Olympic-style torches for baseball gloves (like a catcher's mitt) and then somehow get something alive, an animal of some sort, run out of the forest, and pass these animals on to our team before our rivals come out of another forest. As I run along I feel confused with the complicated rules and ask my running mate to explain. He's huffing, puffing, can't talk. He points to a pile of gloves under a tall pine tree and we snuff out our torches, grab two mitts, and keep running. He gasps to me that he doesn't know how we're supposed to find any animals. I look up into the trees and see these little shivering, furry animals hanging by their tails, their big yellow eyes glittering. I thought they looked cold and scared. "Koala bears?" my partner asks. But I think they are marmosets. (In real life, I've never seen a marmoset, but I may have read about them somewhere.) He uses his mitt like a club, knocking one of the little creatures down. I shout to him, "No! Don't hurt them! We have to bring them out alive!" and then I reach up and use the glove to slowly pull one off, trying to be gentle. It wraps itself around my arm and goes to sleep. Then I can't find my partner. He's vanished. So I run, thinking maybe the other team didn't get any animals and so we might still win. (Then I woke up, feeling very puzzled yet pleased with myself.)

When Lou gave us his associations to the major elements of his dream, he realized that its general theme was his frequent frustration with his colleagues. "They're very competitive," he explained, "symbolized by the race we were having in my dream. That attitude keeps us ahead financially, but sometimes it seems to me it also prevents us from doing the very kind of work that attracted me to the law in the first place—helping people who are victimized (like the marmosets in my dream). My partners usually raise cain whenever I want to take on a *pro bono* case, and I think the dream is showing my feelings about that with the different ways my partner and I handled the little monkeylike animals."

Our group suggested that Lou's exchange of the dream torch for a glove might also be a metaphor related to his career conflicts, with the torch being a Freudian symbol for the penis, and the glove a symbol for the vagina. Lou agreed. "Maybe the torch is a symbol of masculinity, and I'm willing to put it down to put on a more sensitive, feminine attitude, like the glove, in our efforts to win," he told us.

Lou's dream showed him that, in contrast to his colleagues, he is not concerned that being compassionate and gentle will make him appear weak or unmanly. "What I must do is to find some way to get my partners to be more charitable without their feeling they're becoming a soft touch," he said. Eventually, Lou resolved this conflict with Florence's help, by providing his partners with charts and statistics which showed that most of the costs of *pro bono* cases could be written off as losses and tax deductions.

EXTRAVERTED, LEFT-BRAIN WOMEN. Those women who choose the challenges of a corporate structure and are able to compete well with their male cohorts are probably linear thinkers. Unlike the men in this group, these women have often had to develop the special, left-brain thinking processes required in their jobs.

As I have explained in this book's Preface, recent scientific research shows that most females fall behind most males in mathematical abilities after age eleven. These findings are based on examinations of thousands of test results. While this seeming lack of success may be due in part to the fact that boys usually have more acutely developed spatial abilities—which may help them in grasping such concepts as those taught in geometry—it can be argued that even spatial ability is a learned skill.

In other words, females can be taught to excel in math just as easily as males do. However, at the present time the fact is that most women today usually have to exert extra effort in order to excel at these and other linear-type skills. As a result, these efforts may have caused women in this group to sacrifice the ability to openly express their feelings.

Such women are sometimes politically conservative, although many others have joined the ranks of women's rights organizations after experiencing sex discrimination or harassment firsthand. These career/personality conflicts are often mirrored in their dreams. For instance, Terry, a supermarket cashier and mother of three, reported the following:

> Dreamed I went to the day-care center to pick up Missy, our three-year-old daughter. She was building a tower of blocks and every time she added a block, she would stop and make a mark on a piece of paper with a crayon. I thought, "She's actually counting! This is amazing!" and then a little boy grabbed her paper and tore it up. When Missy hit the kid, the teacher came over and told her she couldn't play any more. I felt really angry and started yelling at the teacher and woke up.

Terry told us that, just before she had this dream, she'd been informed by her supervisor that her application for promotion to store manager had been denied. "Our present manager is being transferred," she said, "and everybody in the store knows I'm qualified. But they're bringing in a man from another town. Then when I asked about the accounting department they told me not to be so ambitious, that I should be satisfied where I am, just being a cashier." Terry thought her daughter in the dream represented herself. "I've been good at math since I was little," she told us, "and it usually got me into trouble. Hugh, my husband, is the only man I ever met who didn't feel threatened by my being smart that way."

Terry's dream reflected her left-brain abilities (deftly manipulating objects in space such as the blocks, crayon, and paper, and being able to count at an early age) and her difficulties in expressing these skills (the hostile actions of the little boy, who probably symbolized most of the men in Terry's life, and the teacher, representing authority figures at work who refused to acknowledge her qualifications for what they considered "male" positions).

EXTRAVERTED, RIGHT-BRAIN WOMEN. Of course, men have no exclusive claim to extraversion or introversion, or to right- or left-brain thinking styles. Women who have predominantly right-brain thinking processes can be found in any occupation, in almost all walks of life. However, unless their jobs offer outlets for their creative drives, these women are more likely to be freelance artists, musicians, actresses, or writers—jobs which don't require their leaving home for the rigors and linear skills of the business world.

Some may express their talents and special nurturing traits as homemakers and mothers, preferring to remain at home until their children are on their own. These homemakers can be just as extraverted as their career women counterparts, delighting in get-togethers with a wide variety of personality types.

Women whose gifts and openness were supported and praised as children are likely to have become as self-confident and assertive as their left-brain sisters. Such women are unusually compassionate, sensitive, and concerned about such matters as endangered species, famine, the homeless and civil rights, and are usually liberals politically.

Moreover, women in this typology may have more nightmares than their more conservative counterparts. They seem to fit the group described by Dr. Hartmann as having what he calls "thin boundaries." Such people are especially sensitive, usually very creative, and may have difficulties distinguishing between unconscious data (such as daydreams, fantasies, or dreams) and the "realities" of conscious, waking life.

Suzanne (the artist whose dream of the "dingo dogs" was described in Chapter 3) said, "Before going to sleep I was feeling sadness around the thought, 'My man (Jerry) needs other women besides me. I'll never be enough for him,' and thinking about my Mom and Dad and how Dad needed to sleep with more than one woman." Then Suzanne had this nightmare:

> Jerry and I are in a huge, deserted public building (a school or courthouse) late at night. I somehow get separated from him, end up on a basement floor with high ceilings and lots of marble. There is a woman friend . . . at times, there's a guide—the actor

Gregory Hines. Hundreds of strange men come from back rooms and approach me and the woman. Our guide explains they're dead! I figure if they're ghosts they can't hurt me and I let them touch me. Then I get both afraid and turned on. I run, they follow, chase me up and down steps, through the halls. Finally one catches me, ties me up with my legs spread apart, naked, and begins to examine me. He'd been a prisoner before he died and hadn't seen a woman for years. I'm really getting turned on. Then the guide comes and releases me. I woke up feeling very frightened.

Suzanne, whose emotions are eloquently expressed in her sculpture, paintings, music, acting, and dancing, has dreams which typify the extraverted, right-brain woman. Like the nightmare quoted above, her nightly visions take place in complex settings and are often peopled with numerous bizarre characters such as this nightmare's hundreds of strange men, ghosts, and celebrity-type guides. As in this dream, Suzanne is usually emotionally involved with all her dream elements rather than being an observer, and her feelings are generally quite extreme—either deliriously happy, terrified, furious, deeply sad, or highly aroused sexually. All these vivid, imaginative details are characteristic of this personality type's dreams.

Suzanne thought the ghost men in her nightmare might have been memories of being raped as a teenager by a young ex-con who told her he'd dreamed of a woman like her, in jail. She also thought her Dream Power was telling her that, like her lover Jerry, she herself sometimes has erotic fantasies about others. "That doesn't mean we don't love each other," she continued, "or that either one of us will actually be unfaithful."

Suzanne was probably correct in her understanding of sexual fantasies and dreams, which usually do not indicate that either the dreamer or the person dreamed about is disloyal or unfaithful. Such dreams may have a variety of meanings, depending upon the dreamer's personality and waking circumstances.

For example, dreams of sexual intercourse may symbolize a union or fusion of conflicting aspects of one's personality, such as Frank or

Bert's struggles (described in the section above about macho men) to integrate their anima or feminine sides, their right-brain abilities, with their masculine traits. Sometimes a person who fears loss of a mate for any reason, such as poor health or conflicts not involving sex, may dream of that person's infidelity—a symbol for the feared loss.

On the other hand, erotic dreams and waking fantasies may indicate an unexpressed desire to explore a sexual activity which seems to be illicit or forbidden. In such cases, these visions can be safely explored. Chapters 7 and 10 will provide more information on ways you can use your erotic dreams and fantasies to keep your romance alive. For now the essential point is that the extraverted woman who is right-brain dominant will usually have dreams which portray her abilities to express emotions and imaginative, often fantastic scenes and characters.

EXTRAVERTED, BILATERAL WOMEN. My observations and research indicate that modern women are becoming increasingly bilateral in their thinking, which means that they access both sides of their brain simultaneously. Such women are equally comfortable with logical, linear thinking and with creative, intuitive thinking. Further, they are often assertive, unafraid to state their needs, and expect them to be met. Long before Women's Lib, there were women who asserted themselves—although society was inclined to view them as "too pushy," "tomboys," or "unfeminine." Today, such women may still have a difficult time in their relationships with men, especially those traditional men who may feel threatened by women they cannot control.

Despite a measure of success, women's battles to overcome sexism have not progressed as much as their leaders had hoped. As Dr. Warren Farrell points out in *Why Men Are the Way They Are*, the cigarette ad proclaiming, "You've come a long way, baby!" is only true in a qualified sense. Farrell examines all the major American women's magazines, comparing the overt and the covert messages in their articles, photos, and ads. While the overt message may be, "Don't play games; be yourself; go all out for a career for the sense of achievement"—the covert message in the text of all the articles and ads is: "play games" (successful flirting strategies, old-fashioned love, how to make him *earn* it); emphasis on clothes and cosmetics rather than career skills; and how to use your career to get a man to make commitments.

Nevertheless, there are men in growing numbers who appreciate a poised, assertive woman. After interviewing scores of men aged nineteen to seventy, Alexandra Penney, author of *How to Make Love to Each Other*, says that most contemporary men are especially attracted to self-confident, self-assured women. While one need not be aggressively assertive to be self-confident, the woman who is not afraid to express emotions and ask that her needs be met may be more appealing to the opposite sex than those covert messages in magazines imply.

Further, many women who are assertive, outgoing, and extraverted have a lot of fun. Self-assured and relaxed, such women often love parties and social gatherings where their company is most welcomed because they're genuinely interested in other people's ideas and activities. Usually, they're also sensitive and understanding regarding others' feelings, so that they have many close and trusting friends. Their dreams frequently reflect this poise and sincere interest in others.

Betsy, the secretary (whose "inky" dreams before she began dating Richard, a black man, were described in Chapter 3), had no difficulty expressing herself and was quite popular with both men and women. Here is another of Betsy's dreams:

Dreamed I was at this great party. Everyone was in costume and I'd gotten myself up as an astronaut but the helmet was hot so I took it off. Several women, wearing masks, came over and said I shouldn't show my face but I just laughed and told them I didn't care who recognized me. One woman, in a black sequined cat outfit, began to hiss. She said, "You ought to play the game. That's what this party's all about." Then she grabbed a man dressed as a lion and pulled him onto the dance floor. I saw Richard across the room, also in an astronaut's suit, and I thought, he and I really are alike. He'd taken off his helmet too and he winked at me. I was going over to him when a little girl ran into the ballroom, yelling and crying. She was so cute, with a blond ponytail and little "bunny" pj's with feet. The cat woman stopped dancing and went to the little girl and slapped her. She said, "This is a grown-up party. Now go right back to your room!" and then the poor child really bawled. I could see the cat woman was about to hit her again so I activated the launch switch on my suit and flew right over, scooped up the child and flew right out the French doors, holding her in my arms. She stopped crying and hugged me and I woke up.

Betsy thought the disapproving women in her dream were some of her friends in waking life, who constantly advised her to "play the game" by using feminine wiles to attract men. "They think I can't do any better, and that's why I've settled for a black guy," she told us. "But I know my own heart, and he is the best for me. Even my dream told me so, by showing me a Richard in the same costume." She thought the cat woman symbolized the way she herself had behaved in her teens, and also might represent her mother. "Mom never approved when I stopped being manipulative with men," she explained. "And she did slap me a lot when I was little, when I showed my feelings." Betsy was certain the little girl in her dream was herself as a child. "Also, she's the child inside me now," Betsy went on. "This dream reminds me that I must take care of that little girl part of myself, the part that needs to be protected and reassured."

Betsy's dream and her comments while discussing it give evidence of a personality which is balanced, neither overly right- or left-brain. Betsy shows this bilateral thinking by her typically left-brain, detailed descriptions of the dream party and then her ease in moving to a right-brain grasp of the entire picture or theme of the dream, the portrayal of her need to take care of her "child within," and her determination to follow her heart rather than her head.

Sharon, a computer programmer in a large corporation and one of my students, was an extraverted, bilateral woman who tried to mold herself into her mental image of the way a "brainy" woman should feel and act. Believing she "should" be attracted to men whose business skills matched her own, Sharon continually dated men who were strongly left-brain oriented. Following is one of her dreams which depicts her inner conflicts:

Dreamed I was on a date with Fred, a guy who works in my office. We went to a movie in one of those avant-garde theaters. It was in German with no subtitles and I couldn't understand much but I suffered through it because he seemed to be enjoying it. Then when he took me home I gave him a big kiss at my apartment door, and he disappeared! Then I saw a slimy little animal, something like a frog, flopping around on the floor. I thought, "Oh no, this is all backwards. When the Princess kissed the frog it turned into a Prince, not the other way around!" And I woke up.

Sharon had this dream the night after complaining to our group that the men of her dreams were never available in waking life. Evidently her Dream Power took her remarks quite literally, giving her (in Fred) a demonstration of the typical men she chose, who could never meet her emotional needs because their thinking styles were so markedly dissimilar.

As we discussed her dilemma, other members of the group suggested that Sharon's expectations might be unrealistic. "You keep going out with these intellectual types you meet at work," Peter told her, "when really you're looking for someone sexier and more open about his feelings." Frank objected. "Those other computer programmers may be sexy, too. It's just that they're a little slower about it than you may want or need."

Sharon agreed. "Guess I keep imagining they're just like me, underneath. You know, enjoying logistics and all the computer analyses we do on the job, but all the same, romantic and needing to be close and share everything. But they never are. They either want sex and then back off when we start getting close, or they expect me to be just as uptight as they are." With the group's encouragement, Sharon began trying to meet a different type of man. Peter and Lisa invited her to one of his gallery openings, and she quickly became popular with their more right-brain friends.

Even though Sharon was above average in her left-brain skills, she felt most fulfilled with partners who helped her achieve more balance with her right-brain needs. In the dream quoted above, her date, Fred, showed distinct left-brain traits with his choice of an avant-garde, "intellectual" movie in a foreign language, which compelled the audience to focus on content more than feelings. To compound the discomfort the movie caused Sharon, Fred next literally turned into a repulsive "flop" (the slimy frog) when she kissed him.

Since Sharon was obviously quite adept with many left-brain skills required by her work, her strong need for and pleasure in right-brain activities indicate that she is bilateral and will probably be happier with men who meet her desires for right-brain companionship which she rarely finds in the workplace. Introverted, left-brain men like Fred no doubt do have sexual needs, as Frank suggested. Yet women like Sharon seldom build lasting relationships with that type, who are often quite shy about expressing such feelings.

INTROVERTED, LEFT-BRAIN MEN. This type of man usually has a strong tendency to think by taking each part of a concept or problem and connecting it to the next until arriving at a satisfactory solution or conclusion. He learned in early childhood that these natural, left-brain abilities brought praise and approval.

Such a child might have also discovered that, when he attempted more playful, imaginative, or emotional thinking and behavior, the rewards were less gratifying. Sometimes these more spontaneous, right-brain-inspired actions even resulted in pain or punishment.

For example, I saw a little boy rush into his father's study, throwing himself at Daddy with joyous abandon. But Daddy was writing the monthly checks, and crossly pushed the boy aside with, "Not now, son. Can't you see I'm busy?" The next time I saw that little boy and his father, the child stood by quietly while the adults talked. When the conversation turned to politics, this tiny four-year-old said, "Mr. Bush is a good president. My Daddy voted for him!" and got a hug and chuckles for his precocity.

These linear thinkers often excel in scientific and legal pursuits which require mathematical and logical skills. Further, they tend to be conservative politically and socially, since these positions are usually less risky or emotional.

Jason, whose dream of the woman falling twenty-one stories portrayed his worries about his recovering alcoholic wife, typifies this type of man. A biochemist in a large pharmaceutical company, Jason enjoyed his work, yet seldom shared his thoughts about it with his wife Christine, or even with his coworkers. As he became involved in a group for codependents, which he'd joined as a result of Christine's alcoholism, Jason began to confront his fears about being more open with both his family and his colleagues. During this period he had the following dream:

I saw a boy about ten years old playing with dominoes. He was setting each piece on end, in a long line. I asked what he was doing and he touched the end piece, causing all the others to fall, overlapping each other. "It's the domino effect," he said, grinning in an evil way. I thought, "This kid is more than he seems." Then the dominoes grew into skyscrapers on a busy city street. I sensed a great danger here and ran around trying to tell people not to touch the first building since that would cause the domino effect. They backed away and a woman who looked like my mother called a cop. He told me to move on, that I was disturbing the peace. "It's not me," I tried to tell him. "The peace will really be disturbed unless you help!" And I woke up.

Jason parsed his dream by underlining the action words and circling these important nouns: I, boy ten years old, dominoes, end piece, others, domino effect, evil way, kid, skyscrapers, street, danger, people, first building, they, woman, my mother, cop, he, peace, me, him, peace, you.

As he made associations to the circled words, Jason decided the boy was himself as a child. "I remember having these secrets I thought were evil," he told us. "All they were, my big secrets, were feelings I had about my parents and teachers. I wrote them all down and hid them in a box with a trick drawer no one could find. What I wrote down was stuff like 'I hate my Mom when she says just wait till your father hears about this.' And, 'When Dad punishes me I know he's sad and it makes me sad when he can't take my side.' They weren't really such big secrets, but I thought they were."

These associations led Jason to this explanation of his dream: "I grew up thinking my 'negative' feelings, like anger and pain, were evil. Now, when I'm trying to express emotions, I'm afraid this will cause a sort of 'domino effect.' If I let out these primary feelings (symbolized by the first building), the whole world, all I've built up (the skyscrapers) will come toppling down. My mother could never accept those feelings. In the dream she called a cop. In real life, she would call my Dad and he'd be so sorry, I could tell, but he'd say I was upsetting Mom ('disturbing the peace'). I'd try to tell him I didn't mean to (in the dream, asking the cop for help), but he'd go ahead and ground me or take away TV watching, and then I'd feel like crying but would go and write it down instead."

Although he will probably remain a basically withdrawn, cautious person, Jason began to develop his right-brain traits and to feel more comfortable with groups and social gatherings. With the support of his new friends in Al Anon, he learned to express his emotions more easily. This also helped his wife Christine in her recovery. "I used to sedate my feelings by drinking," she said. "Now, I can share it with Jason instead. He kept his emotions bottled up, and I used the bottle to hide mine. Guess we're more alike than either of us imagined."

INTROVERTED, RIGHT-BRAIN MEN. This type of man, like many shy females, has often experienced pain or ridicule when he attempted to express right-brain abilities. Rather than attempt learning left-brain thinking processes, he may have become convinced early on that he is inferior. Still, he may secretly express his creative or intuitive ideas by retreating into lengthy daydreams and fantasies. Or, he may adopt some hobby which is an "acceptable" male pursuit yet satisfies his right-brain needs—such as the intricacies of handcrafting fishing lures or becoming a fund-raiser for some artistic organization, thus putting himself a bit closer to people with similar thinking styles.

Claude, a thirty-year-old accountant and an Adult Child of Alcoholics, fits this personality type. Born in French Canada and later becoming a naturalized U.S. citizen, Claude still carries emotional scars from his childhood, when the safest means of survival was to hide during his parents' violent quarrels.

Claude's dreams consistently mirrored both his feelings of low self-worth and his right-brain talents, which he tried vainly to squelch. The following nightmare, mentioned in this chapter's section on the way parents affect our preferences in mates, illustrates Claude's characteristics:

Dreamed our house had been burglarized, everything was a mess. (When I got home last night, found a lot of melted frozen foods on the kitchen counter where Monique had forgotten to put them away.) I walked from room to room, feeling frightened and depressed. (The house seemed something like one I lived in with my folks in Canada, but in the dream it was our house, mine and my wife Monique's.) I felt angry with Monique for some reason, as if it was her fault that someone had broken in. Then felt guilty for blaming her. Felt really dazed, scared, upset. Sat down on the kitchen floor and started fooling around with the mess of spilled food there, and then realized it looked like a child's finger painting. Got excited and I recall thinking, "Wow! I've discovered a new art medium!" and I really got into it, with both hands. A strange yet beautiful abstract painting was coming to life right there on the floor as I swirled the foods around, mixing colors and shapes. Then, I heard the front door slam and I thought, "Oh, no. Monique will see this and think I'm crazy!" And I woke up shaking with fear.

Claude thought the messy house was both a representation of the way he'd found the kitchen upon arriving home the night before this dream, and also a memory of his childhood—where the kitchen was always untidy. Our group helped him see that the entire nightmare might have been about those painful times, when his creative expressions (symbolized by the finger painting) were ridiculed.

Next, Claude decided that his feelings about Monique in the dream actually are his waking feelings about his mother, since he believes she was to blame for allowing his father to "break in" upon his private, safe world of childhood fantasies. Claude also agreed with another group member's suggestions that the food he began feeling excited about symbolized the nurturance of self-expression which is missing in his life, and that his fear of being found out and told he is crazy is often the way he feels about himself as an adult.

In later chapters, more of Claude and Monique's story will unfold. For now, the main point is that dreams of this sort may reveal traits indicating the dreamer is an introverted, right-brain type.

Other introverted, right-brain men have often achieved greater success than Claude in their efforts to express their creativity. Many of these enjoy occupations such as being artists, musicians, writers, and poets, which are outlets for their right-brain talents. Many also find mates who understand their need for privacy and introspection.

Alan, the forty-three-year-old journalist whose dream of being trapped on the highway between a van and a semi was described in Chapter 3, was one of these introverted, right-brain-dominant men who had not only come to terms with his introversion, but preferred it. "Guess I've been lucky," he said, "because I've got a job where they give me plenty of space, and Patty, who's a lot like I am. Oh, I make adjustments, and have gotten pretty good at interviewing people, even though I still feel drained if I have to deal with crowds. Then I simply seclude myself awhile, get busy writing, and find I bounce back fairly quickly." These are the typical reactions of introverts, who often need time alone after being around large numbers of people.

Alan was fortunate in that his partner, Patty, was also an introvert, so that they were able to make accommodations for each other's needs for privacy in their daily lives. However, this couple encountered some difficulties when their opposite hemispheric styles came into conflict. Their problems will be discussed further in the section devoted to Introverted, Left-Brain Women. For now, it's important to understand that, while some introverted, right-brain men experience frustrations in their attempts to adjust to a lifestyle where their skills are not acknowledged, many others, like Alan, do achieve both careers and relationships which fulfill their needs.

INTROVERTED, BILATERAL MEN. This personality type is somewhat unusual, because most people who have equal access to both hemispheres tend to feel revitalized by the stimulation of sharing ideas and feelings with others—so that they generally exhibit extraversion traits. However, David, one of the expectant fathers in my research for *Pregnancy and Dreams*, was an introverted, bilateral man.

An electronics engineer and computer expert, thirty-nine-year-old David is also an accomplished musician who combines his knowledge of electronics with his right-brain talents by playing an electric guitar and organ. His and his wife Jackie's home in California's Sierra foothills is filled with both his own and his family's songs and the full-bodied sounds of high fidelity stereo equipment he has built and installed.

In recent years, David has also discovered that he is a "trance channel," and has developed a large following of other "New Age" men and women who come to him for counsel and spiritual guidance. The following dream illustrates David's introverted, bilateral personality traits:

> I am lying on my bed and seem to be hypnotized, which causes me to be unable to move. Hovering around me are four or five beings I realize are extraterrestrials, aliens. They're wearing white smocks with hoods which shade their faces so I cannot see their features, and white gloves. These clothes are shiny, like some

sort of plastic. At first I feel a little scared, knowing they are examining me. Then I begin to feel uncomfortable, thinking there's something odd or wrong about this and that I'd better come out of the trance, so I do—and then I woke up.

Discussing this experience, David told me it was so real, so vivid, that he believed it may have really happened. "If it was a dream," he said, "I think it probably reflects my recent worries about stories of UFOs and aliens taking human form and infiltrating our civilization." David thought the dream's message was that he need not fear being "taken over" by extraterrestrials, since he has become quite skilled at controlling his self-hypnosis abilities and is able to come out of a trance, returning to waking consciousness with ease.

David's dream portrays his right-brain skills by having him in a hypnotic trance for most of the vision. Biofeedback research at San Francisco's University of California and UC Medical School provides convincing evidence that subjects whose electronically monitored brain waves indicate a trance state are accessing right-brain abilities, usually more completely than they are able to do when they are not hypnotized. Thus, David's trance state as the aliens examined him represents his strong right-brain abilities. The dream also depicts a common fear among those involved in channeling and psychic counseling—that they may lose contact with the "real" world and their left-brain thinking processes.

David thought the white-garbed aliens symbolized his perception of many scientists and physicians, who sometimes regard people as "specimens," ignoring their feelings. Thus, the aliens symbolized David's awareness that he could not always accept or trust his highly developed left-brain talents and knowledge. The fact that David felt uncomfortable and different in the presence of a group is also typical of the introverted personality, who often feels he or she is being "examined" or critically scrutinized by others.

INTROVERTED, LEFT-BRAIN WOMEN. While many assertive women may be successful in their careers and social lives, this is not always the case. Some career women may need to learn more assertive skills, even though they may be quite accomplished in the business world. Women of this sort usually achieved high marks in school because of their left-brain abilities, yet since they were girls they probably got little praise or attention from their peers, who may have called them "teacher's pet" or ignored them in favor of more outgoing playmates. Although they may have overcome these negative responses by the time they became teenagers or young adults, many women of this group harbor the same fears and feelings of low self-worth they experienced as children.

Patty, the forty-four-year-old social worker whose conflicts about moving to a strange city with her lover Alan are described in Chapter 3, does not at first glance appear to be introverted. Her choice of occupation is also unusual for left-brain thinkers, who tend to gravitate toward work which involves them less with people and more with abstract, logical ideas (such as the work of attorneys, computer programmers, scientists, and engineers).

However, when Patty introduced herself to our dream study group, her traits became quite clear. She told us, "In my job, my colleagues depend on me to keep track of all their case history files, welfare payments, and so on, so I do a lot more administrative work than actually getting out in the field, and that suits me just fine. I'm not very comfortable with strangers. I never dated much before I met Alan—just never went in for high fashion or party-going or the things most women I know like, the things that attract men. But Alan and I share a lot—we both like books, the theater, and I especially admire his writing talents."

This couple seemed to have few conflicts until Alan accepted a job out of town. Then, Patty's fears about change began to surface in her dreams. Read more about the ways they used dreams to resolve their problems in future chapters.

INTROVERTED, RIGHT-BRAIN WOMEN. This is the woman who was probably scolded as a child for her right-brain activities, especially for daydreaming or "not paying attention." Often, this right-brain thinker has been scolded so much in childhood for her imaginative play, daydreaming, or her inability to conform, that she's become shy or demure and introverted. She might have been compared to other, more left-brain children, and urged to be more like them—but when she tried, she usually failed miserably since she simply could not learn in the accepted, left-brain fashion. As a result, she may have retreated further into fantasies. As she grew older, she may have discovered outlets for expression of her make-believe world by writing fiction, painting, or sculpting.

Such women also may find fulfillment in domestic life, which provides them many opportunities for creating through cooking, decorating, sewing, as well as the deep fulfillment which comes from childbirth and nurturing others. However, as they observe other, more assertive women, introverted, right-brain women frequently begin to feel oppressed and resentful, focusing their anger upon their mates.

This leaves the man feeling bewildered and hurt, since their relationship began under different circumstances, with the woman making him feel she needed his guidance and direction. Suddenly confronted with this change of heart, these men may have no idea why their mates have "turned" on them.

This was the case with Rosemarie and Jim when they first joined my couples' dream study group. Rosemarie's dream of the "monster in the pot," quoted in Chapter 1, is typical of the frightening dreams introverted, right-brain women may have, especially when they are experiencing consciousness-raising about their roles as homemakers. "I'm not eager to leave home and start another career," thirty-eight-year-old Rosemarie explained. "It's just that I want recognition that keeping house, being a hostess, and raising a family *are* a career."

INTROVERTED, BILATERAL WOMEN. As in the case with introverted, bilateral men, this personality type does not appear to develop very often. Women who are able to access either hemisphere with ease are generally quite comfortable with others, who respond to their combined left-brain logic and right-brain sensitivity with acceptance and friendship. However, when some bilateral women experienced rejection (especially for their exceptional left-brain traits which males may have seen as threatening) they may have become introverted. Whatever the cause, women of this personality type do develop deep friendships with a few people, despite their introversion tendencies.

Greta, a forty-eight-year-old widow, youthful grandmother, and a commercial photographer, is a woman of this type. She describes her late husband as an ambitious, overly stressed man who was often "dominating, always had to be right." Although she claims she loved him deeply, Greta's emotional wounds during this marriage, plus the fact that she was born in war-torn Germany, may account for her introversion traits. Essentially demure and a bit self-conscious, Greta nevertheless has a small circle of close friends who are mostly painters and sculptors. These predominantly right-brain companions seem to be attracted to Greta's somewhat cautious left-brain thinking style as well as to her sensitivity to their own creative aspects.

After joining an art class with some of these friends, Greta began experimenting with unusual arrangements of flowers and other natural objects in her photographs, was asked to give a one-woman show, and is now well on her way toward recognition in the field of creative photography. The following brief dream occurred when she was in the midst of this new career direction. It depicts both Greta's introversion and her bilateral characteristics:

Dreamed I was with a group of people, none of whom I knew. I didn't feel too comfortable with them, but I was happy to get to see this wonderful place. We were all visiting my art instructor's home. The walls of his house were not attached to each other; there was no roof, no floor. A gravel path was filled with many century plants, some of them fully grown, others just budding. My instructor told everyone to take all the plants they wanted. I really wanted one, but I held back, didn't want to be greedy.

Both in her dreams and waking life, Greta is seldom assertive. "When I was growing up," she told us, "the worst thing you could be was greedy, since sometimes there wasn't much to go around. Now, I still find it's hard to take what I want. Maybe my dream was showing me that." Greta also thought the artist's home with no roof indicated the surge of creativity she'd experienced after enrolling in his class. "Many things are opening up for me, like the beautiful openness of his house in my dream—new ways I can express so many ideas in my photographs," she explained.

Personality Tests and Measurements

After Dr. Carl Jung published his descriptions of extraverted and introverted personality types, his disciples developed rather lengthy questionnaires and tests with somewhat complicated scoring procedures, based on his theories. These tests were designed to measure their psychoanalytic patients' qualities of extraversion-introversion as well as the degree to which they relate in thinking or feeling modalities. One such test, given to clients at the San Francisco Society of Jungian Analysts, has eighty-one questions which indicate the testee's most typical tendencies.

In the 1950s, psychologists Isabel Myers and Kathryn Briggs devised another test based on Jung's theories, titled the Myers-Briggs Type Indicator. Accurate use of this test is still taught in premed and psychology courses, and it is still widely used as a method of determining personality types by many clinical psychologists.

A simplified version of the Myers-Briggs test is provided in *Please Understand Me: Character and Temperament Types*, by David Kiersey and Marilyn Bates. This quiz is called the Kiersey Temperament Sorter, has 70 questions similar to the Jungian test, and again, a somewhat complicated scoring procedure.

While these tests are available to the public, they are usually difficult for the lay person to interpret. Further, they do not take into account more up-to-date information about right- and left-brain traits. Based on my own observations of these hemispheric abilities as well as my experience in administering the Myers-Briggs test, I have created a Quiz to use in my own practice. My students find it useful in identifying personality types, but please keep in mind I have not scientifically validated the test under valid experimental conditions. Therefore, when you try my Quiz, please keep in mind that it is provided here merely as a guide, and is not intended as a diagnostic tool. (If you feel you need or want a scientifically formulated diagnosis, it's advisable to go to a counselor qualified to administer such tests.)

Part I of my Quiz helps you decide whether you are extraverted or introverted, and is based on my knowledge of various psychological tests and measurements, some of which are described above. Part II assesses right- and left-brain traits and is based on my observations of more than one hundred women and men in my dream study groups, seminars, workshops, and research projects. I believe my Quiz is easier for the lay person to score and interpret than the more complex psychological tests.

It's fun and revealing to take my Quiz yourself and then guess what your partner might say. Then have your partner take it, also trying to guess what you might have answered. By comparing results you can discover how well you understand one another, and the areas where you both may wish to work on your modes of thinking and expressing emotions.

A Quiz to Identify Personality Types

First, check the answer, (a) or (b) which *most closely resembles your style, tendency, or choice*—even though you may not agree entirely. After entering your responses on one of the answer sheets at the end of the Quiz, score according to directions which follow. There are no right or wrong answers, and no personality type is better or worse than any other.

Part I

1. **At a social gathering do you** —(a) mingle with everyone, even strangers —(b) stay with a few, familiar people
2. **At a party do you feel happier if** —(a) you stay, feeling better the later it gets —(b) you leave early to avoid getting tired
3. **When making a telephone call do you** —(a) say whatever happens to occur to you —(b) rehearse what you intend to talk about
4. **When you meet strangers do you** —(a) have very little to

say, feel uncomfortable —(b) talk with them quite easily

5. **In a group do you usually** —(a) start the conversation —(b) keep quiet until someone else speaks first or asks you a question

6. **Would you rather have** —(a) a few friends and see them more often —(b) a lot of friends whom you don't see so often

7. **If the doorbell rings unexpectedly, are you usually** —(a) interested, curious —(b) annoyed

8. **When you travel do you usually like** —(a) unexpected events —(b) planned events

9. **In a class, would you rather have** —(a) instructor's informative lecture —(b) lively class discussion

Part II

10. **Are you drawn more to** —(a) originality —(b) prestige

11. **Is it better to rely on** —(a) deliberate reasoning —(b) immediate inspiration

12. **Is it better to be** —(a) fluid —(b) stable

13. **Are you more attracted to** —(a) sensible people —(b) imaginative people

14. **Is it more dangerous to** —(a) have your head in the clouds —(b) be in a rut

15. **Would you describe your thinking as usually** —(a) abstract —(b) objective

16. **Do you trust** —(a) original expression —(b) precise memory

17. **Are you attracted more by the** —(a) logical —(b) creative

18. **Are psychics** —(a) a bit annoying —(b) somewhat fascinating

19. **Are you attracted to those who are** —(a) reasonable —(b) fascinating

113

20. **Which quality is more important** —(a) ingenuity —(b) stability
21. **Which word do you prefer** —(a) composition —(b) component
22. **Would you rather have things** —(a) settled, decided —(b) unsettled, undecided
23. **Are you more drawn to** —(a) the inventive —(b) the consistent
24. **Is it better to have** —(a) consensus in theory —(b) consensus in facts
25. **Do you prefer** —(a) possibilities —(b) realities
26. **Are you more interested in learning about** —(a) theory —(b) certainty
27. **Are you more attracted to people who are** —(a) insightful —(b) practical
28. **Are you the kind of person who is usually** —(a) cool-headed —(b) sentimental
29. **Do you like to read** —(a) newspapers —(b) novels
30. **Do you work better when** —(a) there is a deadline —(b) You can do it at your own pace
31. **Is it better to** —(a) have a schedule —(b) just let things happen
32. **Are you ruled more by** —(a) your head —(b) your heart
33. **Are you usually more** —(a) practical —(b) fanciful
34. **Which appeals to you more** —(a) innovative performance such as modern dance or abstract art —(b) established performance such as classical ballet or representational art
35. **Are you more attracted to the** —(a) traditional —(b) off-beat
36. **Would you describe yourself as** —(a) organized —(b) impulsive
37. **Are you more interested in** —(a) ideas —(b) facts

Answer Sheets for Personality Quiz

Check either (a) or (b), next to the corresponding number of each question.

Answer Sheet Number One (for yourself):

No.	(a)	(b)	No.	(a)	(b)	No.	(a)	(b)	No.	(a)	(b)	No.	(a)	(b)
1			2			3			4			5		
6			7			8			9			10		
11			12			13			14			15		
16			17			18			19			20		
21			22			23			24			25		
26			27			28			29			30		
31			32			33			34			35		
36			37											

Answer Sheet Number Two (for your partner):

No.	(a)	(b)	No.	(a)	(b)	No.	(a)	(b)	No.	(a)	(b)	No.	(a)	(b)
1			2			3			4			5		
6			7			8			9			10		
11			12			13			14			15		
16			17			18			19			20		
21			22			23			24			25		
26			27			28			29			30		
31			32			33			34			35		
36			37											

Extra Answer Sheet (for you to guess your partner's type):

No.	(a)	(b)	No.	(a)	(b)	No.	(a)	(b)	No.	(a)	(b)	No.	(a)	(b)
1			2			3			4			5		
6			7			8			·9			10		
11			12			13			14			15		
16			17			18			19			20		
21			22			23			24			25		
26			27			28			29			30		
31			32			33			34			35		
36			37											

Extra Answer Sheet (for your partner to guess your type):

No.	(a)	(b)	No.	(a)	(b)	No.	(a)	(b)	No.	(a)	(b)	No.	(a)	(b)
1			2			3			4			5		
6			7			8			9			10		
11			12			13			14			15		
16			17			18			19			20		
21			22			23			24			25		
26			27			28			29			30		
31			32			33			34			35		
36			37											

Directions for Scoring Personality Quiz

Remember that there are no right or wrong answers; this quiz is designed to indicate Extraversion-Introversion and Right- or Left-Brain Traits. Now, follow these directions to discover what types you and your partner fit best:

Part I. Extraversion-Introversion: If you checked 5 or more of the following answers, you are probably an extravert, in that you relate to your environment by reaching outward, receiving energy from contact with others. If you checked only 3 to 4 of these, you are often outgoing, but tend to be shy in some situations. If you checked less than 3, you are probably an introvert who relates to the world around you by turning inward to your thoughts and feelings, needing privacy and time to be alone.

1. (a) 2. (a) 3. (a) 4. (b) 5. (a) 6. (b) 7. (a) 8. (a) 9. (b)

Part II. Right- and Left-Brain Thinking Styles: If you checked 15 or more of the following answers, you are probably left-brain in your thinking style, logical and accustomed to arriving at solutions to problems in a step-by-step fashion. If you checked 13 or 14, your style is probably bilateral, able to access either left- or right-brain abilities with ease. If you checked 12 or less, you probably tend to be right-brain dominant, so that you are in touch with your feelings, and usually solve problems by looking at the entire picture rather than its parts.

10. (b) 11. (a) 12. (b) 13. (a) 14. (a) 15. (b) 16. (b) 17. (b) 18. (b) 19. (a) 20. (b) 21. (b) 22. (a) 23. (b) 24. (b) 25. (b) 26. (b) 27. (b) 28. (a) 29. (a) 30. (a) 31. (a) 32. (a) 33. (a) 34. (b) 35. (a) 36. (a) 37. (b)

After scoring your answers, you may wish to review the descriptions of the personality type you resemble most. For instance, if you're female and your score indicates you are an extravert with a bilateral thinking style, review this chapter's section describing "Extraverted, Bilateral Women." Be sure to keep in mind that most people have tendencies which may fall into more than one category. However, even with the many exceptions this causes, you can get a general idea of your own and your partner's personality type. Using this knowledge, many of my students and clients have been able to resolve conflicts and improve communication skills.

PRACTICING YOUR UNDERSTANDING OF PERSONALITY TYPES. Now, it's time to discover ways to use what you've learned about the differences most people have, and their tendencies toward extraversion-introversion and hemispheric thinking styles. Please bear in mind that either style of thinking carries no value judgment. These thinking processes are the result of both genetics and environment, and are neither right nor wrong. Further, many people may exhibit traits which apply to several types, indicating that they employ different modes for different situations.

If you and your partner have diametrically opposite thinking styles, therein may lie the root of your conflicts or disappointments. Most such differences can be reconciled, since those who are strongly one way or the other usually benefit from attempts to develop the less dominant sides of themselves. For instance, Florence, a left-brain type, delighted in the discovery of her right-brain abilities when Lou, a bilateral thinker, persuaded her to join him in exploring their dreams. Frank, whose initial resistance to right-brain activities frustrated his wife Sarah, learned to enjoy these pursuits and became closer to his wife in the process. On her part, Sarah became more confident and self-reliant as Frank accepted her opinions and interests.

After you've determined your own personality tendencies, notice those of your partner or the men or women you usually date. If you like right-brain activities and your partners usually lean toward left-brain pastimes, you may wish to adopt tactics like Lou's to persuade them to try out your favorite concerns. Or, you may find that having your left-brain partner teach you some of the special skills that type accesses so easily may draw you closer to one another.

The important message behind all descriptions of personality traits is that every individual is different. Understanding how these differences developed, and how essential they feel to the person who has them, can help you become more accepting and less judgmental.

When you can't decide which type one of you may be, sharing dreams will usually provide additional clues. Simply talking about a dream, with the traits of each type in mind, can help you spot similar traits in yourself. Most importantly, knowing a dreamer's type will help you interpret that person's dreams.

Summary

In this chapter you've learned how dreams can provide clues which can deepen your understanding of your partner, or help you find a compatible person if you're still searching for your ideal mate.

Sometimes our expectations concerning true love are unrealistic. We may mistake the fleeting feelings of "being in love" for a relationship that is based on trust and an abiding commitment to continue to love the partner no matter what happens, no matter what faults are revealed when the first blush of those "in love" sensations fades. (However, this does not preclude the fact that couples who remain together happily almost always have learned how to keep the fires of passion and sexuality alive.)

To understand your partner more thoroughly, or to find another person who "matches" your own personality type, you can get valuable clues from dreams. Observe your own dreams to find out which general category your personality fits. Notice dream themes which may indicate masculinity and femininity, with particular attention to female dreams during different reproductive cycles. By becoming familiar with the kinds of dreams women have during different times of the month, you can determine the reasons which may cause you or your partner to behave in seemingly illogical ways.

In addition to gender differences, dreams offer valuable clues to the possibility that you or your partner may be experiencing stress which temporarily affects behavior and judgment. The stress of fatigue, and both minor and major transitions, may cause such emotional upheaval that one's usual reactions become distorted. Some transitions are obvious, such as childbirth, divorce, and aging. Others may seem temporary and thus be less easy to uncover, such as career or environmental changes. One's background and value systems may also influence behavior and attitudes toward a lover.

Do you always seem to be attracted to the same type of person? If so, this may be due to your preference for lovers who remind you of your parents. This is not always self-destructive. It may simply mean

119

that your earliest role models are the ones you still trust and who make you feel most comfortable.

On the other hand, if your relationships generally result in severe conflict or situations which make you feel inferior, you may be choosing partners who continually repeat the unresolved issues of your childhood or adolescence. If this appears to be your pattern, it may be time for you to begin looking for a partner who has the *opposite* traits, someone who will boost your self-esteem rather than sabotage it. However, before making such a decision, simply sharing your new understandings of your previously unconscious motives may be all that's needed to help you and your partner build a new climate of trust between you.

All these usually unexpressed motivations can shape our dreams. With all these wonderfully varied personality traits in mind, review your dream notebook, looking for some of the patterns and differences discussed in this chapter.

Check out your own and your lover's ways of relating to the world around you by understanding the theories held by psychologists since Jung classified people as extraverts or introverts. This method is quite similar to hemispheric classification—determining whether a person is right-or left-brain dominant. After studying all the traits of each type and learning to spot clues in dreams, try my Quiz for Identifying Personality Types.

By learning the sorts of dreams these various types usually have, you can identify yourself and potential partners. (However, when studying the personality descriptions in this chapter, it's important to understand that these are broad profiles, so that most people will have traits from more than one group.)

As you review your own dreams now, with all this information about personality types in mind, you may discover some surprising clues to your own recent behavior. As you are becoming more skilled at dream interpretation, sharing the insights your dreams reveal can lead to the honest communication and deeper trust which is the foundation of lasting romance.

Interpreting the
Dream Language of Love

Now that you've been introduced to Conversational Dream Language and the Basics of Dream Structure and Interpretation, you're ready to learn what some of the best minds of the twentieth century have had to say about the meaning of dreams. As a foundation for this information, you'll learn the ways former civilizations attempted to understand their dreams. Although modern technology has dispelled many of the old myths about dreams, we can still learn from ancient wisdom.

After a brief history of the evolution of 20th century dream theories, Part II will also introduce you to the best of current dream interpretation techniques. These are especially appropriate for lovers, since all these methods stress the importance of sharing your dreams with another.

Having learned these easy yet effective interpretation styles, you'll be prepared to explore the many ways you can use this knowledge to enhance your love relationship. After a fuller discussion of "the Dream Dyad" and discovering each other's "Hidden Agendas," you'll find out how to learn from each other's sexual dreams. By openly and frankly sharing these often ecstatic dreams, lovers can discover new ways to deepen intimacy and keep romance alive.

Chapter
FIVE

A Brief History of the Dream Language of Love

Around 200 B.C., a poet of the Chinese Chou dynasty wrote of a noble prince: "On the rush mat below . . . he sleeps and awakes, [saying] 'Divine for me dreams. What dreams are lucky? [Mine] have been of bears, cobras and other serpents.'" In the 2nd century A.D., Artimodorus of Ephesus wrote that when a young woman dreams that she has milk in her breasts, if she is "a maiden in the bloom of youth, it means marriage." It is also written that Caesar's wife Calpurnia begged him not to go to the Senate on that fateful Ides of March day, because "she had dreamed terrible things and feared something monstrous would happen."

These historical quotes are evidence that mankind has ever been fascinated with the mystery, beauty, and power of dreams. Ordinary people, scholars, priests, poets, prophets, and kings—all have attempted to fathom these mysteries and to explain their cause, their purpose, and their meaning.

While knowledge of the history of these attempts to decipher dreams is not necessary for you to interpret your own sleeping visions, a brief overview of what has gone before will enhance your appreciation of this fascinating field. Further, as you learn of the trials, errors, experiments, and theories of centuries of study, you'll see the logic of the interpretation techniques you've learned so far.

This chapter provides a brief overview of the dream theories of ancient cultures as well as the interpretation methods which developed from the time of Freud to the present.

Ancient Wisdom

Until the 20th century, dreams were generally believed to be messages from some divine power outside ourselves—ancient gods, spirits from another place, demons, even Satan himself. Although we may find such superstitious explanations amusing, it's actually possible that some of those notions come as close to the truth as some of the so-called scientific theories proposed today. For instance, the Jungian concept of the "collective unconscious" and its effect on dreams is not far removed from ancient beliefs that dreams are messages from the spirit world.

Clay tablets dating back to 3000 B.C. show that the Babylonians and Assyrians believed dreams were caused by devils and evil spirits. Egyptians, on the other hand, thought dreams were messages from the gods. Their god of dreaming was Serapis. A papyrus, the Deral-Madineh, gives instruction on ways to obtain a dream from the gods. Dating back to between 2000 and 1790 B.C., this may be the oldest existing "book" about dreams.

The Greeks and Romans also put much store in the power of dreams. The Greek islands had many temples to Aesculapius, god of healing. Pilgrims to these temples underwent special rituals in order to have special dreams which would give them suggestions for healing a variety of ailments. Modern medicine is just now recognizing some of the healing properties of herbs used by the ancients, remedies which were often inspired by their dreams. Contemporary dream psychologists also recognize that it is possible to induce or "incubate" dreams about a specific topic, just as did the mendicants at the Aesculapian temples.

Most people are familiar with Biblical dreams, such as the Jacob's Ladder Dream described in Genesis, and the tortured, plague-predicting dreams of Pharaoh as he resisted Moses' warnings that he must release the Jews from slavery. Dreams have consistently played a major role in the legends and lore of most religions.

In Buddhist legends, Queen Maya, said to be Buddha's mother, dreamed that a sacred white elephant entered her body through her side. This dream was interpreted as a prophecy of the fabled leader's birth and is the subject of a famous 19th century Chinese painting, *Birth of Buddha*.

Other paintings have commemorated dreams throughout history. These include an illustration for a 16th century French poem, *The Romance of the Rose*, which describes a dream of a lover who enters a garden where he attempts to pick a rose, and is prevented by figures who symbolize Danger, Scandal, and Modesty. The 18th century artist and poet William Blake also found dreams fascinating; one of his most famous illustrations, *Queen Katherine's Dream*, shows the queen envisioning "a blessed troop/Invite me to a banquet, whose bright faces/Cast thousand beams upon me, like the sun." Some art historians believe this visionary ink-and-watercolor drawing is the forerunner of the style Blake later used for his famous illustrations of Dante's *Divine Comedy*.

Closer to home, both North and South American Indians have left us incredibly beautiful sand paintings and handwoven fabrics depicting dreams. Indians depended upon their dreams for divine guidance, which affected every aspect of their lives, from planting and harvest times to choice of a mate.

Theories of Dream Interpretation

While modern science has changed our beliefs about the origins and the physiological causes of dreams, their interpretation has taken a different route. The ancient Greeks and Romans, primitive societies, and American Indians in particular frequently used their dreams to predict the future or to heal afflictions of the mind, body, and heart. These techniques are still applicable today. While psychologists rarely believe that dreams are messages from the gods, many do believe that our godlike inner self does attempt to communicate with us via our dreams.

The modern approach to dream interpretation has its roots in the early 1900s when German scientists theorized that the human mind has strata or layers of consciousness. Since then, dream interpretation theory has evolved mainly as:

- Freudian theory
- Jungian theory
- Gestalt theory
- Eclectic approaches

While the first three of these are the major theories which emerged when scientists began to view the mind as having both conscious and unconscious aspects, there were many other variations and adaptations of these principal schools of thought. However, to have a general knowledge of the history of dream theory, these first three main groups are sufficient. The group I have called "eclectic" is made up of theories which are combinations or offshoots of the Freudian, Jungian, or Gestalt theories.

Freudian Theory

Before Freud, one method of determining a dream's meaning was to take each dream element as a sign and then consult a dream manual or authority for its meaning. Today, dream "dictionaries" are considered invalid because they do not take into account the individual dreamer's personality and lifestyle.

Another pre-Freudian method of interpretation involved looking at the entire dream and attempting to find some context other than the actual dream elements for the intended message. For example, in the Old Testament, when Joseph dreamed, "My sheaf rose on end and stood upright, and your [Joseph's brothers'] sheaves gathered round and bowed low before my sheaf," the brothers interpreted this to mean that one day Joseph would rule over them as a king.

Freud's classic *The Interpretation of Dreams*, published in 1900, changed these notions that dreams were divine, good, or bad. Freud theorized that our wishes, especially those which are morally unacceptable to our waking consciousness, find expression in our dreams. He believed these wishes correspond to our earliest stages of development, from infancy to early childhood. Freud named these developmental phases the oral, anal, phallic, and genital stages.

Thus, the adult whose infantile needs for oral gratification (sucking, nursing, breastfeeding) were not satisfied may dream of greedily eating, drinking, or sucking with great pleasure, a fulfillment perhaps not acceptable in waking life. In a like manner, the other developmental phases may be represented in dreams. Had Freud interpreted Joseph's dream, he probably would have seen the sheaves of grain as phallic symbols, and Joseph's more erect one as an infantile wish for dominance over his brothers.

Since Freud claimed that, during phallic and genital stages of development, the child longed for sexual fulfillment with the parent of the opposite sex, his theory met with shocked protests from both the public and the academic community. Yet his belief that certain dream elements were sexual—a snake or candle symbolizes the penis; a door or tunnel, the vagina, and so on—was indeed the representation many of his female patients visualized. Since Freud put forth his theories during the Victorian era, public reaction was all the stronger since it offended the prim and rigid sexual mores of the times. However, it was those very attitudes which were causing the hysteria syndrome Freud observed in so many females. His work no doubt influenced the eventual liberation of both women and men from the Victorian taboos which prevented natural expression of sexual drives.

Freud's complex and highly developed system of dream interpretation contained much more than this concept of dreams as fulfillment of infantile wishes. In *Working With Dreams*, Ullman and Zimmerman point out Freud's emphasis on the ingenious and artful ways dream images express meaning, as well as the ways dream themes provide links to our past and an understanding of the ways we carry childhood conflicts into adult life. Further, Freud introduced the method of free association as an avenue to the meaning of dream images—a method most modern dream psychologists still use. He also advocated the importance of sharing one's dream with another person when attempting interpretation. However, Freud did not believe that a lay person was capable of dream interpretation.

Jungian Theory

When Dr. Carl Jung, one of Freud's early associates, broke off to begin his own system of dream work, he revolutionized psychoanalysis. Jung believed that dream symbols expose rather than hide our inner selves. Jung disagreed with Freud's wish-fulfillment theory, and claimed that many dream elements tell us about parts of ourselves which we may not be expressing. He saw our dreams as allies, rather than as a dark force which attempts to hide unacceptable desires from our waking consciousness.

Jung also encouraged his clients to write down both their dreams and their waking fantasies, and to actively participate in interpretation. This approach is contrary to Freudian discipline, which holds that only the psychoanalyst is trained to unravel the dream's meaning. Further, Jung urged therapists to approach each client's dreams with an open mind, with no preconceived theories or structures. By eliminating the limitations of Freudian therapy, Jung opened the way for dream interpretation by nonprofessionals. Although he did not actually surrender dreamwork to the dreamer, his insistence on the importance of the individual's interpretation eventually led to the refinement of many of the techniques you've been learning in this book.

Jung's belief that our dreams show us unrealized parts of ourselves is the basis of his concepts of the *anima* and *animus*. In Jungian terms, the anima is the feminine side, the animus is the masculine. Thus a female dreamer may discover her animus, her stronger, more masculine side, represented in her dreams and become aware of a need to encourage this part of her nature to expand. Similarly, a male dreamer may discover his anima, his softer, more feminine side. Further refinements of the Jungian approach involve the dreamer's becoming aware of her or his "shadows," or the darker aspects of personality. This knowledge helps the dreamer bring heretofore dormant potentials into conscious, waking life. For example, Bert (whose dream of a talented young man named Albert was described in Chapter 4) told me about the following dream and the way his Jungian therapist helped him interpret it:

> We were transferring these beams to a waiting flatbed truck. We had to balance each beam on a forklift for transferring . . . I was an expert on handling forklifts (2nd segment): We were in this room and I was taking down all of the many pictures on the wall around the fireplace. We were going to repaint, start fresh, discard some of the old. It seemed as though I was doing more than my share of the work, but no matter. (I do take responsibility, but not always with great grace.)

In discussing his dream, Bert explained that he and his wife Annette are building a new house. At the warehouse connected to his office, Bert has been storing some beams which must be forklifted, loaded on a truck, and taken to the building site. In the past, Bert at one time drove forklifts, just as he's doing in the first part of his dream.

Further, once the house is finished, Bert and his wife will have to remove their belongings from their present home. While this may have explained the dream removal of the pictures, Bert thought it also meant that "I am now clearing some of my preconceptions relating to religion, mind, soul, body, and may be able to come to see a separation between mind/body and psyche/self. The latter might not die with the mind/body. May be just a part of the universal collective unconscious, and have a life of its own in which I can learn to participate."

Bert told me he had long been troubled by a fear of being alone, a common fear among people his age, which may actually be a fear of death. Bert continued, "I was also thrilled to have [Bert's Jungian therapist] point out that my invisible partners (animas, shadows, etc.) do have collective intelligence for which I have not given them credit, not communicated with them about, so there is a richness within which remains unexplored—and I do not have to search in others for wisdom, information, intelligence. A lot of that is available to me for the asking. So I should be able to, through active imagination, solve the previous excruciating fear of being alone. This may be a breakthrough that the second part of my dream confirms."

Bert's mention of the "collective unconscious" refers to another Jungian concept. Jung believed our dreams tap into this merging of the human race's higher selves, and that these forces produce what he called "archetypal images." Such images have similarities to myths, legends, and folk tales. Jung called dreams portraying these archetypes "big" dreams and claimed that such dreams denote major changes in the dreamer's unconscious. While Bert's Moving Day dream was probably not an archetypal one, it did appear to him to indicate that an important change was occurring within himself, one which might resolve his fear of being alone, and his fear of death.

While most contemporary dream psychologists applaud Jung's emphasis on the dream as a challenge to the dreamer to develop his special potentials, many do not agree with his concept of archetypes and the collective unconscious. As Dr. Richard M. Jones points out in *The New Psychology of Dreaming*, there are many difficulties involved in attempts to assess the merit of Jung's theories. Obviously, there is no scientific way the reality of a collective unconscious can be shown to exist. However, such a theory goes far to explain the remarkable fact that certain groups of dreamers seem to envision the same motifs and images, regardless of the dreamers' culture or century. For example, pregnant women in primitive societies dream of small animals as symbols of the fetus, just as do modern American expectant mothers. This "universality" of dream themes may be an inherited trait or may come to our dreams via the synthesis of humankind's dreaming thoughts. More likely it simply indicates that people have common experiences simply because they are human.

Gestalt Theory

Dr. Frederick S. Perls, author of *Gestalt Theory Verbatim*, introduced the group therapy method of dream interpretation. With this technique, the dreamer has a dialogue with each element of a dream, with other group members role-playing each part. Perls believed that each dream element portrays an uncompleted or unexpressed part of our past, parts he called "emotional holes."

When we tried out the Gestalt technique in one of my dream study groups, we used Patty's recurring dream of the hallway and the frightening, closed door (described in Chapter 3). Patty and Alan lived together, and at the time of this dream, they were confronted with Alan's opportunity to transfer to another city for a better job. Here is Patty's dream:

> I am walking down this long, rather dark hallway. It has plain wooden walls and a wood floor. At the end, I face a door. It's just an ordinary door, nothing special about it. Has a regular doorknob. But suddenly I am terribly afraid. I feel I'm being pressured to open it and I don't want to. I reach my hand out and see I am trembling, shaking. Cannot bring myself to touch the doorknob. I don't know what may happen, and I always wake up at this point, feeling very scared.

To "role play" Patty's dream, several group members formed two lines, representing the dream hallway's walls, while another stood at the end, as the door. As Patty walked between the "walls," they asked her, "What do we remind you of?" She replied that they seemed familiar, comfortable, ordinary, like the walls and hallways of her home as a child. "But where are we leading you?" one part of the hall asked. Patty came to a quick halt, and looked apprehensive. She told us she was remembering sitting in the corner of a long hallway when she was a child, so we urged her to do the same, now. Curled up in almost fetal position, Patty (who is actually forty-four, and quite athletic) took on the appearance of a frightened little girl. She told us, "When I was about six, we moved to a new neighborhood. There were some really nasty kids outside. They were bullies. Mom kept telling me to go out and play and I would hide in the front hall, praying she'd think I'd gone outside."

Relating this experience to her current situation, Patty was able to understand more clearly why she was having this nightmare so frequently. "I guess I'm afraid to make this move, because my experience with moving has always been scary," she explained.

Critics of the Gestalt technique say that, while it helps the dreamer discover unexpressed emotions perhaps symbolized by the dream imagery, it tends to break the dream up into such small parts that the overall meaning may be lost. On the other hand, this method does provide an effective way for a group to participate in interpretation, and to help the dreamer discover new meanings.

Eclectic Approaches

As all these theories of dream interpretation have evolved, each innovator seems to have retained some concepts of his predecessors, discarded others, and then added his own innovations. Just as Jung accepted Freud's belief that each element of a dream symbolizes something in waking life, and then branched off into new concepts which assumed that each dream is healing rather than concealing, so today's dream psychologists have incorporated some of the Jungian and Gestalt ideas into their own methods.

Dr. Albert Adler was another Freudian disciple who broke away. However, his methods offered little that was new or different, with one important exception: he put forth the idea that dreams reflect the dreamer's waking lifestyle.

Some of the more recent theorists made more substantial contributions to our knowledge of the meaning of dreams. These include Drs. Samuel Lowy, Thomas French, Erik Erikson, Calvin Hall, Medard Boss, Walter Bonime, and Montague Ullman. Recent innovators, who have explored new dimensions of dreams, are Drs. Stanley Krippner, Milton Kramer, David Foulkes, Robert Van de Castle, Ernest Hartmann, and Stephen LaBerge.

Dr. Samuel Lowy was more interested in the physiological causes and the functions of dreaming than in interpretation. Like Jung, he believed that the primary function of dreaming is to help the dreamer reach psychic or emotional balance. However, Lowy departed from other theorists radically in that he claimed our dreams perform this function whether we recall them or not. If we do remember a dream or portion of it, and can use this knowledge to improve our waking life, so much the better. Lowy's departure from the by then established authority of the analyst as interpreter thus paved the way for other innovators.

Dr. Thomas French, who collaborated with another renowned dream psychologist, Dr. Erich Fromm, emphasized his belief that every dream has a "focal conflict." French agreed with Freud that wish fulfillment is symbolized in dreams, but he went further by theorizing that these symbolic wishes are aroused by a current problem, and that the entire dream converges on this conflict in order to help the dreamer resolve it. If we look at Patty's recurring dream of the hallway and the door from French's perspective, we might conclude that both the hall and the door symbolize her vagina, which she is "afraid to open" to her lover, Alan. In other words, Patty's conflict might have gone deeper than her childhood fear of moving. Perhaps she was resisting the move because this would mean total surrender to Alan. By going with him to the city where his new job was, Patty had to give up her own job and friends for his sake, a more total surrender than she had yet committed herself to in their relationship.

Although Dr. Erik Erikson remained within the framework of Freudian theory, he contributed many original ideas to dream interpretation methods. Like Lowy, he believed that the "manifest" dream is of primary importance to the dreamer. The term "manifest" in this case refers to the dream report as it stands, without any attempt to unravel its meaning. In 1954, Erikson wrote one article, "The Dream Specimen of Psychoanalysis" for a psychiatric journal. After that, his interest turned to other aspects of personality. He is especially noted for his works on the identity crisis which adolescents undergo, and for his creation of "inner" and "outer space" concepts of the ways women and men think of themselves in relation to the world at large.

Dr. Calvin Hall also investigated the manifest dream. In fact, he compiled one of the largest collections of facts about dreams and dreamers ever accumulated. With Dr. Robert Van de Castle, he wrote *The Content Analysis of Dreams*, which presents a system for "quantifying" or counting almost every possible dream element or image. Using this rather complex analysis system, a researcher can determine the percentages at which certain images appear in groups of dreamers.

Dr. Medard Boss takes what is called the "existential" approach to dreaming. He argues that the experience of the dream is the only important factor in dreaming. He does not so much disagree with any scientific approach to dream interpretation as he simply disagrees with any approach at all. Dr. Richard Jones points out that, if we were to take Boss' position, then in order to truly understand a dream we would have to remain asleep. However, Boss has contributed to dream psychology in that he emphasizes the special, altered states of consciousness we experience while dreaming.

Dr. Walter Bonime, a clinical psychiatrist in New York City, has refined Samuel Lowy's concepts. Author of *Collaborative Psychoanalysis*, he has brought new clarity to dream interpretation while remaining within the classical framework.

Dr. Montague Ullman has made enormous contributions both to our knowledge of the causes and functions of dreaming and to interpretation methods. Ullman was the first major psychoanalyst to take into account the importance of the discovery of REM sleep. He noted that, when dreaming occurs, the body is in a state of semiarousal. Unlike Freud, who thought dreams serve to keep us asleep, Ullman claims that dreams keep the mind alert as we sleep. Like Jung, Ullman says that dreams reveal, rather than conceal. With Dr. Stanley Krippner, who was the Director of the Maimonides Sleep Laboratory which Ullman founded in 1966, he conducted some of the earliest experiments on dream telepathy. His theories of dream functions in contrast to Jung's are detailed in *Working With Dreams* and include his belief that dreams can be a source of emotional healing. Ullman's novel group interpretation process is described in the next chapter.

Our most recent group of innovators are noted either for having explored groups of dreamers whose dreams differ from those of most people, or for experiments in areas which were formerly thought incapable of being measured. Dr. David Foulkes examined the dreams of children, while Dr. Milton Kramer has written a number of articles for professional journals which offer new insights into dream study, especially with people suffering from post-traumatic stress disorders. Dr. Robert Van de Castle has extensively investigated women's dreams during the various reproductive cycles, and has participated in some recent experiments in dream telepathy. Dr. Stanley Krippner has also investigated telepathic dreams as well as other altered states of consciousness, and has devised a method of interpretation which helps the dreamer become aware of a "personal mythology" which motivates actions and attitudes in waking life. You are already familiar with Dr. Ernest Hartmann, author of *The Nightmare*. He has investigated the biology of dreaming and the effects of drugs on sleep and dreams.

One of the most unusual of these recent innovators is Dr. Stephen LaBerge, author of *Lucid Dreaming*. LaBerge has devised a special electronic "sleep mask" which flashes a yellow light when REM sleep begins. This alerts the dreamer that a dream is taking place, and frequently causes a "lucid" dream. When the yellow light appears in the dream, the dreamer usually remains asleep, and yet knows he or she is dreaming. By awakening laboratory subjects after such dreams, researchers are able to obtain immediate reports of lucid dreams in a way never before possible.

Women in Dream Research

Women generally recall their dreams more often than men, with the result that their dreams have been studied more frequently. Yet there are comparatively few female researchers among those who have made significant scientific contributions to our understanding of dreams. This may be due to the difficulties women have had, until recently, in entering the graduate levels of study which would qualify them to achieve notice in this rapidly growing field.

Among those who have made important investigations, Dr. Patricia Garfield and Dr. Rosalind Cartwright are outstanding. Garfield's books include *Creative Dreaming, Pathway to Ecstasy, Your Child's Dreams*, and *Women's Bodies, Women's Dreams*. The first of these, *Creative Dreaming*, has inspired the public and the scientific community alike with its groundbreaking discussion of the ways we can use the methods of primitive dreamers to control our dreams today. In *Pathway to Ecstasy*, Garfield describes her own dreams of love and sexuality.

Cartwright, director of a sleep laboratory in Chicago, was featured in a recent issue of *Psychology Today* as being representative of the latest directions on dream research. Her work in analyzing the dreams of divorcing couples is a landmark study.

My own research on the psychology of expectant mothers, detailed in *Pregnancy and Dreams*, was probably the largest, most in-depth study of that topic ever published. There are a number of other popular books about dreams written by women, the most notable of which are those by the British psychologist Ann Faraday (*Dream Power, The Dream Game*) and California psychologist Dr. Gayle Delaney (*Living Your Dreams*). Delaney's interpretation techniques are described in the next chapter. Dr. Jayne Gackenbach has been a pioneer in the field of lucid dream research. Her findings are described in Chapter 8.

Summary

This chapter has given you some of the highlights of the history of dreaming since earliest times. Humankind has ever been intrigued with this puzzling phenomenon of the human mind. We have seen that, despite early 20th century derision of the old ways, many ancient beliefs about dreams are after all not so different from our so-called modern concepts.

Although the ancients believed dreams were divine messages, Freudian theory held that dreams are messages from the dreamer's unconscious. Both the ancients and contemporary dream psychologists held that dream images are not what they seem; rather, they are symbols for something else. Joseph's brothers thought his dream of his sheaf of grain standing tall above theirs symbolized his ruling over them in the future. A Freudian might interpret the same dream as meaning that Joseph's penis or masculine power was larger and stronger than his brothers'. Thus, both interpretations have the same underlying meaning.

The major departure from Freud arose with the ideas of Dr. Carl Jung, who emphasized the importance of the dreamer's personal associations to each dream element. Jungian theory also advanced the idea of the "collective unconscious" with its archetypal dream images which occur to dreamers in distinctly different cultures and across time. Jung paved the way for nonprofessionals to take responsibility for their own dreams, without dependence on experts, authority figures, or therapists to interpret for them.

This idea gained added acceptance with the Gestalt group therapy approach, wherein the dreamer and other group members reenact the dream, helping the dreamer view the experience more objectively. Most of the more recent techniques are eclectic in derivation, drawing methods from Freud, Jung, the Gestalt approach, or combinations of these.

This chapter has also acknowledged the work of women in the field of dream research, a comparatively recent development. Since women usually recall their dreams more easily, and have thus contributed a great deal to dream research, their work as scientists promises to give us a better understanding of the still mysterious world of dreams.

As you become more practiced with interpretation of your own dreams, you may find it helpful to look at them from some of the viewpoints of the methods this chapter describes. Perhaps your dreams indicate some early childhood lack of fulfillment—a typical Freudian approach—and you'll find that by nurturing yourself in these areas, you'll feel more self-confident. Or, your dreams may reveal an opposite aspect of your personality, in Jungian terms your anima or animus. By allowing yourself to express these traits more fully, you may find that you've grown emotionally, and that this self-expansion makes you all the more enticing to your lover.

Chapter
SIX

Learning from Modern Experts

At a recent reception for Dr. Stanley Krippner in the posh San Francisco Metropolitan Women's Club, a dozen smartly dressed couples sat around a large table, having coffee and dessert and discussing their dreams. When Krippner requested that someone relate a very brief dream, Annette (a well-known society woman and Bert's wife) volunteered:

> Dreamed I was staring at a large bottle of makeup. Its label read, "Spiritual Center." There was nothing else in the dream. I recognized it as the makeup I use every day, by its shape and size. That strange label was the only thing different about the bottle, since of course my makeup has another name. It seemed I concentrated on the bottle for a long time, and then I woke up.

After the group heard Annette's dream, Dr. Krippner invited them to "Tell the dreamer what you would think this dream meant, if *you* had the dream." The group member speaking should not try to imagine what Annette might have thought it meant. Rather, the association should be the personal reaction of the speaker, imagining that she or he had experienced the same dream.

Another fashionably attired woman commented, "If *I* had that dream, I'd think my dreams were telling me I spend too much time on my appearance and not enough on my church's affairs." This woman's husband remarked, "If *I* had that dream, I'd think it meant my true feelings, my spiritual self, are all bottled up inside."

His wife gave his hand a loving pat while someone else said, "Well, if *I* had that dream, I'd think there's some sort of pun or play on words, with the idea of makeup as being a clue to the type of personality or makeup I have."

Dr. Krippner, the well-known author and lecturer on dreams, was teaching the San Francisco gathering a group interpretation process. This chapter will provide you with details of these modern interpretation techniques:

- The Ullman group method
- Krippner and Feinstein's Personal Mythology process
- The Delaney-Flowers method
- The Maybruck method

The Ullman Group Method

At the reception for Krippner, the San Franciscans were introduced to Dr. Montague Ullman's process for group dream interpretation. After listening to the comments of the group, the dreamer gives her own interpretation, feeling free to use any of the suggestions made by her audience. In this case, Annette decided that her true "makeup" or personality was spiritual. Despite the glossy, glamorous facade she presents to the world, she felt herself to be a deeply spiritual person.

This technique is often quite effective when used between couples as a means of gaining insights into each other's attitudes. This result was clearly demonstrated in Krippner's party setting, when various partners began looking at each other with new understanding after hearing comments such as that of the man who admitted his feelings are "all bottled up inside."

I sometimes use an adaptation of the Ullman technique in workshops and dream study groups for couples. In my workshop called "Reunion of the Sexes," the women tell their dreams and discuss them while the men listen. Then the men do the same, with the women listening. In the third workshop session, we have a discussion about the insights we've gained with this process.

For example, during a California workshop, Kate shared this recurring dream:

I am back in college during the first days of my freshman year. Have a schedule of courses and classes in my hand, and a map of the campus, but I feel overwhelmed. I'm looking for my chemistry class and can't find the room. I blunder into a philosophy class and the teacher, annoyed, tells me I'm in the wrong building. Bells are ringing and I realize I'm late, probably won't make it to the first class. I run out and across to another building and race up some steps but still can't find the room. I feel confused and anxious and think I am just too stupid to be in college and I wake up.

Kate told us she usually had this recurring dream at the beginning of a relationship. "I remember having it after my first date with my ex-husband, and also during our divorce," she said. "Now, I'm going with Guy, whom I really love. But I've had this dream twice in the past month, and I'm wondering if it means our relationship will go sour, just like my marriage did."

Using the Ullman technique, the other women in our group commented. "If *I* had that dream," said one, "it would happen every time I felt out of control. I remember well how confused I was those first days in college, with the overload of new places, classes, and faces. I felt just totally out of control. So if I had a dream like that now, I'd think it meant I'm not in control of something going on in my real life."

Another participant said, "If *I* had that dream, it would indicate I am feeling inferior. Especially the part about thinking I was just too stupid to be in college." A third woman remarked, "If *I* had that dream, I would notice the part about not making it to my first class. That might be a pun or metaphor about my not being first rate, first class, or good enough. And I do feel that way sometimes with my husband, because he's so much smarter than I am in some ways."

After listening to all these comments, Kate said, "Oh, yes! I really relate to that idea that I may not be 'first class.' Because sometimes I do feel inferior to Guy. He's a biochemist with all kinds of degrees. Oh—and in my dream I was late for chemistry class! I want very much to understand his work, which I think is just fascinating. I guess I'm afraid he'll think I'm stupid. Not that he ever, in any way at all, puts me down."

Indeed, Guy was quite surprised that Kate harbored any such feelings. In the men's session of our workshop, he told this dream:

The dream begins in my lab. A very important woman doctor is inspecting us. She comes and looks over my shoulder as I pour some concoction with formaldehyde and other ingredients into a test tube. I explain that it will help me observe some forms of life without actually harming them. She says, "Let's see if it works." She pours some of the liquid onto the top of my head and the next thing I know, I am in the test tube, swimming around in this thick cloudy stuff. I have shrunk! (Last night we saw the movie *Honey, I Shrunk the Kids*.) This doctor is turning the tube round and round, examining me. I feel dizzy and manage to get my head up in the air and yell, "Hey! Let me out! This is awful!" So she shakes the tube and I fall out with a thump, feeling glad to be back to normal. (Then I woke up and I had almost fallen out of bed, with one foot on the floor.)

Using the Ullman technique again, the other men told Guy their reactions. "If *I* had that dream," said one, "it would mean I feel very small and insignificant when one of my superiors at work evaluates me. I just went through a job evaluation, in fact. I came out fine, even got a promotion, but I sure hated going through it."

Another man said, "If *I* had that dream, I would notice the fact that a woman was inspecting me, looking me over. My Mom used to make me feel that way, especially on Sunday mornings. We had to get all slicked up for church and she'd inspect us like an Army sergeant." And a third workshop man remarked, "If that were *my* dream, I'd think being in the test tube meant I feel confined, imprisoned, in my relationship. That's actually the way I feel sometimes about our marriage, and it's the reason my wife and I are here for this workshop."

Taking all these comments into consideration, Guy told us his associations to his dream: "I do agree to some extent with what everyone has said. But I don't feel small or inferior with Kate—not exactly. It's just that, sometimes I do feel she's so worried about making the same mistakes with me that she did with her ex, that she tends to examine and analyze everything in our relationship too much. I think the dream was showing me that. Also, my mother sometimes made me feel the same way, as if I were under a microscope, being observed. I was rather bright," Guy said modestly, "and I think my mother was just being amazed at some of the things I said and did. I know women who do that are usually expressing love and pride—but it can make you feel damned uncomfortable!"

During the last session of that workshop, when both men and women came together to discuss their reactions, Kate and Guy told us that they'd discovered they were more alike than either had suspected. Kate said, "I've been acting like Guy's Mom used to, I'll admit. We both think he's such a genius we often sit back and say things like, 'Isn't he incredible?' and 'Notice how he solved that problem so easily!' I had no idea we made him self-conscious by doing that." Guy added, "And I had no idea Kate felt inferior in any way. She has so much to offer, I learn so much from her, especially about emotions and interacting with others. Those talents are more important to me than whether she's a whiz at chemistry. Even in that area, she knows more than any other woman I've ever met." Guy and Kate vowed that they would continue to share their dreams in order to avoid unnecessary misunderstandings.

You can use the Ullman technique with just one person, preferably your partner. After listening to your lover's dream, instead of making suggestions as to its meaning, say, "If *I* had that dream . . ." and then explain what it might mean if it had actually been a dream of your own. The beauty of this process is that it gives both the dreamer and the listener an opportunity to reveal their own attitudes and problems. It also permits the listener to suggest possible interpretations without imposing on the dreamer's ideas and feelings.

Krippner and Feinstein's Personal Mythology Process

Dr. Krippner, collaborating with Dr. David Feinstein, details the theory of "Personal Mythology" in a recent book of the same title. This interpretation process is based on the idea that we each have a myth about our goals, potentials, and capacity for creativity. Further, this myth, usually adopted early in life, resists change even though we may grow with experience and knowledge. (This concept is similar to my idea of "Hidden Agendas," described more fully in the next chapter.) Krippner and Feinstein call the emerging self-image the counter-myth, which attempts to help us overcome past fears and mistakes. The resulting inner conflicts are reflected in our dreams.

Krippner has been developing this process for a number of years, teaching it to graduate students and psychologists in all-day seminars at conventions of such organizations as the Association for Humanistic Psychology. In these workshops, participants pair off (forming what I call the "Dream Dyad") and share dreams. Each partner in the pair helps the other determine personal myths of the past, attempting to identify dream clues to the new, improved self-image mirrored in recent dreams. When the entire group reconvenes, Krippner uses a dream from one volunteer to demonstrate her or his personal mythology.

For example, in one such workshop a woman told a dream about secretly leaving home to explore a strange town by herself. Krippner rephrased the dream as if it were a fairy tale, with the dreamer as an overly protected princess who escaped the confines of the castle, proving she was quite capable of being self-sufficient. This woman's personal myth was that she was a fragile little girl who couldn't take care of herself and must always rely on the opinions of others. Her counter-myth was that she is now an adult with valid opinions of her own.

At the conclusion of a typical Personal Mythology workshop, participants formulate a brief slogan which captures the essence of their new myth, which usually synthesizes the best elements of both the old myth and the counter-myth. Then each one asserts his or her "slogan" to the applauding group. For instance, the woman whose dream showed her escaping the bondage of her myth that she was nonassertive might avow, "I can make my own decisions!" or "I can do it myself!"

While this technique is very effective in all-day seminars and workshops, it does require considerable effort and dedication on the part of the dreamer, and may be most effective when undertaken in a group with a charismatic therapist such as Krippner as leader. One of its many assets is that it helps the dreamer become aware of self-defeating attitudes and behavior, as well as alerting one to dream clues which suggest alternatives.

The Delaney-Flowers Method

Dr. Gayle Delaney's *Living Your Dreams* describes her technique of thinking of your dream as a movie, with yourself as scriptwriter, set designer, director, and each of the characters. In a dream study group, Delaney's clients "interview" the dreamer about the dream "movie" from the viewpoint of director, actors and actresses, and so on.

One of the interviewing techniques in Delaney's book involves having the dreamer pretend she is defining a dream element or image to "an alien from Mars" who has never heard of that item. In this way the dreamer is encouraged to extend the imagination in search of synonyms and associations to the dream image. Dr. Loma Flowers, a

San Francisco psychiatrist, has been working with Delaney for a number of years. Together, they have refined this method of helping the dreamer make associations to dream elements. They now colead workshops in the U.S. and Europe, where this technique is emphasized.

For example, when we tried this method in one of my dream study groups, Suzanne, the artist (whose dreams of wild dogs and of being chased by ghost men were described in previous chapters), shared the following:

I'm with my friend Jane in a San Francisco hotel room . . . She says, "No one could love you like *I* do. No one could know me like *you* do." Suddenly an earthquake begins . . . I know the place will crumble. I tell her we need to take off. On foot, we reach an intersection. Watching some buildings fall, we head in one direction together. Suddenly she's gone and a lost lion runs toward me, terrifying people. I stroke it and calm it. It clings to me, slightly hurting my hand sometimes because of its fear, but I can handle it. I run into a coffee shop, emptying my pockets in which are two twenties, a ten and some ones. I say, "Just give it *something*! Some meat, a doughnut!" A waitress gives me a large bowl of condensed milk. The lion laps it up hungrily and then is a bit more mellow and tame. I go to pay the bill and the male owner of the restaurant says, "I've got the waitress here to testify against you about bringing that lion in here, if you don't pay the full bill. It's fifty-three dollars." And I start yelling, "Fifty-three dollars! You have no right! I took this lion in to help people!" and I woke up still feeling angry.

Using the Delaney-Flowers method, we asked Suzanne to describe various parts of her dream as if we were aliens from outer space. In describing Jane, Suzanne said, "She's a friend who, in my waking life, represents sexuality. And danger. Because my lover Jerry seems attracted to her. I'd like to be like Jane, who isn't afraid to show her sexiness." Next, we asked Suzanne if anyone else reminds her of Jane. "Well, we are alike, actually," Suzanne admitted. "Just as she said in my dream, we understand each other. We both have strong sex drives."

In describing her dream's hotel room, Suzanne said, "Jane and I were shaken out of it by the earthquake. That's a jolt. In my waking life, the day before I had that dream, Jerry and I had been at our therapist Bill's office, and in talking about my sexuality I did feel jolted, because I got an impression that Bill might have thought I sometimes come on too strongly. But when I went to bed, I was feeling happy that both Bill and Jerry had seemed to understand about my recent feelings of power and self-confidence."

When asked to describe a lion, Suzanne told us, "A large jungle cat; I think of it as female. It represents power, grace, sexuality, and magnetism. It can be dangerous, too." In relating this description to her waking life, Suzanne said, "This must be a symbol of my own female energy and power."

Suzanne went on to describe her dream's restaurant owner as an authority figure, like her therapist, Bill. She said, "In my dream, after feeding my power (the lion) the owner tells me my bill (another reference to Bill in waking life) is too much. I would have to give up all my money (also a symbol of my power)." She thought the overall message of her dream was, "You have no right to tell me I have to give up all my power. The reason I took on this female energy was to help other people."

You can use the Delaney-Flowers method with your partner quite easily. Simply listen to a dream, and then ask the dreamer to describe each element as if you were an alien who had never heard of that particular item before. Then, ask if anything in the dreamer's waking life is also like that description. The advantage of this method is that it enables the dreamer to make associations to each dream image without feeling pressured. Even people who claim they "have no imagination" can usually define a dream element quite easily—and in so doing they are, in fact, providing the listener with associations and clues to their true feelings about that specific image.

The Maybruck Method

You have already been introduced to my own technique of parsing the dream report, and then making associations to all the important nouns and action words. This method frankly borrows from the Delaney-Flowers process in that the listener encourages the dreamer to describe and define each dream element, and then relate these to waking life situations. Both Dr. Delaney and Dr. Flowers urge other professionals to attend their training workshops, as I have done, and to use or adapt their methods as they see fit. I am in debt to these effective therapists for their willingness to help others like myself.

My method differs in that by using it you can interpret your dreams alone, without a partner. While I agree with most other dream psychologists that dream sharing is a vital part of interpretation, at times when you cannot discuss a dream with someone else, you can still use this easy technique.

For instance, when her husband George was out of town, and she was unable to attend her usual dream group session, my student Cynthia interpreted the following dream by parsing it:

Dreamed I was standing outside our house, which we've been remodeling for the past year. Inside I could see George and several workmen, moving around with their hammers and other tools. The house was on a beach, with an ocean view (actually, we live inland, in a valley). Suddenly a gigantic wave of sand began rolling toward the house, which began to wobble at the impact. George and the workmen suddenly flew out of the house. They looked like little elves or cartoon characters, shooting up into the sky, tools flying after them. Then the house toppled over, the wave of sand rolled over it, burying it completely, and I woke up. Even during the dream I <u>felt more surprised</u> than upset, and

when I awoke I <u>felt relieved and relaxed</u>.

Cynthia telephoned me after she had parsed and begun translating this dream without any help. She had circled all these important nouns: their house, George, the workmen, their hammers and tools, the beach, the wave of sand, elves, cartoon characters, and the sky. Then, she underlined the verbs, the action words: was standing, have been remodeling, could see, moving around, began rolling, began to wobble, flew out, shooting up, toppled over, rolled over, and burying. She also highlighted her emotions during and after the dream by underlining "felt more surprised" and "felt relieved and relaxed."

Cynthia thought her dream house represented all the turmoil she and George had recently undergone as they remodeled their house. Further, some career setbacks had caused George to take a new job which involved travel away from home for weeks at a time.

She thought the workmen symbolized "helpers"—all the friends who'd tried to help the couple during the past year of distress. In describing the wave of sand, Cynthia said, "It reminds me of sand flowing through an hourglass. I think it represents time passing."

As she described her emotions and feelings during this dream, Cynthia said she'd felt a sense of release. "The tension and worry rolled off of me, just the way the sand was rolling," she explained. At this point, Cynthia exclaimed, "That's it! That's the meaning of this dream! I've let go. I'm no longer attached to all those problems. It's all in the past, and George is out of it, too."

Cynthia and George were also learning how to recognize other dimensions of their dreams. In addition to the parsing, and making associations to the highlighted dream elements, I teach my students to notice the following:

- Patterns in dreams
- Levels in dreams

Now that you've learned my basic interpretation method of parsing and making associations, you're ready to learn these refinements which are the mark of an advanced dreamworker. To learn these easy techniques, you'll need records of your dreams over a period of at least several weeks.

PATTERNS IN DREAMS. My term "patterns" refers to a repetition of a general theme or motif in two or more of your dreams. Jung called this an examination of the "dream series." By reviewing your dream notebook, you can discover possible patterns in your own dreams. To get a true picture of the issues you may have been neglecting or ignoring, it's necessary to examine dreams over a period of several weeks, since it usually takes that long for these repetitions of themes or motifs to become apparent. Look for a recurrence of similar feelings or concerns. Such patterns usually indicate that the unexpressed emotion or the conflict your dreams are reflecting has not been resolved and needs to be confronted.

For instance, after George returned home, Cynthia shared her dream of the sand wave with him. Together, they reviewed their dream notebooks for the past several weeks, discovering that nearly every entry contained references to their reconstructed house or George's career problems. After Cynthia's dream experience of "letting go," her dreams began reflecting other concerns and images.

LEVELS IN DREAMS. To glean every possible message your inner self may be sending you in a dream, an understanding of the way your unconscious can imply several meanings with one symbol becomes important. In this case, the word "levels" refers to the possibility that one dream image may have several interpretations, all of which may seem appropriate. For example, Cynthia's rolling wave of sand symbolized time passing as well as the way her tension and worries "rolled off" of her when she had the dream.

To explore this concept further, let's consider this dream George had around the same time, while he was traveling:

Dreamed Cynthia and I were at a ski resort, waiting in line for the lift. I was warmly dressed but saw that Cynthia was wearing a sundress and sandals and was shivering. I suggested she go back to the lodge and get a proper outfit. Then the lift came and she got on with me, anyway. When we got to the top and got off, I said, "I don't see how you can keep the skis on with no boots, just sandals," and then I saw she was wearing boots, ski pants, parka, gloves—everything she needed. (At that point I knew I must be dreaming, since something like that couldn't happen in real life.) I felt amazed. We started down a steep slope and I lost my balance, crashed into a tree, and couldn't move. No pain, but thought I must've broken my leg. Heard a whooshing sound and looked back to see an avalanche of snow rolling toward me. Down the slope I could see Cynthia. She didn't seem to be in the path of this big wave of snow that was coming. Somehow I managed to grab a tree branch and pull myself out of the way as the avalanche roared past me. Then I let go, fell back into the snow, and felt very relieved. Kept telling myself it was only a dream yet I was hoping (rescuers) would come soon. (Then I woke up,

feeling quite relaxed in spite of the scary parts of the dream.)

After parsing his avalanche dream, George could see that his high-lighted words pointed to this interpretation: "While Cynthia and I were waiting, she seemed unprepared—but when our plan finally went into action, she was ready. But I crashed and almost got overtaken with an avalanche that would have meant big trouble!" In other words, George thought his dream was a review of the past year, reminding him to praise his wife for the way she had stood by him, even though she was a bit frightened (shivering), and for proving herself quite capable of handling whatever happened. Further, George was able to see that, even though he "crashed" (symbolizing the loss of his earlier career), he was able to "pull himself out" and to avoid further disaster (by getting a new job).

As we discussed his dream, George also concluded that the mass of snow rolling toward him in the dream might have symbolized, at another level, the same theme as Cynthia's sand wave—the rolling by of all their past problems and worries. He thought this additional meaning for the avalanche was especially appropriate because he re-called feeling relieved and relaxed after the snow passed by. Then he commented, "But I guess I'm still waiting for somebody to 'rescue' me, just like I was in the dream, even though I know it's not realistic." As a matter of fact, George was "rescued" in that his success as a traveling salesman soon got him a promotion to manager of a nearby local office, so that he could again be at home with his family.

George's and Cynthia's dreams might also be classified as what I call "symbiotic," since they both dreamed of similar images (the rolling sand and the rolling snow). Moreover, they both experienced the same dream emotions of release from tension as these massive forms moved by. Symbiotic dreams appear to happen most frequently to couples who, like George and Cynthia, are undergoing some type of crisis or important transition. It may be that such events cause partners to rely upon each other so deeply that they begin to think alike. Then, this closeness appears in their dreams as remarkably similar images. However, these symbiotic dreams are quite rare. If you and your partner are not experiencing such dreams, don't feel that anything is amiss. On the other hand, if you'd like to have such dreams, you may be able to do so by practicing the incubation techniques in future chapters.

Meanwhile, the essential point here is to learn to discover possible alternate levels of meaning for your dream symbols. The following excerpts from dreams of other couples provide additional illustrations of this concept:

- *Penny, whose dream of her 1st husband is quoted in Chapter 4*: In a shopping mall, going from store to store . . . trying to get a "new look" and can't find what I want.
- *Ward, Penny's 2nd husband, the same night*: A strange, beautiful redhead is making love to me . . . then she strips down and I see she isn't a natural redhead.
- *Marcia, whose menstrual dream is quoted in Chapter 4*: Opened the back door and all kinds of birds flew into the house . . . I didn't care about the mess—they were wonderful.
- *Herb, Marcia's husband*: Dreamed I walked out into the lake and then floated on my back . . . it was so peaceful, I wanted to stay there forever.

When Penny had her dream of shopping for a new look, she'd been feeling rather self-critical and worried about getting older. "Just before we fell asleep, I told Ward I was thinking about getting a face-lift, or doing something drastic to feel better about myself," she explained. "So I think my dream was about that." At another level, Penny's dream might have been showing her that she was still feeling unsure about her relationships with men, and that this second marriage was perhaps another failed attempt to find what she wanted.

Her husband Ward's dream of making love to a strange redhead might have reflected their bedtime conversation. "I love Penny just the way she is," Ward told us. "It won't matter to me if she changes her looks. Like the fake redhead in my dream, she'll still be the same, underneath!" As our discussion continued, Ward realized the redhead might symbolize something else, at another level. "I think of redheads as being especially sexy," he said. "I guess I'm wishing Penny would be a little more assertive in bed. I wish she would initiate sex, once in a while."

Ward's admission led our group into an honest talk about their secret sexual desires. Most of the men admitted to fantasies similar to Ward's. One of the women remarked, "But if a woman is already feeling insecure, like Penny's dream showed us she feels about herself, it's not going to be easy for her to make the first moves." Then Penny said, "Well, now that I know how Ward feels about it, I feel better already. Until now, I didn't really believe he loved me that much."

Both Marcia's and Herb's dreams indicated the changes taking place in their relationship since Herb discovered that Marcia's distrust of men stemmed from her brother's cruelty during childhood. Marcia's beautiful dream of her home being filled with singing birds of many shapes and colors mirrored her happiness about her new domestic harmony. At another level, she thought the birds symbolized her desire for children. "I never wanted the responsibility and extra work, before," she explained. "Now, I'm so in love with Herb, I really want to have his child and fill the house with lots of excitement. In my dreams, the birds were leaving droppings on the furniture but I didn't care, because they made me so happy. I'd feel the same way about children, now."

Herb's dream of floating on a calm lake also reflected his contentment about their life in general. At another level, he thought these dream feelings, especially his "wanting it to go on forever," might indicate his resistance to Marcia's desire for a child. "We've only just started enjoying our life together," he said. "I want a little more of this before everything gets turned upside down with a crying baby, diapers, all that." Herb and Marcia did wait another year, and then went through a stressful time when they were unable to conceive. At this writing, I'm happy to report they have a little girl, and another baby on the way.

To put these finer points of dream interpretation into practice, take a few moments right now to review your dream notebook. To search for dream patterns, review a series of dreams, looking for recurring themes by noting the symbolic meanings you assigned to various dream elements. Note the repetition of emotions—especially anxiety—to find out which feelings you may have been repressing or avoiding. Next, look for deeper meanings for the dream elements you've already interpreted. Discussing any additional levels of your dream symbols with your partner will often help you uncover ideas you may not have considered. This introspection can aid you in self-exploration, and simply letting your partner know your thoughts may help both of you express feelings which might otherwise erect barriers between you.

Summary

This chapter has provided you with descriptions of four well-known dream interpretation processes: Ullman, Krippner-Feinstein, Delaney-Flowers, and a fuller description of my own method. These are the techniques I have found most helpful with my students and workshop clients, and they are especially effective with couples who wish to understand their dreams in order to improve their relationship.

The Ullman group interpretation method involves: (1) a dream told to the group by a dreamer; (2) various group members offering their associations as if they had had the dream themselves; and (3) the dreamer taking note of the group's ideas, and then presenting her or his own interpretation. Ullman's method has the advantage of allowing the listeners an opportunity to share their own perceptions about dream images, thus revealing their personal attitudes and thinking styles.

With the Krippner-Feinstein Personal Mythology process, dreams help the dreamer to: (1) identify the still operative, old myth; (2) identify or create a counter-myth which challenges the old one; (3) produce a new myth which is a synthesis of the old and the counter-myths; and (4) resolve and rehearse, putting the new myth into action.

In essence, the Delaney-Flowers method has the dreamer first report a dream and then "define" or describe each dream element to the group. Next, the dreamer is asked, "Does anything in your waking

154

life remind you of that definition?" Thus, the dreamer is gently encouraged to make personal associations to dream images and to decide how these symbolize waking concerns.

The Maybruck method consists of: (1) writing the dream report and parsing it by underlining action words and those indicating emotions, and circling important nouns; (2) making associations to the highlighted words, with special attention to feelings during the dream and upon awakening; and (3) relating these associations to waking life. Although it's preferable to share your dream with your partner, close friends, or a group, this method is also effective when used alone.

Further refinements of my techniques include noticing the patterns and levels in your dreams. Dream patterns are often revealed when you examine a series of dreams over a period of several weeks. When similar themes or symbols appear in several dreams, this may indicate that your inner self has not yet resolved some issue or concern of your waking life. If you give your conscious attention to this conflict or problem, your dreams will probably change, and will begin reflecting other images and ideas.

Although the first association which pops into your mind about any dream element is frequently the correct one, sometimes the same image may reveal more than one level of truth about yourself. Although Marcia's wonderful house full of birds indicated her pleasure with her marital relationship, it also symbolized her desire to have babies now that she and her husband had resolved past misunderstandings.

Now is the time to reexamine your own dream notebook for additional clues to your emotional growth and to deeper understanding of your partner. Having practiced these advanced dream study techniques, you'll be prepared to use this new understanding to increase your sexual intimacy.

Chapter
SEVEN

Loving with Dreams

On a foggy Saturday morning, thirty-eight-year-old Christine and her thirty-nine-year-old husband Jason are enjoying sleeping late. Snuggled together spoon fashion, they seem to be swathed in a cocoon of bonded bliss. Even their breathing is synchronized, as if they are one body. Indeed, they are so entwined it's hard to tell which arms belong to whom.

Christine awakens first. Without opening her sleep-laden eyes, she wiggles still closer to Jason and lazily reviews the dream images still clear in her memory. Jason stretches and yawns. "Shh!" Christine whispers. "I'm still in my dream." Jason lies still, blinking, also trying to hold in mind his own rapidly fading visions of the night. He carefully slides to his side of the bed, reaching for his dream notebook. Sitting up in exaggerated slow motion, yawning and rubbing away the last vestiges of sleep, Jason begins writing. Christine sits up too, smiling impishly.

Jason pauses, eyeing his wife's body as the sheets fall away, revealing her full breasts and slim waist. "That must've been some dream," he says, putting his notebook aside. "What makes you think that?" she murmurs, tickling his ear with the tip of her tongue. "Because of that kittenish, just-ate-the-canary grin on your face," he laughs.

"Well, as a matter of fact," she giggles, "I was eating. But not a canary. I was eating *you*." Jason moves closer and begins stroking her. "Tell me more," he whispers. Then Christine relates this dream:

It must have been a Wednesday night, because Connie was visiting and you weren't home, so I guess you were at your weekly bowling game. Anyway, Connie said, "We don't have to sit around while the men are out having fun. Let's go have fun, ourselves." I told her okay, but reminded her I don't like to go anywhere there's drinking. She said, "I know just the place, trust me." So we left. Connie was acting mysterious and wouldn't tell me where we were going. We were in a taxi with a woman driver. "See, this really is 'Women's Night,' complete with a female cabbie," Connie said. I asked her if we could eat where we were going because I was starving. Then we pulled up to this dimly lit house with the blinds closed. The cabbie made some suggestive remarks and winked at us as we got out. "What are you getting me into?" I asked Connie, but she just pulled me along to the door where she gave several knocks in a kind of code. The door swung open, we went in, and it closed automatically. Creepy! Inside there were little cubicles with curtains. Each one had a table and two chairs and everything was candlelit. We sat down and a woman in a black negligee brought us a menu. It was all in some strange language with letters that looked Chinese or maybe Russian or Greek. Connie told me not to worry, she would translate. She said she'd order the appetizers for us. She pointed to something on the menu and the waitress left. On the table was a bowl of what I thought were flowers and then when I looked closer I saw they were condoms on little sticks. "Now, wait a minute," I told Connie. "Whatever you have in mind, I'm not going to do it. I don't cheat on Jason." She told me to relax, that nothing would happen that would upset me. Then the waitress came back with two plates of what looked like Chinese egg rolls. I tasted one and it was really delicious, sort of honey filled. After I'd eaten two, Connie told me they were aphrodisiacs. I knew that already because I was feeling aroused, but it was weird, almost like being drunk. Then Connie told me to order whatever I wanted. I said, "All I want right now is to be with Jason," and the next thing I knew there you were, lying naked in the middle of the table, grinning at me. Connie was gone but I hardly noticed. I got up onto the table and started kissing you. I told you I was really hungry and I started licking your neck. I could feel these ripples of excitement running through my whole body like electricity and then we both just floated up from the table. We were flying and I was still hungrily licking and nibbling you when I woke up.

Listening to Christine's description, Jason has been gently pushing her down under the covers. "If *I* had that dream," he murmurs, "I'd think it meant I really wanted to make love to you." Christine smiles. "That's what I think it means, too."

Christine confided this little scene to me the following week. "That dream was so personal, I couldn't report it at our group," she said. "And, Jason and I never did try to interpret it, to see if it had any other levels of meaning. We just got too carried away. At the time, I couldn't care less about writing it down or parsing it! Anyway, I think it meant just what Jason said, that I wanted to make love."

This couple were enjoying one of the most delightful ways to share their dreams. I agreed with Christine that her dream of the sexy nightclub probably indicated her desire for intimacy. As a recently recovering alcoholic, Christine had spent a number of months feeling unsure about her ability to respond to Jason sexually, without the aid of alcohol. "That dream taught me that I can feel 'high' without any booze," she said. "And it was actually even better than really being drunk, because there was no hangover!"

Of course, most dreams are not usually as erotic as Christine's. Nevertheless, telling your dreams to your partner immediately upon awakening does help build an atmosphere of intimacy between you.

Some couples speak their dreams into tape recorders every morning, and then play these back for each other in the evening when they have more time for discussion. Personally, I still recommend keeping a dream notebook, since this method gives you the opportunity to review your dreams for additional nuances (such as patterns in a series of dreams, or the various levels of meaning an image may have) at a later date. However, if you find another method more convenient or enjoyable, by all means use it.

This chapter will show you how to use dreams to increase the intimacy of your own relationship by:

- Forming a Dream Dyad
- Discovering Hidden Agendas
- Understanding erotic and sexual dreams

The Dream Dyad

Christine and Jason's awakening exchange is a good example of a Dream Dyad, which simply means that two people share their dreams and help each other interpret them. Although any two people can create a Dream Dyad, we're concerned here with the special closeness you can achieve with your lover by using this process. Before you begin, it's a good idea to be clear about a few "ground rules":

1. Listen without interrupting
2. Withhold your opinions
3. Encourage associations
4. Accept emotions and offending attitudes
5. Suggest alternate interpretations

THE ART OF DREAM LISTENING. Allow your partner to relate an entire dream without interrupting or commenting. After the report, if the dreamer is silent, ask, "What do you think this dream means?" and then listen again. You can show your interest by listening attentively. However, if you find yourself reacting negatively, try to maintain a "poker face" for the moment so as not to inhibit the narrator.

ROMANTIC DREAMS

For example, Florence, the C.P.A. whose dream of "76 trombones" is described in Chapter 4, told Lou this dream as he listened quietly:

I'm in the living room of the house where I grew up, only now I am my adult self. I'm practicing "walking like a dancer," just the way I did as a teenager, trying to balance several books on my head. I have pinned my hair on top of my head so it will make a better surface for the books. My younger brother is there (but he's still a toddler in the dream), playing with his blocks in the corner. I walk all the way to one end of the room, turn slowly, and then my brother pulls at the hem of my skirt, making me lose my balance. The books fall on his head and he starts to howl. "You hurt me!" he cries. "I didn't mean to make you mad! I just wanted to play!" and I feel really angry with him. An older woman I don't know comes in and picks him up. She scolds me and I feel frustrated because she won't understand that what I was doing is important, too. Then I woke up.

After Lou heard Florence's dream, he asked, "What do you think it means?" She said, "Well, I think it has something to do with my work as a C.P.A.—the part about 'balancing books' is an obvious reference to that. Maybe this dream is telling me that I need to make others understand that my work is important to me, even though it may not seem that way to them."

WITHHOLDING OPINIONS. This does not mean that you should repress your feelings. Rather, you should simply refrain from expressing any emotions or your own ideas about what your partner's dream may mean, until she or he has had a chance to arrive at a personal interpretation. Remember that every individual's inner self is different, as unique as a fingerprint or snowflake—and sometimes as delicate. If your mate suspects that your reaction will be negative, or if you impose your own opinions too soon or abruptly, an emerging idea or association may be thwarted or squashed. Later, you'll have the opportunity to present your own ideas. Right now, it's important to build the same climate of trust and acceptance you yourself would like when it's your turn to relate your own dream.

When Florence told Lou her first associations to her dream, his natural reaction was to feel defensive. In the past week, he and Florence had disagreed several times about her working overtime on a difficult case. "I don't take my work home with me," he explained, "and I resent it when she does. I feel we need our few leisure hours to relax, not to work. And, I can't help because her work is so specialized. So, I feel left out even if she brings her papers home to do while I'm there." Nevertheless, Lou refrained from repeating these objections as Florence explored her dream.

ENCOURAGING ASSOCIATIONS. After the dreamer responds to your question about the dream's meaning, you may next guide her or him to make associations to each element of the dream. This is easier if the dream has been parsed. If not, mentally review the dream and ask, "What is a (name the dream element)?"

For instance, Lou suggested, "Tell me about your little brother. Describe him to me as if I knew nothing at all about him." Florence said, "He's never been as serious as I am. Oh, he made good grades, but his fun-loving qualities were what made him popular in school, and he's still like that. And, I do admit that when I let my hair down, I always have a good time with him."

Then Lou asked, "Does anyone you know remind you of him?" and Florence exclaimed, "Of course! *You* do. I guess my little brother in the dream symbolizes you, and our relationship right now. You're forever wanting me to stop work to play, and you don't seem to understand how important it is to me to balance my books."

ACCEPTING EMOTIONS AND OFFENDING ATTITUDES. Even when your partner's dream feelings or the attitudes the dream reveals make you feel uncomfortable, it's important to accept them. Should a dream reveal that your lover is angry or hostile toward you, remember that it's better to get these feelings out in the open than to allow them to go unexpressed. Repressed emotions often lead to resentments which can sabotage your relationship.

161

At this point, you may be asking, "What about *my* feelings? Don't I have a right to express myself, too?" You most assuredly do have that right. However, this is not the time to react. Doing so might destroy the trust your partner has given so far. Bear in mind that, whenever someone shares a dream, she or he runs the risk of revealing a very private, personal part of the inner self. This makes the dreamer feel unusually vulnerable. At this point, it's crucial for you as the listener to respect the trust your partner has offered. A negative response now may inhibit future communication. Your chance will come later, as the dream sharing dialogue continues.

Instead of defending himself, Lou commented noncommittally, "That's interesting," and then went on to another dream image. "Who do you think the older woman in your dream might symbolize?" Florence replied, "She's probably my mother or the baby-sitters who were always taking my brother's side, always blaming me. He was so cute, and charming—and still is—he made me feel sort of awkward by comparison. And, I guess I sometimes feel that way with you, too."

SUGGESTING ALTERNATE INTERPRETATIONS. Sometimes the dream itself will suggest a resolution to the conflict it portrays. Often the dreamer may be so caught up in explaining her or his position that these alternatives escape detection. This is where you as the listener can make a difference, without destroying your partner's trust.

Using the Ullman technique, Lou said, "If *I* had that dream, the part about my hair pinned up would interest me. And, I might pay more attention to what my little brother was saying, that he didn't mean any harm, he just wanted to play." Florence then admitted, "Yes, I did say, didn't I, that whenever I 'let my hair' down, I had fun with him." Smiling, she added, "And I do have fun with you, Lou dear. Guess I have been grimly serious, lately. And, I do know you're not really at all like my mother." Lou agreed. "You're right. I'm on your side. I just hate to see you get too stressed out and overworked. And, I do miss your company lately."

Hidden Agendas

Florence's dream revealed her "Hidden Agenda"—which was that her role was to be serious while others, such as her younger brother, were the ones who could have fun and play. In a Krippner workshop, this would be termed Florence's "Personal Myth."

Almost everyone has and acts upon these attitudes and belief systems—often without being aware that such reactions and behavior stem from a self-image which is usually outdated. Frequently these beliefs are the result of childhood experiences or distortions of reality.

Florence had always been a perfectionist and an overworker. Although this attitude resulted in her success, it caused her to sacrifice many of life's pleasures. When she first fell in love with Lou, she was so overwhelmed with unexpectedly romantic feelings that she temporarily ignored the pressures of work. "The first couple of months, I went around feeling giddy, my head in the clouds half the time," she said, "and I almost lost a few clients. It was their complaints that brought me back down to earth with a thump!" Here we can see that what Feinstein and Krippner would term Florence's "Counter-Myth" was coming to the fore. Then, just as she was beginning to take life less seriously, her Hidden Agenda asserted itself again, and she once more focused most of her energies on what she perceived as grim reality.

Unfortunately, it took the onset of illness to make Florence change her lifestyle. Despite her conflicts with Lou, she continued to pursue her career to the exclusion of all else, when she suffered a mild heart attack. She told me, "Lou was watching TV, I was working at my desk nearby. Then the next thing I knew, I was in the hospital. Lou said he looked over and I was slumped over. He thought I'd fallen asleep. Then he couldn't rouse me, my pulse was very faint, so he called the paramedics."

Had she paid more attention to her dreams, Florence might have noticed warnings that she was subjecting herself to too much stress and tension. For example, a few nights before the heart attack, she had this dream:

I'm on a Greyhound bus, checking my watch because we're run-ning late. I have to be at an IRS office in a distant town. Looking out the window, I see we're going in the opposite direction. I get up and ask the driver, "Doesn't this bus go to Battleford?" (In real life, I never heard of any of these towns in my dream.) He tells me we'll get there eventually, but first we have to go to Pleasantville to take some teenagers who're in a rock band. Then we have to make a stop at a hospital in Safety Harbor where he's picking up some doctors who're going to a convention. I get annoyed and tell him this isn't fair, that they told me in the station this bus would get me to Battleford on time for my appointment. He just shrugs and tells me the other stops are more important. Then I woke up feeling frustrated and annoyed.

While she was recuperating, Florence and I discussed this dream. She thought the town named Battleford symbolized her "battles" with the IRS. "Every time I had to go for a client's audit," she said, "I got anxious and tense, as if I were a soldier going into battle. From now on, I'm just going to let my partner handle those audits. She doesn't get nervous about them the way I do." Florence thought the other dream towns, Pleasantville and Safety Harbor, symbolized the changes she now had to make in her life. "When I had the dream," she said, "I couldn't understand why the bus driver thought a rock band or some doctors going to a convention were more important than my appointment. Now, I see that my dreaming self was giving me a message, to detour and have some fun (in 'Pleasantville'), to stop and take care of myself (in 'Safety Harbor')." She also thought the mention of the stop at a hospital might have foretold her illness.

On her doctor's advice, once she was on her feet again Florence drastically curtailed her heavy work load. She hired a bookkeeper to take over many details, and expanded her computer system so that her secretary could handle some of the "busy pencil pushing" she'd been doing. Now, she and Lou spend all their evenings and weekends together. "When five o'clock comes," she said, "I simply stop whatever I'm doing. My life is more important than any amount of success. The funny thing is," she went on, "even though I raised my fees and have a waiting list, it seems I now have more clients than ever. I guess it pays in business to be hard to get!"

It's also interesting that, once she made efforts to change her Hidden Agenda, Florence's dreams changed as well. She experienced several "flying" dreams and thought these exhilarating visions were evidence of the new freedom she was feeling. Both she and Lou also began having more sexy, erotic dreams—further evidence that their intimacy was deepening now that Florence had changed her Hidden Agenda.

Now is the time to examine your own and your partner's dreams for clues to your attitudes and belief systems. Dreams of your past, of yourself as a child or in a childhood setting such as a house you grew up in, or even dreams of friends or relatives you may not have seen for years, may all be indications of outdated Hidden Agendas. Following are excerpts from dreams bearing such messages:

- *Gina, nurse whose dream of having a penis was quoted in Chapter 2*: Went into recovery room to find a heart patient with doctors and nurses all around him. (Why wasn't I notified?) . . . felt paranoid . . . a nurse told me I really should be careful what I share with people. She said, "It's embarrassing!"
- *Kirk, Gina's lover, whose dream of chasing a blonde through tall grass is quoted in Chapter 2*: Old, familiar recurring dream segment—A sort of dance between myself and whatever animal, this time a snake. It knows I'm afraid and will not leave me alone . . . I fight the paralysis of fear . . . nonchalantly move away . . . I jump safely out of the way only to find . . . a much smaller but deadly snake. Dream ends.
- *Monique, whose dream of finding the parking lot changed into a zoo is quoted in Chapter 3*: On vacation with Claude . . . I am driving and no matter what turns I make, we're on the wrong highway . . . I start to cry but Claude turns away and goes to sleep.
- *Claude, Monique's husband, whose dream of their burglarized house is quoted in Chapter 3*: At an important conference with my employers . . . mentioned I didn't like some aspects of his

proposal . . . my boss wrote me this note, "You're fired for saying that!"

Gina's dream of suddenly finding herself replaced in her usual workplace indicated her feelings of insecurity about her hard-won position as Recovery Room Nurse. However, this dream had another, more important message, a clue to Gina's Hidden Agenda: she feared that when she shared her feelings and innermost thoughts she would meet with strong disapproval. Just as her colleague told her she should be more careful about sharing, so might be the reactions of all those closest to her.

Her lover Kirk's dream of the frightening snake revealed that he had a similar Hidden Agenda. Kirk told me, "The snake was about eight feet long and seventy inches around, yet I saw it was not dangerous. Even so, I was fearful, but decided to repress that fear. I told the others it was harmless and they began playing with it. But the snake sensed my fear and came right to me."

Kirk's Hidden Agenda was that he must not ever admit being afraid. As a child, he'd been told that "big boys" aren't scared, being afraid is sissy, and so on. Now, although he knew the value of being honest about all his emotions, he believed that when he compulsively hid his feelings, someone would sense his fears and become a threat to him. This fear stemmed from being told over and over that his parents "always knew" when he was lying. When Gina and Kirk shared these dreams, they were able to see that both of them yearned for the trust and acceptance which comes from true love. Gradually, they were able to learn to trust each other enough to share their emotions without the expectation of rejection.

Monique and Claude had another conflict. She believed she had to handle every domestic situation perfectly, felt inadequate when she could not, and believed she could never ask Claude for help. Her dream of being lost on the highway portrays her dilemma clearly, with Claude ignoring her distress and falling asleep.

Claude, on the other hand, was convinced that whenever he "interfered," even with good intentions, his intrusion was resented. When Claude dared to comment somewhat negatively at his dream business conference, he was fired. In waking life at home, Claude rarely offered to help while Monique often felt overwhelmed. Both husband and wife in this unhappy situation were rapidly building resentments because neither suspected the other's Hidden Agenda. As we discussed these dreams, it developed that both had come from dysfunctional families. Monique's mother had become a widow quite early in life and had depended on Monique to shoulder many responsibilities which were inappropriate for the young girl. Claude's parents had both been alcoholics who argued incessantly and sometimes violently. As a small boy, he'd learned to hide when his parents quarreled, and never risked taking sides for fear of reprisals and abuse.

Although both Monique and Claude were in private therapy, they agreed it was the sharing of these two dreams which helped the most in the eventual resolution of their conflicts. "I don't care if Claude doesn't always do a professional job with something around the house," Monique said. "It's just so nice to have him trying to help, and not feeling I have to manage everything alone." Claude agreed. "I really like helping, now that I know she likes it too. It's a wonderful feeling to know you're needed."

Sexual and Erotic Dreams

Several of the couples described above began to have sensual, erotic dreams after the resolution of conflicts which were preventing them from being deeply intimate. Such dreams are often the mark of the lasting love which develops from honest communication and trust.

However, the fact that you or your partner are having sexual dreams does not necessarily mean that you are aroused by each other. Such dreams can be reflections of feelings of general well-being, or can be merely the result of hormonal upsurges during sleep. Erotic dreams are usually one of several types:

- Dreams of physiological origin
- Explicitly sexual dreams of psychological origin
- Symbolic, romantic, or euphoric dreams

Erotic Dreams of Physiological Origin

Dream researchers are still unclear as to whether or not sexual dreams are actually caused by the deep stages of sleep which characterize the REM phase. These dreams are somewhat different for females and males.

MALE NOCTURNAL ERECTIONS AND "WET" DREAMS. Most males have at least one erection during a typical night's sleep. The dreams which accompany this arousal period in males are usually sexually explicit. Dream researchers have not yet established whether the dream causes the erection, or the erection causes the dream. However, evidence points to the dream as at least partly the cause of the erection. Dr. Ernest Hartmann, author of *The Biology of Dreaming*, reports that the erections which occur when the dream is highly sexual are larger than is the case when the dream is less explicit. Further, when the dream content is aggressive or portrays threats to the dreamer's masculinity, the erection may subside entirely. Nevertheless, most physicians proceed on the assumption that erections during sleep are evidence of normal sexual functions.

According to Dr. Bernie Zilbergeld, author of *Male Sexuality*, these nocturnal arousals are often used by both urologists and sex therapists to determine the cause of male impotence. The patient puts a type of paper "collar" on his penis at night; if the collar is broken when he awakens, he probably had an erection while asleep. This helps the physician decide whether the origin of the impotence is physiological or psychological. During a recent TV talk show, Dr. Ruth Westheimer suggested to a frustrated woman that she "take a peek" while her lover slept, to see if his lack of response was a physical or an emotional problem.

Following are excerpts from male dreams accompanied by erections:

- *Hugh, the construction crew boss whose dream of an earthquake is quoted in Chapter 3*: Dreamed I was having a few beers . . . this unknown gal comes over and pushes me back onto the bar, tearing my clothes off . . . she was all over me, in front of everybody . . . I was in heaven!

- *Peter, the painter who moved to New York with Lisa*: This drawing just seemed to spring from my pencil, without any thought on my part . . . a very sexy scene, an orgy with bodies entwined. Saw that I was one of them . . . Then I was in the scene, and having a big orgasm.
- *Guy, the biochemist whose dream is quoted in Chapter 6*: I was in an old-fashioned brothel during the Gold Rush . . . a "Diamond Lil" or Mae West type unzipped my jeans and I ejaculated all over the front of her red satin dress. Everyone was laughing but I didn't care. It was great!

These explicitly sexual dreams are quite typical of what is commonly called the "wet" dream. However, more teenaged boys probably ejaculate during such dreams than do adult males, who are more likely to awaken before orgasm. You may have noticed that the men's dreams quoted above all describe sex with unfamiliar characters. This is another typical trait of men's erotic dreams.

FEMALE SEXUAL DREAMS DURING OVULATION. Women also have sexually explicit dreams, and these usually occur more frequently during ovulation. In this case, the physiological origin of the dreams appears to be more clearly defined. While women have sexual dreams at other times, those reported during ovulation are usually the most explicit. The erotic dreams of other phases of women's reproductive cycles are more likely to be symbolic in nature.

In *Women's Bodies, Women's Dreams*, Garfield explains that both men and women are somewhat aroused sexually whenever they dream. However, numerous studies of thousands of women's dreams have found that females consistently dream of sexual activities in a more symbolic manner than do men.

There are many theories which attempt to explain this phenomenon. One likely theory is that, despite the so-called sexual liberation movement of the seventies, many women are still inhibited by sexual taboos, so that they often do not allow themselves to think consciously about either their own or the male genitals. Thus, most women are more likely to dream of objects which resemble female genitalia or indicate their function, such as containers (vases, purses, boxes, circular objects), objects or animals whose names are a pun (a cat or "pussy," a chick, a beaver, a doll, a bird), or another body part which resembles the vagina (mouth, ear, eye). Women also dream symbolically of male genitals (snakes, elongated vegetables and fruits, knives, swords, keys, upright structures), animals with slang names for the penis (such as a rooster or cock), or dream characters with suggestive names (such as Peter or Dick).

These extensive studies of women's dreams have also shown that females are more friendly to males and more easily aroused sexually prior to and during ovulation. These attitudes are consistently reflected in their dreams. Indeed, although women's dreams may become more explicit and less symbolic concerning sexual activities as women become less intimidated by cultural taboos, it is unlikely that the cyclic intensity of their erotic dreams will change. Women are naturally more easily aroused around ovulation time, and their dreams portray this passion.

Following are excerpts from the dreams of ovulating women:

- *Tammy, the actress whose dream just before her period is quoted in Chapter 2*: Dreamed John, my director, was tickling my navel but this made my clitoris throb . . . I came, and woke up to find my nightgown all wet and wadded up between my legs.
- *Sarah, Frank's wife, whose dream just before she caught a bad cold is quoted in Chapter 2*: In the dream our next-door neighbor was making love to me . . . I had one orgasm after another. (I don't even like him, in real life!)
- *Patty, the social worker whose recurring dream of the hallway and closed door is quoted in Chapter 3*: A long, involved dream . . . some terrorists had tied me up and left . . . Alan came home and instead of untying me, stroked me and played with me until I came, and then we [had intercourse] and I came again.

Although women sometimes dream of having sex with unknown characters, this is rare. When Tammy dreamed that the director of a play she was rehearsing tickled her navel, she told me, "At dress rehearsal the day before this dream, John was showing the wardrobe people how to make my costume so my navel would show, and he touched my waist. But I don't find him attractive at all." Tammy thought the director symbolized her husband, Ben, who was out of town at the time.

Sarah also dreamed of another man, her next-door neighbor. "I felt so aroused that night," she said, "I might have dreamed about sex with anyone. That often happens to me around this time of the month, and I think it's my body's way of letting me know I'm fertile."

Patty's dream of being tied up by terrorists brings to mind a common daydream or fantasy many women indulge when they're awake and masturbating. In *My Secret Garden*, author Nancy Friday comments that such fantasies may be some women's method of achieving orgasm without feeling guilty. After all, if one is bound and helpless, "illicit" sex is unavoidable. In Patty's case, her dream may have been helping her reenact this delightful feeling of total surrender, and the dream even conveniently provided her true lover, Alan, to consummate the act.

Sexually Explicit Dreams of Psychological Origin

Although the dreams discussed above appear to be related to the dreamer's physical state, nevertheless, like most dreams, they portray emotions and waking life situations. However, these psychological implications sometimes appear in sexually explicit dreams which do not seem to have any relationship to the dreamer's body state.

MALE SEXUAL DREAMS REFLECTING WAKING LIFE CONCERNS. Men's dreams sometimes contain highly sexual content which seems to have more to do with some waking life problem or conflict than with the normal tension-release cycle which generally accompanies male "wet" dreams. For example, Ralph, an avid sports fan, had the following dream of his lover Peg's best friend Louise:

I was at a ball game with some buddies. We were all yelling when our team made a run. In my excitement I pounded on the shoulders of a blonde in front of me. She turned around and I saw it was Louise. I grabbed her and kissed her. She started to moan in a definitely sexy way. I felt very aroused so unzipped my pants. Louise knelt down and started sucking me. Then our team hit a homer and I was screaming with joy. None of my buddies noticed what Louise was doing. They were all jumping up and down, shouting, clapping each other on the back. I couldn't believe it— the next batter hit a homer! Just as he hit the ball with a loud crack, I came. Then I looked down and Louise was gone. Sitting in her place was another woman who looked like Peg from the back. I thought, oh no, I hope she doesn't know what Louise did! Feeling guilty and anxious, I woke up.

When Ralph and Peg discussed this dream, Peg managed to refrain from voicing the jealous comments which immediately sprang to mind. Instead, she asked him to describe his impressions of Louise. "She always laughs at my off-color jokes," he said, "and I do get a feeling she'd be willing to experiment a bit more than you are." At that point, Peg told Ralph that she herself sometimes fantasized about oral sex. "But you never make any moves in that direction," she pointed out, "so I thought you'd be shocked if I suggested it."

This frank and intimate exchange led quite naturally to some very satisfying and exciting sexual adventures between Peg and Ralph. When they confided their new intimacy, I told them what Alexandra Penney has to say about the topic of oral sex in *How to Make Love to a Man*. Penney claims that when a woman kisses a man's penis, it makes him feel his masculinity is truly adored. Hearing this, Peg commented that, when Ralph made love to her this way, she had similar feelings. "While he's doing it," she said, "I keep thinking, 'he loves me, he *really does* love me!' and it's positively thrilling."

FEMALE SEXUAL DREAMS REFLECTING CONFLICT RESOLUTION.
The women I've studied rarely had dreams of a highly sexual nature which appeared to portray some other problem or concern. However, when they effectively resolved a waking sexual conflict with their partners, their dreams often mirrored the feelings of pleasure brought about by the new intimacy. For instance, after Peg and Ralph threw inhibitions aside about oral lovemaking, she reported this dream:

> I'm flying or floating in the air—yet somehow I feel surrounded by a soft fluffiness. I'm nude and these soft fluffy things are caressing me all over. It feels marvelous! I love the way they slip delicately over my breasts, my rib cage, my stomach, my lips and cheeks, all at once. I feel warm and lazy. I stretch and these fluffy things continue to stroke me no matter which way I move. I open my eyes a moment and then close them because the light is too bright. But in that second I saw hundreds of beautiful, vividly colored butterflies swarming all over my body. I roll over onto my stomach and let them tickle my back. I spread my legs and they flutter over my buttocks and the inside of my thighs. I feel something like sweet honey oozing out of my vagina and I taste it in my mouth at the same moment. Delicious! It's the most ecstatic sensation I've ever felt. (I woke up thinking of Ralph and how wonderful it was when we made love last night.)

Symbolically Erotic Dreams

Just as explicitly sexual dreams usually contain many images which refer to emotions other than sexual ones, so do seemingly unsexy dreams often reflect sexual desires or arousing situations. The images which Freud saw as sexual (such as long, cylindrical objects symbolizing the penis, or tunnels, gates, or doorways symbolizing the vagina) may in fact represent genitals. However, it's always important to bear in mind that the dreamer's personal associations to any symbol are nearly always the correct interpretation, regardless of any "authority's" version.

For instance, Kirk's dream quoted earlier, of his attempts to hide his fear of a large snake, might have indicated a fear of sexuality in some manner, with the dream snakes as symbols of a penis. Yet Kirk believed his fear of the snake symbolized his problems in expressing his innermost feelings.

MEN'S SYMBOLICALLY SEXUAL DREAMS. Although Kirk's associations to snakes were not sexual, other male dreamers in my classes and workshops have reported typically Freudian interpretations of dream images. For instance, Alec, the man in his seventies whose sexy dream of topless women is quoted in Chapter 4, had this dream of snakes which did appear to be phallic symbols:

> Dreamed Georgia and I were in the reptile house at the park, when someone yelled that the snakes were all loose. Another tourist grabbed an axe next to the fire alarm box and started chopping away at the floor where some small garter snakes were coiled. I ran over and was trying to stop him, because those were harmless. Then other tourists pulled me away and a cop put handcuffs on me. "I'm arresting you for endangering women," he said, and I woke up feeling puzzled and a little angry.

When asked if snakes reminded him of anything in his waking life, Alec immediately responded, "I think they're phallic, definitely." It developed during our discussion that Alec had been worried about becoming impotent, having lost his erection unexpectedly the night before this dream. "I've been bragging about how aging hasn't arrested my virility," he told me, "and then it seemed I was a victim, too." As soon as he made this comment, Alec exclaimed, "Of course! That's what the cop arresting me in the dream was all about. I've been thinking of my sex as 'being arrested.' And, I guess I feel like I'm 'endangering' at least one woman, my wife Georgia, by not being able to satisfy her the way I always had before."

Before our discussion, Alec had already talked with his doctor, who assured him nothing was physically wrong. "It just may take me a bit longer nowadays," he said, "but with patience and Georgia's help, I can still make pretty good love." Georgia smiled. "I keep telling him

I like it better this way, anyhow," she said. "We have plenty of time to fool around, there's no rush, and really no need to worry. I'm a very lucky—and satisfied—woman."

Georgia herself tended to have symbolically erotic dreams. The following is replete with typically "Freudian" symbolism:

Dreamed I was in this fabulous high fashion store. It was an enormous room with walls of mirrors. When you touched a mirrored panel, a door swung open, and behind it were models showing various designer outfits. The amazing thing was that the models all looked like me, or rather, younger versions of me. They were on revolving pedestals with a Greek column in the center, which they held onto to keep from losing their balance. Soft violin music was playing. The displays were very sensual. One I thought was divine was a slinky black- and gold-sequined, tight-fitting gown which was split up the front from hem to waist, so when she moved the model showed her legs in black stockings. She stroked the column and sort of draped herself over it. As I watched her, I became the model, felt I was actually in her body. The dress was lined with satin and felt wonderful on my skin. I woke up feeling very aroused.

Georgia thought the mirrored panels or doors were symbols of femininity. "And the night before this dream," she said, "I was looking at myself nude, in a full-length mirror, and thinking that, even though my hair is gray, my body is still in pretty good shape." (In fact, Georgia is a very attractive and fit woman who has every right to be proud of her excellent physical condition.) She also thought the Greek columns the dream models were leaning against were phallic symbols, commenting that she herself "leans on" her husband Alec for emotional support as well as physical intimacy.

VOYEURS IN EROTIC DREAMS. Although no recent statistical studies have been made regarding the comparative frequency of symbolically sexual dreams of women and men, such dreams are more usual with my female students rather than with the males. Additionally, men are usually the central characters in their own erotic dreams, whereas women often dream of other people making love. For example, Shirley, a homemaker in her early forties, said that as she fell asleep one night, she told herself, "I'm going to have a romantic dream." She awoke the next day with this memory:

My husband Norman, his sister and her husband, and another couple were at a big house under real stressful circumstances. We were waiting for something (I don't recall what it was) to happen . . . There were three bedrooms in the house. I looked into the first one and the man (of the third couple) was having sex with a strange woman. I walked on to the next room and Norman's sister was having sex with a strange man. I proceeded down the hall and looked into the third bedroom and Norman was having sex with a strange woman. None of this seemed to bother me at all as I thought, "That will make them feel better." Then I saw my brother-in-law was working in the garden, hoeing weeds, watering flowers, and I thought, "Oh, hope he doesn't know what's going on," as it would upset him . . . went outside hoping to keep him from going in the house and catching them all . . . He had a big smile on his face . . . He nodded toward the house. I said, "Have you been in there?" He said, "Yes and I think it's great. They'll feel a lot better." (Then I woke up.)

As she discussed this dream, Shirley commented, "The general feeling I had was that the sex partners were just there for sex, that's all, and it didn't count. All this was just fine with me, in the dream. Awake, I know I'd feel differently, especially about Norman and a strange woman!" The day before this dream, Shirley's in-laws had stopped by for a brief visit.

When Norman heard his wife's dream description, he said, "My sister wouldn't say the word sex, much less do it like that!" Both Shirley and Norman were very amused with her "romantic dream," saying that their in-laws are "very uptight, possessive," and the most unlikely people to behave so outrageously.

Sometimes men have these "voyeur" dreams, too. For example, Jim

(Rosemarie's "controlling" husband who is described in Chapter 1) reported this dream of himself and his wife as "Peeping Toms":

> Dreamed Rosemarie and I were coming home from a party. I parked in the driveway and before we got out, she pointed to our next-door neighbor's house and said, "Jim! Look what they're doing!" The neighbor and his wife were in their bedroom with all the lights on, making love. Rosie and I got out of the car very quietly and went closer. We whispered to each other that we shouldn't be doing this, but we did it anyway. We got right up under their window and looked over the sill. Rosie gasped when the woman got on top, riding her husband like a horse. I started kissing her and I woke up, feeling very excited and wondering if she'd be upset if I woke her. Finally I did, told her about the dream, and we tried out the same position.

Jim explained that his and Rosemarie's attendance at our dream study group had helped him realize that he did not really want to "play the dominant role" he had assumed in their relationship. He thought this dream pointed the way to a delightful experiment in which he could "let Rosie take over the reins." Although she blushed a bit as Jim related his voyeur dream and its aftermath, Rosemarie had a definite air of more confidence and self-esteem than she'd exhibited in past weeks as she and Jim struggled to reach more honest communication.

Summary

In this chapter we have explored the ways dreams can assist you in loving and being loved. By forming a "Dream Dyad" with your partner, together you can listen to and learn from each other's nightly visions.

When beginning your Dream Dyad, it's important to agree upon basic "ground rules." These should include listening without interrupting, withholding your opinions until later, encouraging the dreamer to make associations to each dream element, accepting offensive or hostile emotions or attitudes, and suggesting alternate interpretations when your partner appears to be avoiding facing issues the dream seems to suggest. You may wish to add other agreements to your Dream Dyad contract. The important point here is to establish an atmosphere of trust so that, when either of you is describing a dream, you'll feel confident that whatever you reveal about yourself is met with loving, unconditional acceptance.

The mere telling of your dream to your lover will often make the experience more objective, so that you will comprehend dream messages which may have baffled you before. Be especially on the lookout for your own and your partner's "Hidden Agendas." These are old, often outdated attitudes and belief systems formed in the dreamer's past, usually in early childhood. These dream revelations will often clear up a variety of misunderstandings between partners.

Sometimes these Hidden Agendas account for sexual inhibitions or an inability to communicate one's true preferences in lovemaking. Our secret fantasies or wishes for various sorts of foreplay may be mirrored in our dreams. Discussing such dreams together eases the way toward making such wishes known to each other.

Sexual and erotic dreams may arise from the dreamer's physical state, may be purely psychological in nature, may be a combination of both, or may be suggested symbolically so that, at first glance, a dream may not appear to be erotic at all.

Explicitly sexual themes frequently appear in men's dreams, and may accompany a nocturnal erection. Teenage males tend to ejaculate during these dreams, although adult men sometimes reach orgasm as well. This normal tension-release function of male dreams may also create a vision which is symbolic of some waking life concern.

Women's explicitly sexual dreams often occur during the ovulation phase of the reproductive cycle—generally about fourteen days after the dreamer's period. Although women are less likely to have these explicitly sexual dream images at other times, such dreams do occasionally occur. However, females tend to have more symbolically erotic dreams than they do these obviously sexy images. When sensual feelings of arousal surface in female dreams, they are often expressed as sensations of flying, floating, or soaring. Many women report being orgasmic during these ecstatic dreams. Further, more females than males report dreams of watching others engaged in sexual activity, although men also have these voyeur-type dreams.

Now is the time to examine your own dream notebook for clues to symbolically erotic dreams, noting in particular the emotions you experienced during the dreams and immediately upon awakening. Share these memories with your lover, using the ensuing discussion to lead into a frank and honest exchange of your sexual fantasies. Such confidences should enhance and deepen your intimacy and romance.

PART
THREE

Fluency in the Dream Language of Love

This section of *Romantic Dreams* introduces you to the fascinating art of creating your own dreams. Such dreams are of two types: the incubated dream, which is a dream about a topic you deliberately choose before falling asleep; and the lucid dream, in which you are conscious that you're dreaming during the dream.

You'll also learn additional ways you and your lover can use both the spontaneous dreams you're already having and your new, self-created dreams, to reach further heights of sexual ecstasy and lasting intimacy. You'll read the actual dream reports from other couples who have experimented with these methods to add excitement and fulfillment to their lives.

Then, you'll read about the ways many of the couples described in previous chapters have used their new powers of imagination and dream control to improve sexual fulfillment. You can adopt these "visualizations" and "creative daydreams" to enhance your own lovemaking, or you can follow easy directions to create your own fantasies and make them a reality.

Finally, the last chapter will demonstrate the ways many couples have learned to use their dreams to keep romance alive. By learning these simple techniques, you and your partner can hope to have a lifetime of the trust, tenderness, and close communication which are marks of a successful, committed relationship.

Chapter
EIGHT

Creating Your Own
Dreams of Love

In *The King of Dreams*, the poet Clinton Scollard wrote:

> Some must delve when the dawn is nigh
> Some must toil when the noonday gleams
> But when night comes, and the soft winds sigh,
> Every man is a King of Dreams.

You are not merely a spectator of your dreams, nor do you need to lie helplessly asleep, at the mercy of nightmare monsters or other demons of the night. Once you and your partner have learned to recall and interpret each other's dreams, you can choose the topic of your nightly visions and can even learn to control the setting, characters, and action. Thus, you can become the King—or Queen—of your own dreams.

While some of these techniques of dream control are not easily acquired, others are so easy that many dreamers are able to achieve them with the first attempt. This chapter will explain:

- Preparation for dream creation
- Dream incubation
- Lucid dreaming
- Benefits of dream creation

Getting Ready

Serious dream students have the most success in creating dreams of their choice. After you've become able to recall your dreams consistently, and have practiced the interpretation methods described in previous chapters, you'll qualify as the type of advanced dreamworker who can create your own dreams. Although people who know little or nothing about dreamwork might be able to create a dream of their own choice, or even to be aware they're dreaming during the dream, it's been my experience that such incidents are rare. On the other hand, my students who feel confident about remembering and translating their dreams frequently have success with these advanced techniques.

However, before falling asleep it's a good idea to learn to be totally relaxed, putting to rest the concerns of the day. Otherwise, any "unfinished business" is likely to intrude upon your dreams, taking priority over your conscious attempts at control. Many people need to use some special method of relaxation rather than expecting their waking minds to simply switch off at bedtime—especially if they've had a busy, stressful, or eventful day.

RELAXATION TECHNIQUES. This book's Appendix lists simple instructions for making your own tape, to play before attempting dream incubation or lucid dreaming. These methods are also effective as preparation for the creative daydreams and visualizations described in later chapters.

Although you can buy audiocassette tapes for this purpose, most do not have a space at the end to permit you to add your own special self-directions for incubating a dream or creating lucidity. Further, these commercial tapes often incorporate other messages designed to enhance a specific skill or behavior, and may not be appropriate for dream creation. The methods I prefer for this purpose are called Progressive Relaxation and Autogenic Training.

Progressive Relaxation is so named because you learn to relax one set of muscles at a time, progressing from head to toes. Concentrating on your body and breathing in this manner seems to quiet the left-brain-type thinking which usually occupies our waking minds, allowing the right hemisphere to receive and act upon the directions you wish to give it.

Autogenic Training teaches you to think of each part of your body as already relaxed, heavy, and warm. This method is so effective that many people fall asleep before they've completed the instructions. If it has this effect on you, try recording your dream control instructions at the end of the Autogenic Training steps listed in the Appendix. Or, you may have to use only the Progressive Relaxation method in order to be sufficiently awake to give yourself the required dream directions.

Dream Incubation

To program yourself to dream about a topic of your choice, follow these simple steps:

1. Write a brief account of the day's "unfinished business" in your Dream Notebook.
2. Choose your dream topic, and write a brief sentence about it. For example, in Chapter 1, Rosemarie is described as incubating a dream which she hoped would explain her nightmare of being in a restaurant where she was served a monster in a boiling pot of oil. Her incubation sentence was, "Tonight I will dream about the monster in the pot, and ask it what it means."
3. Turn out the lights and become deeply relaxed. If this part is difficult, use the relaxation instructions in the Appendix.
4. As you feel yourself drifting off to sleep, silently repeat your

incubation sentence. If your partner is also attempting dream incubation, you can both listen to taped relaxation instructions. Another effective method is to have your partner read the relaxation directions in a calm, gentle voice, and to repeat your dream incubation sentence softly as you fall asleep.

DREAM INCUBATION FOR CONFLICT RESOLUTION. An example of the ways a couple can benefit from practicing dream incubation comes from Marcia, described in previous chapters as a woman who believed all men feel superior to women. In Chapter 4, we read a snippet of Marcia's menstrual nightmare about being violently attacked by her husband Herb and his friends. As this couple attempted to resolve their differences, Marcia tried incubating another dream about her nightmare. As she fell asleep, Herb softly repeated this sentence, "Tonight you will dream about me and my poker buddies, asking us to explain why we hurt you."

Following is Marcia's incubated dream:

(This dream was a sort of combination of two dreams I had before, in that there were characters in it from both the other dreams.) Once again I was in the supermarket watching that nasty boy teasing his little sister. Only this time when I went to the check-out line, Herb and his poker buddies came up behind me. The boy and his mother and sister were behind the men in the line. The men were pushing and shoving me so I almost lost my balance. I felt scared, thinking they were going to attack me, but I got up my courage and said, "Why are you guys trying to hurt me?" and one of them said, "Marcia, we are NOT gonna hurt you. We'd never do that. We're just trying to get you out of here, away from that little brat back there. He's dangerous." And Herb was smiling and nodding. He said, "Go on out, Hon. We'll pay your bill and meet you at the car." And I woke up.

The "nasty little boy" dream Marcia refers to is also quoted in Chapter 4. In that dream, she discovered the clues to the Hidden Agenda which prevented her from trusting men: her older brother had cruelly abused her as a child. Marcia thought the above incubated dream was a reinforcement of her new attitudes about males in general and especially about her husband Herb.

"When I reviewed my menstrual dream about being attacked by Herb and his poker buddies," she explained, "I realized they had not hurt me at all. I'd just *assumed* they did it because I had cuts and bruises. In that dream when they came toward me, I was scared, thinking they were about to hurt me. Now I understand that Herb and our friends really feel protective, so I'm beginning to trust and tell them how I feel." Marcia's incubated dream quite clearly pointed out that, as an adult, she had little to fear from males, and that both her husband and their friends were sympathetic and eager to help.

INCUBATING EROTIC DREAMS. When Peg and Ralph were trying to improve their sex life, they incubated dreams about several aspects of their relationship. You may recall Ralph's spontaneous dream of having oral sex with Peg's best friend Louise, during a ballgame, which is quoted in Chapter 7. Ralph's dream had made clear his wish that Peg would loosen up a bit in their lovemaking.

When Peg admitted she felt overly self-conscious about engaging in such activities with Ralph, she incubated a dream by requesting, "How can I be less inhibited with Ralph?" That night, Peg had this dream:

(Dreamed we were hiking. Ralph was somewhere ahead of me on a forest trail.) I am getting tired and hot, worried because I may have taken a wrong turn at a fork in the path. Then I come to a very high stone wall with an iron gate. A sign says, "Nudists Only—Remove Clothes Before Entering." Looking through the bars of the gate, I can see people in the distance but can't tell if they're really nude or not. What looks like white shorts may be just where their tan stops. They're running around, playing some kind of game and laughing, shouting, but I can't make out the words or if Ralph is with them. Should I undress and go in? If I were sure Ralph was there, I would. But what if he's not? Then I'd really be embarrassed. Finally I decide to chance it and start taking off my clothes. Then I realize I'm sweaty, dirty, and smelly. My canteen is empty so I can't even rinse myself. Naked, I walk through the gate and stay close to the wall. Then I come to a stream and get in. It's a surprise because the water is almost warm, and deeper than it looks. Touching bottom I feel mud and hope I can get it off my feet later. Then I see two men already in the stream. One of them offers me a bar of soap and I start lathering myself. For some reason it seems okay when this man starts soaping my back. Both men are total strangers. The other one starts lathering my breasts. I ask him if he's seen Ralph and he says, "Don't worry about him. You'll find him when you're ready." (And I woke up feeling very aroused and wanted to go take a bath or shower with Ralph.)

Peg told me she did awaken Ralph and lead him to the shower. "It was wonderful," she said. "We couldn't even wait to get out of the bathroom, we were both so turned on." Peg thought bathing with her lover helped her overcome her inhibitions. "Before," she explained, "when I thought about oral sex I felt afraid he'd think I was unclean. Bathing together got rid of that worry, and the warm water relaxed us both." Ralph added, "We also found out that sex in the morning is a great way to start the day!"

If you and your partner have tried unsuccessfully to incubate dreams about a topic of your choice, do not be discouraged. Sometimes it's necessary to make several attempts before such a dream occurs. Congratulate yourself for at least trying. Once your unconscious gets the message that you're seriously interested in this type of dream creativity, you'll eventually be rewarded with the dream you seek.

Lucid Dreaming

The ability to know that you're dreaming while the dream is still taking place is called "lucid dreaming." While many of us may have had such a realization, we typically awaken immediately after the thought, "This must be a dream." Some people appear to be naturally gifted in that they are able to remain asleep while being aware that a dream is taking place. Others have learned to achieve this awareness by using various methods now being taught by dream psychologists. This skill at dream control is not easily come by. It's been my experience that even experienced dreamworkers may never achieve such abilities.

However, if you're willing to devote the time and effort to practicing the techniques suggested by experts, the results are well worth it. In *Control Your Dreams*, Dr. Jayne Gackenbach and journalist Jane Bosveld discuss the rapturous feelings reported by lucid dreamers. These range from emotions of pleasure and happiness to ecstasy, euphoria, and a type of spiritual enlightenment that often defies description.

In *Lucid Dreaming*, Dr. Stephen LaBerge relates similar reactions. Additionally, LaBerge suggests that the ability to dream lucidly helps the dreamer become more "alive" in waking life. He reasons that, when we discover the extra qualities of dreams by being conscious during the dream state, we can carry this awareness into our waking lives, discovering new dimensions of what we call reality.

Dr. LaBerge has devised a method for achieving lucid dreaming which he calls MILD (Mnemonic Induction of Lucid Dreams). This consists of the following steps:

1. When you awaken, review a dream you remember, going over it repeatedly until it's memorized.
2. Go back to sleep, telling yourself as you do, that when you dream again, you will know you're dreaming.
3. Imagining yourself in the same dream you just memorized, see yourself as knowing you are dreaming.
4. Repeat steps 2 and 3 until you are quite sure you intend to know you're dreaming, or until you fall asleep.

Although LaBerge has found this method is very effective with his students and with subjects in his sleep lab experiments, my own students have had only partial success with the use of the MILD techniques. It's important to bear in mind that you must be able to recall your dreams easily before trying any dream control methods, and that people who have already learned to incubate dreams have the highest success rate with lucidity.

Gackenbach and Bosveld describe another method which my students like. This is derived from the work of Dr. Paul Tholey, a West German psychologist, and consists of disciplining yourself to think about your dreams during the day, *while you're awake*, in the following manner:

1. Five to ten times daily, ask yourself, "Am I dreaming or not?"
2. Imagine that you are in a dream, and that everything you're experiencing while awake is actually a dream.
3. Think back to events that took place earlier and ask yourself if those were dreams.
4. When anything unusual occurs, or when you have very strong feelings, ask yourself the same question.
5. If you encounter anything while awake which also appears in your dreams (a dream setting or character, for instance), ask yourself the same question again.
6. Recalling any dream experiences which never happen when you're awake, try to visualize them as actually happening. For example, if you've had flying dreams, imagine doing that while you're awake.

After practicing Tholey's daytime thoughts, when you're in bed and really going to sleep, simply remind yourself that you will know you are dreaming when you do dream. Tholey also suggests concentrating on your body as well as upon visual images as you drift off. My students use the relaxation techniques in this book's Appendix for this portion of Tholey's method.

Notice that both LaBerge and Tholey emphasize the changes which occur in our waking thinking processes when we have lucid dreams. By deliberately raising awareness of illusion and reality while we're awake, Tholey helps the dreamer to be more conscious of the subtle differences between waking and dreaming. When these differences happen during our sleeping visions, we are then more likely to realize we're dreaming.

LUCID DREAMING FOR CONFLICT RESOLUTION. Florence and Lou, the accountant and lawyer whose dreams are quoted in previous chapters, were determined to explore every avenue toward making their romance deep and lasting. After Florence eliminated much of the stress in her life by coming to understand the Hidden Agendas reflected in her dreams, she and Lou next wanted to improve their sex life. At my suggestion, they began using Tholey's methods to induce lucidity. One night when they both tried this, they actually met and made love in their dreams. This is Florence's lucid dream:

Lou and I are in an absolutely gorgeous hotel suite. (I think it was the Fairmont in San Francisco although I've never stayed there in real life.) We have two bottles of complimentary champagne but I am more interested in looking at the suite, going from this sitting room to another sitting room, to a bedroom and then another, then to the enormous bath with two Jacuzzi tubs and two separate showers. There is even a private dressing room just for me, and a similar one for Lou. Then I realize everything is *double* and it strikes me as funny. Before falling asleep, I had tried to take *double* control of my dreams by both incubating a dream and saying I would be lucid in it. At this point I know I am dreaming. I rush back to where Lou is, telling him it's actually happening. Just as I shout, "Look! I'm lucid!"—I wake up.

(When I woke up, I felt disappointed at first, and then made up my mind to return to the dream. So I lay there and reviewed what I'd just dreamed, telling myself I was dreaming it again. Sure enough, there I was, telling Lou I was lucid—only this time I was careful to stay calm so as not to wake up.) Then Lou says, "But I thought you incubated a dream about us making love." Then I feel very confused and feel myself blushing. I want him to initiate sex, not expect me to do it. Then, I suddenly know I can have anything happen that I want, so I silently direct him to come and hug me. He does! It's amazing! Then I have the lights go dim, make soft violin music play, and mentally direct him to lead me to the bedroom. As we lie down on the bed, I then realize that, even though Lou doesn't know it, I am initiating this sex. That annoys me (and I woke up feeling trapped and hopeless about ever changing our sex life).

Although Florence's lucid, incubated dream of so many "double" images obviously symbolized her attempt at "double dream control," it may have had another meaning, at a different level. As we discussed her dream, she realized it was also demonstrating her feelings about a type of "double standard" in her relationship with Lou. "We both want the other one to initiate sex," she said. "I guess this makes us both feel sought after, more desirable. On my part, I still have a lot of sentimental, old-fashioned ideas. I want to be 'swept off my feet' and want Lou to be an aggressive lover. But he likes it when I let him know I'm aroused and eager. This puts me in a kind of double bind— I do want him, sometimes very passionately. Yet I'd like it if he set the mood."

Although Florence's explanation of her first lucid dream attempt did not directly change the pattern of this couple's lovemaking, it did pave the way toward fuller communication about the topic. Eventually, they were able to achieve a better accommodation of each other's needs and fantasies, so that Florence no longer felt pressured to be the one who always "set the mood."

SEXUALITY IN LUCID DREAMS. On the same night that Florence had her first lucidity experience, Lou also had a lucid dream. However, his was more explicitly erotic:

Dreamed we were at the racetrack, behind the scenes, admiring one horse in particular. Its name was Nightingale. The jockey told me I could ride it, so I mounted and the horse just took off. It was a big thrill. Looking down, I realized there was no saddle. I was riding bareback. Then we lifted off the ground and were sort of skimming along, almost flying. Then I knew I was dreaming. I wondered how the horse felt and then I *became* the horse. I could feel Flo sitting on top of me as I raced along. Then my hoofs hit the ground and I was myself again. I was lying on the ground, we were [having intercourse], and Flo was on top, pumping up and down. Her hair flew back in the wind and she moaned. She looked so beautiful! I had an orgasm that seemed to shake the very earth underneath me. It was the most incredible sexual experience I've ever had, and I woke up to find I had ejaculated.

Lou thought the name "Nightingale" for his dream horse was a direct reference to Florence, whose namesake was the famous nurse. This lucid dream did make it quite clear that Florence was correct in her belief that Lou enjoyed sex most when she initiated it, symbolized by her being "on top" and "riding" him.

Notice that Lou began to fly in his lucid dream, until the actual lovemaking began. Then, the couple were quite definitely "grounded." Gackenbach and Bosveld say that sexual activities appear in lucid dreams when the dreamer anticipates healthy sexual pleasure. (This was the case with Lou, in contrast to Florence, whose lucid dream abruptly ended as sex began.) These authors also speculate that flying in lucid dreams may be more prevalent than it is in nonlucid dreams because lucid dreaming requires a special kind of kinesthetic or body "balance," an ability which lucid dreamers learn with practice.

Although Lou wasn't able to fly very high above ground on his dream horse, this was his first successful attempt at lucidity. As he became more skilled at dream control, Lou was able to fly higher and reported that these flying dreams were "every bit as blissful as the lucid sex." Since his intention before falling asleep the night of the horse dream was to have an explicitly sexual encounter with Florence, it may have been that Lou's dreaming self was giving him a brief glimpse of the joys of dream flying, before proceeding to the erotic scene he had programmed.

The Benefits of Dream Creation

One of the most obvious benefits of learning to control your own dreams is the pleasure such dreams can provide. Other benefits include problem and conflict solving, physical and emotional healing, enhancement of your sex life, and discovery of your own and your partner's Hidden Agendas.

Sweet Dreams

Using the simple techniques described at the beginning of this chapter, you can program yourself to have a dream about any topic you desire. Unless you're eager to find the meaning of a particularly puzzling dream or a frightening dream character, your incubated dreams will probably be among your sweetest memories. For example, the following excerpts from self-programmed dreams indicate the happiness they evoked:

- *Sylvia, 52-year-old homemaker*: (After asking to dream about a romantic 25th Anniversary.) Larry and I were on a cruise ship . . . we danced out onto the deck in the moonlight and then as we kissed, we rose up together high into the night sky . . . he said "Happy Anniversary, Darling!"
- *Larry, 56-year-old department store manager, Sylvia's husband*: (Tried to incubate a dream about our upcoming anniversary for several nights and finally had this one.) We were both lying in a big hammock, in our bathing suits . . . A pretty girl in a grass skirt brought us drinks in coconut shells. Sylvia smelled so nice and I felt real content, even though nothing unusual happened.
- *Kate, whose recurring dream of being lost in a college building is described in Chapter 6*: (Fell asleep repeating to myself, "I want to have a happy dream.") It was Christmas morning and I was five years old . . . Under the tree was the Barbie doll I'd been praying for. Every package I opened had another outfit for Barbie . . . I was so happy!
- *Guy, Kate's lover, the biochemist, whose dreams are also quoted in Chapter 6*: Wanted to incubate a dream about Kate and got this instead—in the first part an older woman who I think was my mother was dying. Felt sorry yet somehow detached . . . Next scene I was driving this great Italian sports car . . . Thought

about Mom and that I had inherited money for the car . . .
Woke up feeling so happy I was almost laughing out loud.

Sylvia's incubated dream of her 25th Anniversary is a stereotype of a romantic moonlit scene, while her husband Larry's dream a few nights later is equally sentimental. However, Sylvia was literally "swept off her feet" and "carried away" as their passionate kiss caused them to rise into the night sky. On the other hand, Larry's idea of romance was a bit more mundane—and comfortable—portraying the couple lolling in a hammock while being served by a dancing hula girl.

When Kate asked for a happy dream, she got a scene right out of a TV commercial. "My parents didn't believe kids should have such toys," she explained, "so of course those were the things I wished for. After this dream, I went out and bought myself a Barbie doll just for the heck of it. Guess that was silly, but I'd always wanted one." Guy commented, "I loved it when Kate did that. It's what you psychologists call 'loving the child within.' But, I couldn't figure out my own dream. My Mom is healthy and fine, so why would I dream she died?"

As we discussed Guy's dream, and especially his feelings for his mother, it developed that his attitude had begun to change in recent weeks. "I used to phone her at least once a week," he said. "Now, it's more like once a month, when Kate reminds me. It's not that I don't still care about her. It's just that, ever since I got serious about Kate, there hasn't been much time for anything else but her and my work." As he described these recent changes, Guy realized the meaning of his dream. "Of course!" he exclaimed. "That's it! My attachment to Mom is dying, not Mom herself. That's why I felt 'detached' in the dream. And, maybe the Italian sports car stands for my affair with Kate. And Mom made this possible, in her own way—because Kate is almost a younger version of my mother."

Problem and Conflict Resolution

Dream creation is an extremely effective way to find solutions to your daily problems and conflicts. Such problems do not have to relate to matters between you and your partner—programmed dreams can yield resolutions to a variety of dilemmas.

For instance, Florence the CPA's dream of seventy-six trombones, quoted in Chapter 4, alerted her to the fact that her client could take a deduction for expenses incurred in constructing a building at 76 Main Street. In a similar manner the following excerpts gave the dreamers ideas for problem solving:

- *Marlene, 28-year-old cellist, in a California workshop*: Incubated to dream about a difficult passage . . . Knew I was dreaming and stood aside to watch a great cellist play the same notes . . . asked him for his secret. Woke up and tried it. It works!

- *Peter, artist-muralist whose dreams are quoted in Chapter 4*: (Asked my Dream Power to help me figure out how to retouch some smeared spots at the top of the mural, without damaging the rest of it, which is still wet.) Dreamed Lisa and I were at a movie about Van Gogh . . . Suddenly it changed to a scene with Mary Martin in *Peter Pan* . . . The audience started to boo and complain . . . I woke up knowing just how to reach the trouble spots.

- *Lisa, Peter's wife, new mother*: I incubated this dream to find out if there's any explanation for the baby's colic. Saw a twisted, knotted, tubelike snake . . . untied the knot and heard a lullaby quite loudly. Next day the pediatrician discovered the baby needed surgery to correct an intestinal abnormality. Now, surgery is over, our baby is well and contented, no more colic or crying.

Marlene, a San Francisco symphony musician, had a lucid dream which gave her a demonstration of the exact fingering techniques she needed for a challenging portion of a score she had not been able to master.

Peter's incubated dream gave him the idea for constructing a "harness" which would lift him to the areas of his mural which needed retouching. To engineer the contraption, Peter actually copied one worn by actress Mary Martin in the Broadway musical *Peter Pan* to help her "fly" across the stage.

Peter's wife Lisa also got help from her unconscious about their new baby's inexplicable, "colicky" crying and obvious stomach distress. "I just couldn't pass it off as being only colic," Lisa wrote. "After this dream, I insisted that our pediatrician do further tests, and sure enough, it turned out to be a twisted colon and not colic at all." Lisa's dream directed her toward a healing solution for her baby's illness. Other creative dreams sometimes play a part in the actual healing process.

Healing Dreams

In addition to providing clues to baffling physical symptoms and emotional distress, incubated and lucid dreams sometimes appear to have a direct role in healing. Following are excerpts from such dreams:

- *Georgia, Alec's wife, whose dream of the mirrored store with many doors is quoted in Chapter 7*: The night after my face-lift surgery, tried to incubate a dream to speed the healing . . . Dreamed a hole opened in the ceiling and colored lights streamed through it . . . they were like spotlights of different colors. It was beautiful and peaceful.
- *Monique, Claude's wife, whose dreams of loss of control are described in previous chapters*: Told myself I'd dream of something to stop the migraines I've been having. I was floating in a very large spa, a whirlpool. The waters seemed to draw an energy out of my head . . . my hair stood up like it was electrified.
- *Frank, our dream group's "skeptic," whose dreams are quoted in most previous chapters*: Had another bad cold or the flu . . . dreamed I was at an Indian reservation for a ceremony . . . knew I was dreaming and asked the shaman to heal me. He led me into a cave which was so hot I started to sweat . . . they were chanting . . . I could hardly breathe, the air was so hot. Woke up and my fever had broken.

Georgia's incubated dream as she recovered from cosmetic surgery suggests the amazing healing powers of the mind. She reported that, the day after this dream, her physician was amazed that her facial swelling was completely gone and that she had no bruises or discolorations (common symptoms after this type of surgery). "My recovery was so fast," Georgia said, "all my friends were surprised. I had almost no pain and was able to go out in public in less than ten days."

Monique had decided to try incubating a healing dream as a last resort after two months of extremely painful migraine headaches. "The medications weren't working any longer," she said, "and my doctor refused to prescribe anything stronger. He suggested biofeedback or hypnosis. I was ready to try anything—but after that dream I haven't had the headaches again and it's been three weeks." Monique could scarcely find the words to describe her sensations during her dream of floating in a warm Jacuzzi. She said she could feel and see her hair pulling out and upward, as if her head were "electrified, being drained of a heaviness."

Frank's dream was unusual in that it was a lucid dream in which he was able to stay asleep after he realized he was dreaming, and was even able to ask for help. "I probably had a fever," he said, "so my dream put me in an Indian sweat hut—only in this case it was a cave. The middle of the dirt floor was piled with red-hot rocks. When we crawled inside, it was so hot I thought I was going to pass out." When Frank awoke, he said he felt "weak and shaky," and was drenched in cool perspiration, but his throat no longer hurt. After a hearty breakfast he was able to return to work "feeling as good as new."

Of all the couples' dreams I have collected, these are the only examples of deliberately created "healing" dreams. This seems to validate my belief that programming your dreams is not an easy task. However, the results indicate that attempts to create your own dreams can be well worth the effort. Even those of my clients who were not able to become lucid in their dreams report that simply trying to do so has heightened their abilities to recall and understand all their dreams.

IS DREAM CONTROL DANGEROUS? This question has intrigued dream psychologists and researchers for some time, and has become of more concern in recent years as the public learns the latest methods of dream incubation and lucid dreaming.

Those of us who believe that dreams function to help us become aware of repressed or unexpressed emotions advise taking a cautious approach. While there is no convincing evidence that dream control can harm anyone, either physically or emotionally, it is possible that, if used improperly, such methods might prevent one from experiencing the benefits of spontaneous dreaming.

Attempts to "get rid of bad dreams" or to vanquish dream monsters or other frightening characters may serve only to sabotage the dreaming mind's goal of focusing our attention on unresolved conflicts or problems. Instead, I urge my students to ask puzzling or frightening dream characters what they want, why they are appearing, or what their purpose may be. Usually, this friendly attitude results in the "monster" becoming friendly as well.

Moreover, even when dreamers try to erase distressing dream elements, these issues will often take another form—sometimes in the same dream, or else in another, often more terrifying nightmare. For example, Ingrid, whose pregnancy dream is quoted in Chapter 4, tried to incubate a dream in which she would see her unborn child. Instead, she dreamed of discovering that the family dog had been decapitated. In the dream, she was trying to get her husband Curtis' attention and finally succeeded when she showed him their beloved dog.

In waking life, Ingrid had been disappointed that her husband wasn't as excited about her pregnancy as she was. In fact, he seemed to belittle her concerns and complaints about the discomfort she was feeling as her abdomen grew larger. "He cares more about the dog than he does our baby," she commented. As we discussed her dream, Ingrid came to the conclusion that she needed to resolve this relationship conflict before her unconscious would permit her to "see" her unborn child as a human baby rather than as a symbolic animal. After she persuaded her husband to go with her to their obstetrician and to view the fetus in a sonogram, he began to take more interest, and to treat her with more sensitivity. Having resolved this problem, Ingrid was then able to incubate sweeter dreams about her pregnancy.

Equally important, Curtis was present and extremely helpful during the delivery of their healthy baby girl.

Summary

In this chapter we have explored the various methods now being taught to help us "control" or create our own dreams. Such dreams are either "incubated" or "lucid," or combinations of both.

An incubated dream depicting a topic of the dreamer's choice is relatively easy to achieve. Once the dreamer is able to recall and interpret dreams, an incubated dream can be programmed simply by telling oneself, "I will dream about (the topic of choice)."

However, all attempts at dream control are more effective if the dreamer is able to relax deeply before falling asleep. Once in this relaxed, almost hypnotic state, the unconscious appears to accept and to act upon the dreamer's directions more readily, providing dreams on a desired topic.

After mastering the skill of dream incubation, many dreamers are able to program dreams in which they will be lucid, aware that they are dreaming while the dream is taking place. While this skill is much more difficult, the benefits of lucidity are many. Lucid dreams give the dreamer an opportunity to experience rapturous feelings seldom duplicated in waking life. These include the joys of flying, heightened sexual fulfillment, and a new awareness of the pleasures of waking reality.

Readers are cautioned to approach dream control with discretion, making reasonable requests for a dream topic, and avoiding attempts to erase or conquer nightmarish dream characters. All the elements of our dreams have a purpose. Rather than programming our dreams to eliminate any unpleasant images, the better course is to incubate dreams to discover the meaning of these elements.

It's also important to give yourself approval and encouragement simply for making the effort to create your own dreams. Even if you're unsuccessful, your mind will take note of the fact that you're giving your dreams this serious attention, so that you'll discover a new clarity and understanding of all your dreams.

Chapter
NINE

Making Your Fantasies Come True

In *Spanish Studies*, Act III, Scene 5, the poet Longfellow wrote:

> Is this a dream? Oh, if it be a dream,
> Let me sleep on, and do not wake me yet!

And Shakespeare proclaimed:

> All this is but a dream,
> Too flattering sweet to be substantial.
> (*Romeo and Juliet*, Act II, Scene 2)

> If it be thus to dream, still let me sleep!
> (*Twelfth Night*, Act IV, Scene 1)

201

How many times all of us have longed to remain enfolded in our sweetest dreams, never having to return to harsh awakening! All too often, we must rouse ourselves and get on with daily routines. However, it's possible to recreate those rapturous moments, both with your new dream control skills, and with your waking imagination. Moreover, you and your partner can travel, both in your dreams and your daydreams, to an exotic paradise of your choice—without leaving the comforts of your own bedroom.

This chapter will show you how to:

- Sightsee in your dreams
- Make love with daydreams and visualizations
- Use your dreams to have satisfying sex after fifty
- Make erotic dreams a waking reality

Dream Travels to Paradise

Betsy and Richard, the "mixed" couple whose dreams are described in Chapters 3 and 4, became experts in the ability to travel in their dreams. "It happened by accident," Richard explained, "when we'd been reading some travel brochures. That night, we both dreamed about going to some of the places in the brochures. So, we decided to experiment with the idea. It took awhile to figure out how to dream about specific places, but eventually we learned how."

Betsy laughingly told us about their first attempts. "If you don't tell yourself the precise place you want to go in your dreams," she said, "some very funny things may happen." When they began learning dream travel techniques, Betsy and Richard agreed on the incubation sentence, "Tonight I will dream I am in Venice." After listening to their relaxation tape they repeated that sentence to themselves as they fell asleep. This is Richard's incubated dream about "Venice":

Dreamt I was on a wide, crowded public beach. All the men looked like "Mr. America"—real weight lifter types. They were strutting around, flexing their biceps. One guy came up and asked me where I worked out and I said nowhere, I just run or walk for exercise. He sneered at me and said I ought to find some other beach since this one was only for jocks. Two men were wrestling and this one guy said, "You'd better leave now because the winner will take you on next." And I woke up feeling puzzled about it all.

When we discussed his dream, Richard realized he had, indeed, received the incubated setting he'd requested. "Only, it was Venice, *California*," he said. "Better known as 'Muscle Beach.' Next time, I'd better remember to ask for Venice, *Italy!*"

Richard's dream also gave him a message about his waking life situation. "Guess I still feel I'm an outsider," he said. "Even though I know Betsy loves and accepts me, it sure would make life easier for us if her parents did, too."

Betsy had better luck in reaching her incubated destination. However, her dream also portrayed her parents' disapproval:

It started out exactly like a photograph, or one of those travel posters. A perfect scene of the palaces and crooked streets of Venice, with me in a gondola being rowed by a handsome Italian who was serenading me in a deep baritone with some aria from an Italian opera. I couldn't understand all the words but it was about love, very romantic. It was night and the moon reflected in the waters of the canal. Then the gondola began to rock violently and I fell out. There was a white rose floating by and I grabbed onto the stem. It held me up like a life preserver so I kicked and came up to a pier or dock. Some old women reached down and pulled me out. One of them gave me her shawl as I was shivering. We went into a cafe or bar and my parents were there. Mom said, "You look terrible!" and I started to cry. Dad put his arm around me and told me to have a glass of wine. "You don't understand," I said. "I'm trying to find Richard." Then I asked the bartender if he'd seen Richard and he said something in Italian, meaning he didn't understand. I felt frustrated and a little angry, because Richard was supposed to meet me there.

When Betsy tried to incubate a dream, she had hoped to dream of meeting her lover Richard in Venice. Instead, she was unable to find him in her dream, even though she herself made the trip. However, she did find him there symbolically, in that when the gondola capsized she clung to a white rose. This same symbol had appeared in Richard's dream quoted in Chapter 3, when he stole a white rose from a neighbor's garden. Betsy's dreaming mind presented her with this symbol she knew indicated Richard's presence—even though her unconscious seems to have had another, more pressing message for her consideration, that of her conflicts about her parents.

The next night, Betsy changed her incubation sentence to, "Tonight I will dream again about being in Venice, Italy, and Richard will be there." This time, the gondolier was Richard. When the gondola overturned, they both fell out. "This time, my parents were waiting at the dock," Betsy said. "When we climbed out, Mom told me this was what I could expect if I continued to live with Richard, and I woke up feeling angry again."

Clearly, Betsy needed to come to terms with her worries about her parents' unwillingness to accept Richard. Both Richard's and Betsy's dreams point up the fact that even an incubated dream about a specific topic or setting will often mirror the unresolved issues of one's daily life.

Christine and Jason, whose sexual experience as they awoke from pleasant dreams opened Chapter 7, both attempted dream incubation on the same night, with more rewarding results. This couple decided they wanted to dream about making love in exotic, faraway places. "We were disappointed when our vacation plans fell through," Christine explained, "so we decided to experiment with dream travel to cheer ourselves up. We both went to sleep telling ourselves we would dream about being together on a tropical island paradise." This was Christine's dream:

Jason and I are wading out of an ocean which is very calm, more like a lake except the sandy bottom is white. We're holding hands and we're both golden tan. It's warm, but not too hot. The beach curves around almost in a heart shape and is outlined with palm trees. Jason reaches down and picks up a squirming lobster, saying we can have it for dinner. It's red, already cooked, and I think that's amazing. We're the only people there, yet there is a white tent all set up for us on the beach, with a big white umbrella outside and a table all set with crystal, china, linens, even a vase of tropical flowers. We run up to the tent. Inside there are towels laid out on a wide, soft bed. "E.F. or F.F.?" Jason asks and I start to giggle and can't stop, so he slaps me on the backside and then French kisses me while he pulls off my bikini. Then, I help him take off his suit, and we towel each other off. Wrapping the towels around ouselves, we go outside and sit at the table. The lobster is magically there, a piece on each of our plates. He pours wine and we both talk excitedly about this paradise while we eat. I complain that there's no dessert and Jason says *I* am the dessert! So we go back into the tent and lie on the bed. We're both so hot there's no time for foreplay—we just throw ourselves on each other, and I feel myself coming. It's like being filled with sweet liquid lava which builds up and up until I explode. Feel as if I'm blowing apart from the inside explosion, but we stay together like one body. Suddenly it is night and we are still glued together but we're high above the island, in a dark blue sky, floating up there. I still feel as if I am both myself and Jason, like we are one body. It's the happiest feeling I've ever had in my entire life! Down below I can see the white tent. It has a big hole in the top and I think we must have rocketed right through it! Jason is softly kissing my neck and breasts and I pull him even closer, thinking, "Oh God! I'm getting hot again!" and I wake up.

On the same night, Christine's husband Jason had this dream:

Dreamed we (Chris and I) were sitting on a white, sandy beach, with our toes in the water. Looking around, I realized it was Megan's Bay on St. Thomas, a place I've always wanted to take her. It was really crowded with lots of tourists. Then I saw they all looked like people we know and so I knew it must be a dream. Well, I thought, since this is a dream I can make them all go away—and right then they just disappeared! I was laughing and Chris said, "What's so funny?" and I grabbed her and kissed her. We were rolling around naked in the wet sand with little waves washing over us. I was getting really horny, but Chris said she was hungry. So we got up and walked back into the shade of some palm trees and a native boy brought us a picnic basket. Chris was leaning over it. Her breasts hanging down like that always turn me on. So I said we'd just have to eat later and I pushed her down onto the sand. She had a fish on a stick in her hand and she kept eating it all the time I was [making love to] her. This made me a little mad at first and then I thought it was funny so I took a bite of the fish without ever losing my rhythm. She was responding, thrusting up to me, and eating the fish at the same time and I remember thinking that was something new and then I woke up. After that we made love for real and it was really great, the best ever.

Notice the similarities in Christine's and Jason's dreams: the same island setting (Jason explained that Megan's Bay really is heart-shaped, just as Christine's dream depicted it); the seafood lunch and Christine's determination to "eat first"; and their passionate drive to make love.

Symbiotic Dreams

It's quite unusual for two people to have such similar dreams at the same time. This occurred with several of the couples I studied during my research for *Pregnancy and Dreams*. Since such remarkably alike dreams seem to happen only to people who are very close, I have dubbed them "symbiotic." Dream researchers at Carleton University in Ottawa, Canada, have recently discovered other examples between twins and siblings who were emotionally close.

Since these symbiotic dreams are quite rare, please do not be disappointed if you and your partner are unable to have them. Such dreams appear to happen when the dreamers have similar thinking processes, or when they are experiencing the same, usually stressful, circumstances in their waking life. Christine and Jason were both quite upset that their vacation plans were canceled, so that they were probably in the same emotional state. The expectant couples who reported symbiotic dreams during my research of pregnancy psychology were also undergoing similar anxieties about the approaching delivery.

Sexual Daydreams and Visualizations

My students often ask about possible connections between daydreams and sleeping dreams. I tell them about the extensive investigations of the nature and content of daydreams conducted by Drs. Jerome Singer and John Antrobus, of City University of New York. These researchers say that the waking state of consciousness during a spontaneous daydream is often "split," or operating at two levels.

When we're doing routine or boring tasks, a part of the mind disengages and turns to images and thoughts of the inner self. Examples of such boring situations might be driving a car along a familiar route, listening to a dull lecture, or the monotony of a factory worker's assembly line activities. At such times, a daydream seems to pop into our heads without effort.

Although the images such daydreams provide may arise from the lower brain (as do the pictures we see in REM sleep), daydreams, reveries, and fantasies are unlike sleeping dreams in that these waking visions are more under our conscious control. For instance, if some part of the boring activity claims our attention (an unexpected detour confronts the driver, the lecturer displays slides or asks a question, a defect appears in the assembly line), we can "come back" to the task at hand, and then return to the daydream where we left off.

Contrary to popular belief, most of the daydreams which are spontaneous, seeming to come into our minds "out of nowhere," are not about sex. Further, those which are erotic tend to be rather commonplace.

Erotic Daydreams, Fantasies, and Visualizations

In contrast to the spontaneous daydream, a deliberately evoked sexual fantasy may be elaborate and concerned with "taboo" acts we might never attempt in real life. However, there's usually no reason to hide these fantasies from your partner. Instead, you can learn how to use these private and usually secret fantasies to create safe, dreamlike episodes you can share without shame or worry. Doing this can add new spice to your sex life, as well as deepen the trust and love you have for each other.

GETTING READY. The first step toward achieving the special sexual pleasures of erotic daydreams is to *communicate*. At a time when you feel trusting and emotionally intimate, share your personal (usually secret) fantasies with your partner, explaining that you do not wish to act on these ideas right now, preferring to modify them at a later time, together.

For instance, Ben (the actress Tammy's husband, described in Chapter 4) had a secret sexual fantasy about being seduced by a nurse. "I've had this ever since I had an appendectomy in my teens," Ben said. "I woke up at night and my nurse had her skirts pulled up. She was probably just adjusting her white stockings, but I imagined she was masturbating and it turned me on. Man, I was sure embarrassed when she came over to the bed and saw my erection!"

Until we discussed sexual fantasies in our group, Ben had been afraid to reveal his secret thoughts to anyone, especially his wife. "It's so corny and juvenile," he said, "I thought she'd laugh me out of the house." But when he finally told Tammy, she loved the idea. "After all," she explained, "I am an actress, so this gave me a chance to play a sexy role with my favorite audience."

CREATING AND INTEGRATING THE EROTIC DAYDREAM. As you and your partner communicate about your secret fantasies, you may find that merely talking about them is all either of you need to become highly aroused. Or, you may want to "act it out" in a more formal manner. One way to do this is to actually write a script and then perform it. Tammy did this for Ben as follows:

(*Scene*: Ben, wearing only a pajama top, lies in a hospital bed. Room is lit only by a night light. Nurse Tammy, in white cap and uniform, enters, stands near bed, lifts up skirt revealing white garterbelt and white stockings. As Ben watches, Tammy takes off her white lace panties and strokes herself, all the while smiling seductively at Ben. Leaving skirt hiked up, she approaches bedside.)

TAMMY: Well, young man, how are we feeling tonight? (pulls sheet down) Oh my, is this for me?

BEN: (shyly) Yes, ma'am . . . excuse me, ma'am.

TAMMY: Oh, that's all right, dear. I'm flattered that you like my legs. Now, if you're a good patient, maybe I'll let you see even more. But first, roll over on your tummy, dear. (Ben rolls over. Tammy removes his pajama top, massages his back and buttocks with lotion, then rolls him over onto his back again. She now anoints his neck, chest, stomach and penis with the lotion, gently massaging each area.)

TAMMY; You've been such a good patient, Ben dear, now I'm going to show you more of myself.

(She removes uniform and bra, kicks off her shoes, and climbs up on top of him. He caresses her breasts.)

BEN: Oh nurse, that feels so good!

TAMMY: Now it's time for your treatment, dear.

(She mounts him, and they climax together.)

Ben confided that it was more Tammy's willingness to dramatize his fantasy than the actual action which aroused him so much. However, some people have much more difficulty communicating these very private thoughts to their partners, especially if the fantasy has "dangerous" aspects.

For example, Peg, whose oral sex experiments with Ralph were described in the previous chapter, had a secret fantasy that she was kidnapped and raped. Indulging in this vision while she masturbated inevitably resulted in Peg's reaching orgasm. "Sometimes I even think of it when Ralph is making love to me," she confessed in our private interview. "But, this fantasy really worries me. I believe rape is a terrible crime, and very demeaning to women. The idea that I have such thoughts really upsets me."

Peg was surprised to learn that many women have such fantasies. Sex therapists and psychologists generally agree that these imaginary scenes arise from a woman's fears of being thought promiscuous if she actually expresses her sexual desires. By fantasizing that she is forced, a woman with these inhibitions can rationalize that she "surrendered" without self-blame or guilt. Another explanation may be that the physical release of orgasm is preceded by an emotional feeling of surrender, which many women associate with being dominated physically.

Although I reassured Peg that her fantasies are normal and harmless, she wondered whether her continuing to indulge in them might be reinforcing her sexual inhibitions and the feelings of low self-esteem which kept her from openly asking Ralph for sexual fulfillment. When I suggested that she and Ralph might try "acting out" these secret imaginings, Peg was initially horrified. "I'm afraid to tell him," she said, "and, if I did, and we really did those things—I guess I'm afraid we might go further and get into some really dangerous stuff, like sado-masochism."

Thus it came about that I taught Peg and Ralph how to use her secret fantasies to enhance their lovemaking and, at the same time, change her self-defeating attitudes. By intentionally incorporating affirmative messages into a new, creative daydream, Ralph was able to help Peg reprogram the inner beliefs which prevented her from total expression of normal, healthy sexual desires.

Once they began to communicate about their formerly clandestine imaginings, Peg and Ralph were prepared to compose a daydream or visualization which would permit them to "act out" the erotic elements of Peg's fantasy in a safe manner. First, Peg wrote a frank, explicit description of the thoughts she entertained while masturbating. Next, the couple collaborated on a modified version which would also improve Peg's lack of assertiveness.

Here is the scene Peg and Ralph created, in Peg's words:

Ralph, already naked, pushes me down onto our bed and undresses me, covering my mouth with kisses and telling me I must do as he says. Then he holds my wrists firmly, telling me that no matter how I try, I cannot get away. He tells me over and over how beautiful I am, how sexy, how much he wants me. His kisses move over my breasts, my nipples, and then over my stomach as he pushes my legs apart with his shoulders. Then he says I must tell him what I want. He keeps caressing me until I am so hot I beg him to kiss me *there*. He does and then stops just before I come, to tell me again how desirable and sexy I am, and that I must tell him what I want. I scream, "Oh, yes, yes, take me!" and he enters me. He releases my wrists and I throw my arms around him as we both say, "I love you," over and over with each thrust and lunge. Then we come, together.

By including firm yet loving demands that she tell him her desires, Ralph helped Peg combine her need to be more assertive with the stimulus of her secret fantasy's arousing quality of male domination. By declaring their love as they reached orgasm and integrating these thoughts into their deeper consciousness, Peg and Ralph effectively erased the impersonality of her previous fantasies, a factor which Peg had found especially distressing. Instead of feeling led to more aggressive or violent acts, this couple eventually found that they could achieve the same heights of arousal without any focus on the dominance/submission aspects. "Just knowing that *he knows* what I'm thinking is all I need to turn me on," Peg explained. Ralph added, "All this has made me feel so close. It makes me feel Peg has given me something very precious. It's the kind of sharing I always wanted and never really believed we could have."

To create your own erotic daydream or dialogue with your partner, you may think of other methods. Some couples speak their thoughts into a tape recorder, playing them back during lovemaking. Ralph and Peg carefully wrote out a "script," recorded it, and listened to it without touching one another. Then, they acted it out from memory. After using their taped creative daydream for a few weeks, Peg reported that her private fantasy had changed dramatically. "The other night when I was alone," she confided, "I tried to do that old rape fantasy and it just disgusted me. My mind went instead to memories of the last time Ralph and I were together, and it was pure bliss!"

SOME WORDS OF CAUTION. Whatever your erotic fantasy may be, it's wise to keep it to yourself until you are confident you're involved in a lasting, loving relationship. Had Peg confided her thoughts of being forced into sexual acts to someone she didn't know well, she might have risked physical harm. Since Ralph was her partner of several years, we both knew he loved her and sincerely wanted to share her innermost thoughts. Ralph's biggest pleasure was this mutual revelation of their fantasies; his actions afterward showed Peg that she could trust him without reservations.

This type of sharing is especially effective with couples who have been together many years. When seventy-two-year-old Alec (whose dream of being at a "topless" beach on the French Riviera is quoted in Chapter 4) told his wife Georgia about his erotic musings, she was delighted to experiment with acting it out—with some very definite changes. Alec said he fantasized himself as a sultan surrounded by a harem of voluptuous women. When he shared this with our dream study group, Georgia exclaimed, "I'd love to be in your harem, darling—but you'll have to settle for just one wife!"

Later, Georgia gave me this written description of her "real life" version of Alec's secret fantasy:

One night, before Alec got home from his volunteer work at the Senior Citizen Center, I set the scene by pushing back all the living room furniture and covering the carpet with all kinds of pillows of many shapes and sizes. Dimmed the lights and got all dressed up in a "Harem Girl" costume which I borrowed from a young woman friend who is studying belly dancing. It has a sequined bra, a veil, and low-cut, sheer harem pants. I put on a very heavy, musky perfume, dark eye makeup, and even rings on my toes! Had some of my friend's Greek music on the stereo—not exactly out of Arabian Nights, but it did set the mood. Well, when Alec got home he was sure surprised! He got undressed, put on a turban I'd made, and his silk robe. We had some wine and I told him, "You can pretend you sent away the rest of the harem, wanting only me tonight," and he said, "If I really had a harem, I'd do just that, my dear!" Then I danced for him and we ended up making love on the floor pillows.

This senior couple are an example of the pleasures available to both sexes in later life. These really can be the "golden" years of a relationship, when both partners are well informed about possible physical limitations. By sharing their feelings and insights with our couples' dream study group, Georgia and Alec helped the younger members prepare for the years to come.

Lovemaking After Fifty

It's surprising how many couples believe their sex life will wane or disappear once they've reached the half-century mark. This is not true; on the contrary, many people experience an increase in sexual desire, which is heightened by the absence of worries about pregnancy and the extra leisure time provided by retirement. Men and women who had an active sexual life earlier can look forward to similar enjoyment in their later years.

However, both sexes can expect some physical changes which may alter their lovemaking styles. Recent studies by Masters and Johnson show that most men over age fifty want sex less frequently, take a longer time to get an erection, and ejaculate sooner than was the case in their youth. Women in this age group frequently complain of vaginal dryness, and a few report loss of sexual desire.

During the menopause, some women have bouts of "hot flashes," dizziness, and sweating, which may interfere with desires for intimacy.

These symptoms may appear before a woman's periods have ceased, or after they have stopped. According to experts quoted in *Ourselves Growing Older*, these uncomfortable symptoms are transient, so that most women can look forward to feeling normal again within a year. Meanwhile, it's helpful to dress in layers so that, should a hot flash occur, you can cool off by removing top layers. Since these symptoms are related to sudden drops in hormonal levels, ask your physician about estrogen replacement therapy.

Hormonal therapy also helps correct the common complaint of vaginal dryness. Additionally, this condition can be alleviated with daily use of a hormone-enriched cream prescribed by your physician. Further, there are over-the-counter and mail-order lubricants available, which are safe for use during foreplay and intercourse and do not contain petroleum oils (to be avoided since long-term use increases dryness). Ask your pharmacist about nonprescription, water-based lubricants.

These minor limitations need not put an end to lovemaking after fifty. In fact, recent Kinsey research and that done by Masters and Johnson indicate that many older people discover the joys of oral sex and other expressions of intimacy such as cuddling and manual stimulation for the first time. All these activities provide outlets for emotions, release tension, promote sounder sleep, and make both partners feel more desirable—even when neither, or only one, of the partners reaches orgasm.

Ward, the fifty-one-year-old winemaker whose dream about an incipient ulcer is quoted in Chapter 2, came to me for advice when he and his wife Penny began having sexual problems related to his changing physical state. "At first, I thought I was just overtired," Ward said. "Suddenly I just didn't want sex the way I used to. But then when I got rested and slowed down on the work load, I still just couldn't seem to get interested. Now, Penny thinks I'm having an affair, or just don't love her anymore. Not so! Is this just part of getting older?"

Ward was experiencing one of the most common sexual problems, the syndrome of low sexual desire. Dr. Bernie Zilbergeld, author of *Male Sexuality*, says that there is no such thing as "normal" sexual desire. One man may enjoy sex every day, sometimes twice or more daily, while another may be satisfied with sexual activity once a week. If the couple are content, either frequency is normal. It is when desire drops dramatically, as in Ward's case, that there is some cause for concern. Generally, if a man engages in any kind of sexual activity (including masturbation) less than twice a month, it's probably wise to consult a physician for the source of the problem.

If the cause is *physical*, it can often be corrected with simple hormonal medication. Sometimes the decrease in desire is due to other illnesses, or a side effect of medications such as the diuretics often prescribed for high blood pressure. Adjustments in these medications may be all that's required for sexual desire to return. Overconsumption of alcohol can also inhibit sexuality, in both males and females.

If the cause is *psychological*, both partners can accomplish a great deal toward effecting changes. According to the editors of the newsletter *Sex Over Forty*, the most common psychological causes of low sexual desire are: negative thoughts—especially repressed anger and resentments toward the partner; depression—due to any sort of stress, or fears of aging and death; fear of intimacy—which may not arise until the man retires and finds himself in closer contact with his mate; and relationship problems—especially typical of retired men whose wives are still working.

After Ward consulted his physician, who assured him he was healthy, he agreed to communicate his anxieties more openly with Penny. Acting as mediator, I encouraged them both to express their feelings about sex. It developed that Ward was somewhat bored with Penny, who seemed less attractive than when they first married. Ward commented, "She just doesn't seem to care anymore, and always looks sort of, well, unkempt." Penny admitted she paid less attention to her appearance. "I used to spend hours getting my hair done, dressing nicely," she said, "and Ward was so busy or so tired, he never noticed. So I just gave up." With Ward's reassurances, Penny promised to change this attitude.

Dream Clues to Sexual Problems

When physical dysfunctions are ruled out, your dreams may provide clues to psychological factors which may be contributing to loss of sexual desire. Following is a very revealing dream Ward had during this period:

> Dreamed I was practicing football in high school. On the sidelines, the cheerleaders were practicing. After practice, this one cute cheerleader, Mary Jo, trotted along beside me, flirting and fawning all over me, telling me I was her hero, hinting she wanted me to ask her to the Homecoming Dance. I felt embarrassed, but I must have liked it because I woke up with an erection for the first time in months.

When Penny heard Ward's account of this dream, she exclaimed, "That little bitch, Mary Jo! I thought you couldn't stand her!" Ward protested that he'd never cared for the cheerleader, and couldn't understand why she'd appeared in his dream. "I haven't even thought about any of those guys back in high school, for years," he said.

In times of stress, or when we have waking conflicts which appear to have no solution, our dreams may portray characters and settings from our past. Such dreams often seem to be reminding us of the ways we solved a similar problem in bygone days. When Penny and Ward understood this, they were both able to see the true message from his cheerleader dream. "Oh! Now I get it!" Penny said. "Even though you didn't like Mary Jo, she turned you on because she admired you so much." Ward agreed, adding, "But you're the only one I love, Penny. I guess I've been wishing we could just show each other how much we care, the way we used to."

This explanation was all Penny and Ward needed to bring romance back into their life. When she saw that Ward noticed, Penny began taking better care of herself, as well as verbalizing her appreciation of her husband's many talents. On his part, Ward arranged his schedule so he'd have at least one day of rest each week, during which he and

Penny revived some of the hobbies they'd once enjoyed together. I'm happy to report that Ward's sexual desires for his attractive, youthful wife returned. In the next chapter, we'll learn more about this couple's newly found techniques for keeping their romance alive.

Acting Out Your Erotic Dreams

In previous chapters we've already encountered some examples of the ways couples have "acted out" their erotic dreams—such as Ralph and Peg's experiments with oral sex after her dream of bathing in a stream at a nudist camp. Now is the time to review your own dreams for suggestions of erotic dream innovations that you can make a waking reality.

Lisa and Peter, whose dreams are quoted in most of the preceding chapters, reported many instances of dream enrichment of their waking sex life. "Lisa's dreams are better for this than mine are," Peter, the artist, explained. "Mine are often sort of abstract—swirls of color. Great ideas for my murals, but not as much like real life as Lisa's." Following is one of Lisa's dreams, which she and Peter especially enjoyed recreating in their waking hours of intimacy:

Dreamed I was a stripper in a rather sleazy nightclub. (Last night we saw an old movie about a Broadway dancer who started out as a stripper.) I was draped in furs from neck to floor, and as I moved I would show my legs in a teasing way. I danced out onto a ramp and all these men were leering at me and I was enjoying every minute! (In real life I'm not like that at all!) Then I started stripping, dropping the furs one by one. They were all different kinds, a long white fox boa, a mink one underneath, and finally a short sleeveless kind of fur dress made out of red bunny fur, which unzipped down the side. By that time, some of the men were practically crawling up onto the ramp, throwing money at me, cheering and yelling take it off. I remember feeling very sexy and excited. Then to my horror I realized my body had changed. Under the red fur, my chest was flat and hairy like a man's. I saw Peter in the audience and I thought, oh horrors, he won't love me anymore. And I woke up feeling a little scared.

Lisa thought her sudden change into a man in this dream indicated her reluctance to be sexually aggressive or to take the initiative in lovemaking. "Somewhere I got the idea that it's not feminine for the woman to admit she's feeling excited," she said. "And I certainly would just die if I ever actually went out in front of a bunch of men in a getup like that! But when I told Peter the dream, he loved it—told me he wished I would come on to him when I feel like it."

As a result, Lisa and Peter went shopping for a stripper's costume, complete with g-string, and created their own "nightclub" in the privacy of their bedroom. After they moved from California to New York, Lisa wrote, "We went to a striptease place and it was actually very nice. And, I got some ideas for a new bedroom routine!"

Following are excerpts from other erotic dreams which provided variety to the dreamers' waking lovemaking:

- *Maureen, 42-year-old homemaker, Carl's wife, whose dreams are quoted in Chapters 2 and 3*: Dreamed Carl woke me up from my nap by caressing me. Told him my dream and the next Sunday he did exactly that. It was even nicer than my dream.
- *Claude, Monique's husband, whose dream of his boss firing him for interfering is quoted in Chapter 7*: I was in a Chinese restaurant . . . behind a beaded curtain saw an Oriental couple making love . . . she was on all fours and they were doing it "doggie fashion." (Sounds ridiculous but in the dream they looked beautiful, mysterious.)
- *Margo, whose dream of jewels during ovulation is quoted in Chapter 4*: Dreamed Sean and I were making love in our car at a drive-in movie . . . when they kissed on the screen, we did, too.

These couples took their erotic dreams' suggestions to add some spice to their lovemaking. Maureen and Carl had fallen into a habit of limiting their sexual activities to Saturday nights, when Carl was more rested than during the week. They had learned that they both felt more passionate when they felt relaxed. "I overlooked the fact that Maureen wasn't usually 'in the mood' then," Carl said. "Her Saturdays are anything but restful. But her dream clued me in—after she has her Sunday afternoon nap, when everything is warm and quiet, we have hours to fool around. That dream sure put some new excitement in our time alone together!"

Claude and Monique had gotten into another type of dull routine, by always assuming the same coital "missionary" position, with him on top. Claude's dream of the beautiful Oriental pair on their knees inspired him to try some other positions. "We knew about all the different angles we could do," Monique explained, "but we hadn't tried any for years. Now, we're experimenting with all sorts of positions, and it's as if we're back being newlyweds!"

Margo surprised her Air Force husband Sean the next time they went to the movies. "I put my coat over both our laps and we started 'petting' just like we used to do, right there in the movies," she said. "I couldn't wait until a time when we might go to a drive-in to try it out! Sean got so passionate he didn't even want to wait 'til the movie was over, so we went home and to bed!"

Summary

Once you've learned to incubate dreams about topics of your choice, you can use this skill to visit exotic locales. This "dream sightseeing" is an especially delightful pastime for lovers, who sometimes even have "symbiotic" dreams, in which they experience sleeping visions with similar content and settings. Although such dreams are rare they are possible, and seem to occur when a couple are undergoing like emotional states.

However, even though you and your partner may not be able to have symbiotic dreams, or even have much success with dream incubation, you'll probably find that the powers of your waking imagination have expanded simply because you've been paying more attention to the unconscious aspects of your mind. Daydreams and fantasies are areas of imagination which anyone can explore and control.

Although daydreams seem to "pop into" our minds out of nowhere, you can create reveries which can help you integrate new attitudes to replace self-defeating ones. Further, you can take the ingredients of your secret sexual fantasies and intentionally "rewrite" them into scripts which will enable you to share your fantasies' most arousing qualities with your partner.

This revelation of your private, erotic imaginings should be attempted only with the lover whom you trust implicitly. After the two of you have discussed your reverie in detail, try collaborating on a nonthreatening version which you can "act out" together. Although some couples like to go to great lengths to make their fantasies come to life, costumes and props aren't usually necessary once you have shared the basic concepts with each other.

These mutual visualizations are often especially effective with lovers who appear to have lost their desire for sex as they mature. People over age fifty who are physically healthy sometimes suffer from decreased sexual desire for purely psychological reasons. As in other relationship conflicts or problems, dreams can serve as valuable clues to the sources of this seeming indifference to one of life's greatest and most enduring pleasures.

Additionally, lovers of all ages can examine their dreams for delightful suggestions which can add variety and spice to their lovemaking. Take the time to review your own dream notebook for these very personal messages from your inner self.

Chapter
TEN

Keeping Your
Romance Alive

"We've been married nearly four years now," Diana told me with a little sigh, "and I almost wish we had some of the problems we used to worry about so much. At least life was thrilling in those days." Her husband Bill agreed. "The first couple of years, we focused on each other," he said. "You know, all our differences and whether we could work them out. These days, it's all about child-raising and what we can afford. Seems we're friends and coworkers, but somewhere the love and romance got lost."

Rosemarie and Jim have an entirely different view. "I wouldn't want to return to the first years of our marriage," Rosemarie says. "A lot of that first romantic thrill was actually fear. I didn't know Jim the way I do now, and that both attracted and scared me. Now, we know each other so well, we often don't even have to finish a sentence because we both know the end. This is very comforting."

Jim adds, "Now, when something comes up—and life always gives us new experiences and feelings—we sense the changes immediately. Then we start looking at our dreams for clues about how to cope with any problems those changes may cause between us."

Unlike Jim and Rosemarie, Bill and Diana neglected their dream notebooks and dream sharing, as well as most of the other personal and intimate aspects of their marriage. Becoming parents, with all the new responsibilities that entailed, took priority in their time together. However, when they returned to our dream study group after several years' absence, Bill and Diana were soon able to revive those wonderful feelings of excitement and fulfillment, adding to them the trust and communication skills their years together had provided.

This chapter will show you some of the ways Bill and Diana, Jim and Rosemarie, and other couples have used their understanding and sharing of dreams to cement the bonds of their love. These techniques for keeping your romance alive include:

- Continuing the Dream Dyad
- Using old dreams to create new ones
- Starting a new sex life in your middle years

Continuing Your Dream Dyad

Diana and Bill stopped sharing their dreams when they became parents, rationalizing that they simply didn't have the time. "Then when we both started losing interest in sex," Bill said, "and Diana started complaining that the romance was gone, we realized we'd better *make* the time—or we'd just keep drifting farther apart."

This couple was fortunate in that they recognized the first symptoms of dissatisfaction within their marriage, and were prompt in their attempts to avoid further decline. More than half of all contemporary newlyweds end up in divorce courts. A look at information from the National Center for Health Statistics shows that those marriages which survive the first four to ten years are less likely to fail than those of couples wed for only one to three years.

According to these statistics, Diana and Bill, with almost four years behind them, had a 46.7 percent chance that their relationship would end in divorce. On the other hand, Jim and Rosemarie, approaching their 15th anniversary, faced only a 21 percent chance of a failed marriage. While even these percentages seem high, many couples can feel more confident of their marriage's stability with each passing year.

As we discussed the feelings of discontent Bill and Diana were having, it became evident that they'd lost sight of the goals they set when they were engaged. "We promised each other we'd share everything," Bill recalled. "When we stopped telling each other about our dreams, that was just one more thing we had to pass up, temporarily. Only, the 'temporarily' became more or less permanent."

"It wasn't simply that we stopped working with our dreams," Diana explained. "The real issue was that we stopped paying attention to anything that used to keep us close and sharing. For us, reviving the Dream Dyad activities made it easy. It gave us a place to start rebuilding what we'd lost."

After resuming attendance at our dream study group, Bill and Diana realized that the Dream Dyad is an ideal therapeutic aid because it:

- Encourages compromise and commitment
- Builds trust
- Enhances communication skills
- Reveals "secrets" in a nonthreatening manner

Compromise and Commitment

Another recent study of relationships, conducted at Boston University by researcher Wendy Greene, found that people who appreciate closeness and commitment are more likely to have successful relationships than are those who give priority to independence and assertiveness. Patience and the sometimes compromising attitudes needed in a mutually satisfactory Dream Dyad can help you and your partner strengthen the intimacy and dedication which are hallmarks of a stable relationship.

At first, Diana strongly objected to my use of the word "compromise," reminding our group that her need to hold onto her hard-won independence had been a source of conflict before she and Bill got married. Then Jim explained, "It's more a question of being unselfish, more generous, than one of giving up being independent or assertive."

Jim, whose struggles as he learned the art of dream-sharing conversations were described in Chapter 1, had trained himself to withhold his reactions while Rosemarie related her dreams. "I used to interrupt, telling her exactly how some part of her dream made me feel," Jim went on. "So Rosemarie got to expect that whatever she said would make me mad. That caused her to keep her thoughts to herself, until I learned how to be a good dream listener."

This patient acceptance not only helps couples create an atmosphere of trust during Dream Dyad discussions; it also tends to become a habit, spilling over into other, routine interchanges. Following is a Dream Dyad dialogue between Bill and Diana, demonstrating Diana's attempts to become a better listener:

BILL: Dreamed we were at your sister's house, a seedy, shabby place . . . You arrived with a child, a little boy, who was hungry. I felt great compassion for him. He had meat, but he needed and wanted potatoes . . . I gave the boy potatoes, which he took home. Then I was in a bar, in an awful neighborhood— the bowels of L.A. . . . These two men got up and danced . . . began to fight. One was very powerful, huge . . . I had to get out of there, but couldn't get all my possessions together . . . Out on the street, the car I'd borrowed from your sister was gone. Other cars were crashing into each other . . . Wanted desperately to get back to you, but had terrible difficulty getting all my stuff together.

DIANA: What do you think the dream means?

BILL: I don't know, it just doesn't make sense. No, wait a minute! I used to dream about a little boy, remember?

DIANA: Yes, and you thought he symbolized yourself as a child.

BILL: That's right. It was just before we got married. So, if the child in this dream is me, then I must need "potatoes." But I don't see what that signifies.

DIANA: What do you associate with potatoes?

BILL: Well, this kid had enough meat. Guess that means he had enough protein to keep him alive. But potatoes are carbohydrates, energy. And I like potatoes, always have.

DIANA: So, maybe you aren't getting enough of what you need for energy, or enough of what you like the most?

BILL: Yeah, that makes sense. You've been giving me—our marriage—just enough of yourself to keep things going. But I miss the fun part. Our sex life used to be better, you know.

DIANA: Well, that's not all my fault! It takes two to tango—and you're always too tired lately. If you'd take better care of yourself, you might have more energy!

At this point in their dialogue, Bill and Diana stopped communicating. By voicing her own emotional response to Bill's complaints, Diana prevented Bill from continuing his dream interpretation.

Dr. David D. Burns, author of *The Feeling Good Handbook*, says that the secret to dealing effectively with complainers is not to give advice, but to simply agree, validating the other person's viewpoint. Jim, who had been advising Diana and Bill on Dream Dyad techniques, gently reminded Diana of this all-important concept and the couple resumed their Dream Dyad. This time, Diana managed to avoid expressing her reactions, with this result:

DIANA: Yes, I can tell that you miss the fun, and the energy a good sex life used to give you. Is that what the potatoes in your dream symbolized?

BILL: Exactly. And notice that the child went away once he got his potatoes. So, maybe I'd stop acting so childish if we could overcome these sex problems we're having lately.

DIANA: Okay. I can understand your feelings. Now, would you like to talk about the next part of your dream?

BILL: Well, that's the really puzzling part. Don't know why it took place in L.A. and I don't recall ever even going to the slums down there. Guess I have seen it in the movies.

DIANA: Let's talk about the settings in both parts of this dream.

BILL: The first part was in your sister's house. In the dream it was really run down. And the second part was also in an awful setting. Maybe this symbolizes the way I feel right now, about our whole environment. Oh, I love where we live, in the suburbs. But I certainly don't like the way our life together has gotten so dreary.

DIANA: What about the characters in the second part? What do you think they stand for?

BILL: They were kind of dangerous, and angry. I didn't like them. Just wanted to get out of there. The whole feeling in that part was that I wanted so much to get out and back to you. But it seemed like I just could not get all my possessions together.

DIANA: Yes, I know that feeling, too. Frustrated. Just can't seem to "get it all together."

BILL: Right! But I think the encouraging part is that my main thought was I really wanted to get back to you. And I do, Diana. I love you so much.

Building Trust

By putting aside her need to be right, Diana helped Bill relax. Once he began to trust her, he was able to confide some of his innermost feelings about their relationship. Had she continued to say aloud the defensive reactions which arose when Bill seemed to be blaming her, Diana might never have heard the true message of his dream—that he loved her and wanted desperately to get back to the intimacy they had once shared.

When Diana then described one of her own dreams, it was her turn to reveal the resentments and doubts she had also been feeling. "I had that old nightmare about being smothered," she told us. "Right away, Bill knew I was feeling pressured again to give up a very important part of myself. He suggested we ought to try harder to find some way I can still work and at the same time give both him and our son the attention they both want from me."

This couple did find ways to satisfy their often conflicting needs. Once their son entered preschool, Diana was able to devote more time to her career. The extra money enabled them to take a long-postponed "second honeymoon."

By reviving their trust in each other, the Dream Dyad helped Bill and Diana confront one of the most sensitive issues which frequently plagues long-term relationships, that of mutual sexual stimulation and fulfillment. Later in this chapter, we'll learn how this couple used their dreams and the powers of their imagination to begin what was essentially a new sex life together. The important point here is that they first built a foundation of trust and acceptance, using dream sharing as a nonthreatening way to make each other aware of the concerns which had accumulated during their years of mutual neglect.

Improving Communication

After the dialogue described above, Diana admitted she'd literally "bit her tongue" to withhold her automatic reactions when Bill commented that their life together had "gotten dreary." She said, "All I could think of to do was to change the subject, so I asked him about the next part of his dream."

Another successful tactic Diana used was to simply "reflect" back to Bill whatever he said, rather than interjecting her own emotional responses. This let him know that she had heard and understood his remarks, and was not passing judgment. "Once he got to the end of his dream," she said, "I was so touched by his saying he loved me and desperately wanted us to be close again, that I just forgot how his earlier remarks had upset me."

By daily practice of Dream Dyad techniques, Bill and Diana developed new communication skills which served them well in other situations. "I used to complain that he never told me how he really felt," Diana said. "Guess I had such a short fuse, he didn't want to set me off, so he just kept everything to himself." On his part, once he began to trust that his wife wouldn't take personally his every remark, Bill began to soften some of his comments. "At first," he said, "I was like a kid, testing her to see how nasty I could be before she reacted. Then, when I saw she really did want to hear my side of things, I had to admit that it *does* take two to tango. Our problems were as much my doing as they were hers—maybe more so."

In *Eye to Eye: How People Interact*, Dr. Peter Trower summarizes effective communication skills. These include: a roughly equal amount of give and take in talking so that neither partner monopolizes any conversation; listening by giving your partner supportive feedback both vocally and with body language (such as nodding your head, making eye contact, assuming open and friendly facial expressions); and equal disclosure of increasingly more intimate information.

The Dream Dyad develops all these communication skills. The dreamer talks while the other partner listens, and then gives guiding assistance in the interpretation phase; then the listener becomes the talker, relating a dream while the other partner takes a turn at listening and guiding. Dream Dyad listening skills also include the noninterruptive feedback Dr. Trower suggests. Diana said, "When I let go of defending myself, and really listened to Bill's words and watched his expressions, I just naturally started making eye contact with him and nodding sympathetically."

Revealing "Secrets"

The "disclosure" expertise which Dr. Trower recommends is also a natural outcome of most Dream Dyad sessions. Couples who are skilled in Dream Dyad sharing often discover previously unsuspected "Hidden Agendas," desires, and sometimes surprising belief systems as they listen to and comment upon each other's dreams.

For example, in Chapter 7, Jim's "voyeur" dream about their neighbors made it clear to Rosemarie that he'd enjoy a different position during their own lovemaking. After they experimented with this, Rosemarie had the following dream:

There was a lot of noise outside and I looked to see a parade going by (actually we live on a very quiet street). Jim was very excited and went out to talk to the paraders. Then he came back with all these people in wild costumes. I was very upset because he just brought them right inside without checking with me. The house was a mess and I was running around trying to tidy up. I was in the bathroom wiping off the sink. A woman wearing a tight black miniskirt and a bra came in and just started using the toilet without even speaking to me. I said, "I'm not the maid, you know. This is *my* house!" and I woke up feeling a little bit mad with Jim.

When Jim asked Rosemarie what she thought her dream meant, she said, "It seems to have something to do with privacy. Or maybe my dislike of having people just drop in. I like to know ahead of time. Maybe I worry too much about what others think of me."

Jim then asked, "What does 'privacy' mean to you?" and Rosemarie said, "Well, for one thing it means not doing certain things in front of others. Like that woman going to the bathroom in my dream. I'd never do that! And, I wouldn't ever secretly watch our neighbors. Oh, I know that was a dream and you wouldn't do it, really. But I guess that's been worrying me."

When Jim urged Rosemarie to tell us more along these lines, concerning her associations to privacy, she blurted out, "This is exactly what I mean! I just hate it when you discuss our—you know, our *intimate* times—in front of other people. That feels all wrong to me. These things should be private!"

Jim apologized to his wife, saying he hadn't realized she didn't want to participate in such discussions in our group. Rosemarie telephoned me the next day to explain more. "I don't mind sharing these things with you," she said, "but it did really embarrass me that time when Jim told the whole group about me being on top when we made love." I reassured Rosemarie, telling her she needn't feel pressured to disclose anything she considered private. "I know you asked the group to vote on whether or not to talk about these things," she continued. "But at the time, I went along because Jim was so enthusiastic."

Further private discussion with this couple revealed other levels of Rosemarie's dream about her home being invaded by the paraders. "I've been worried that all that business about watching the neighbors was leading up to something else," Rosemarie told her husband. "Thought maybe you secretly wanted to have some kind of orgy, with other people watching. That would just mortify me!" Then it developed that Rosemarie was quite willing to experiment with different sexual positions, "or a lot of other things. As long as it's just between the two of us."

Even though Jim had considered himself an "expert" in the art of dream conversations, he too had some fine points to learn. Rosemarie courageously risked Jim's disapproval when she revealed attitudes about privacy her husband hadn't suspected. With more practice, this couple was able to recognize the clues both their dreams were giving them about their inner feelings around what would always be a sensitive subject to Rosemarie. Jim restrained his enthusiasm, confining his group comments to topics other than sex. Gradually, as Rosemarie began to trust him, she (privately) reported, "That discussion about my dream of the paraders was a real breakthrough for both of us. Since then, our sex life has gotten really super!"

Reviewing Your Dream Notebooks

Another way to use your dreams to keep your romance alive is to review your dream records. Some couples reminisce over their Dream Notebooks the way many people leaf through photo albums, recalling pleasant scenes and happy times together. The sentimental, nostalgic feelings such memories evoke can arouse dormant sexuality and become the departure point for new lovemaking adventures.

Creating New Dreams from Old Ones

Sylvia and Larry, the couple whose sweet incubated dreams are described in Chapter 8, decided to recreate some of their favorite dream elements. Sylvia had been deeply moved by the dream segment in which she and Larry catapulted up into a moonlit sky during a passionate kiss. Since Larry had never experienced the joys of dream flying, they decided to try incubating dreams about this phenomenon.

As they fell asleep, they repeated to themselves, "Tonight I'll dream we are kissing and flying at the same time."

This is Larry's incubated dream:

(Before we went to bed, I'd been watching a little of a late-night cable TV movie, an X-rated thing called *Emmanuelle*. In one scene, the heroine is on a plane making love with a complete stranger.) In this dream, I was on a plane, squeezed in between two very fat women. Across the aisle I could see Sylvia. When the seat belt sign went off, I got up and went over and sat on the arm of her seat. She was surprised and I told her this was more comfortable than being jammed in with those slobs across the aisle. She laughed and started kissing me. Then the stewardess came to tell me I had to return to my seat. The plane began to roll and I woke up, feeling amused at the tricks your mind can play. I got my flying, kissing dream, all right!

Sylvia appeared to get better results with dream incubation. Further, her programmed dreams were frequently lucid as well. This is her dream on the same night:

I was up very high in our bedroom and I could see both Larry and myself lying on the bed below. It was amazing! Saw Larry roll over and put his arms around me. Then I thought this must be a dream but I kept very still, just floating up there, because I didn't want to wake up. As I watched, I could see us beginning to kiss and make love. Larry was opening my nightgown and I was unbuttoning his pajamas. I thought, "Oh, I wish Larry could fly, too," and then he was up there with me. At the same time, we were still both of us on the bed below. I motioned him to be quiet so we just hung there for a long time, watching ourselves. It was like it was two other people who looked like us. I turned to Larry (the one up there on the ceiling) and we kissed. Then we were both back on the bed and I woke up, feeling both aroused and puzzled.

Sylvia's ability to remain asleep during her lucid dream was probably disrupted by the sexual feelings the dream aroused. Several of my dream group members have reported similar experiences. It may be that the physical changes which take place under such circumstances somehow interfere with the delicate balance necessary to maintain lucidity.

Sylvia and Larry continued their efforts, and eventually were able to fly in some dreams, and to kiss in others—but never in the same dream. "It was worth the trouble, though," Larry told us. "The sensation of dream flying is amazing, just like Sylvia told me. There are just no words to describe how great it feels."

Making Dreams into Waking Fantasies

Florence, the C.P.A., and Lou, the lawyer (whose dream adventures are described in previous chapters) were delightfully open with our dream study group about their lovemaking experiences. "If our sex life starts getting monotonous," Lou told us, "we get out our Dream Notebooks and relive some of the best times we've had together."

Two dreams they especially liked were the lucid ones which are quoted in Chapter 8: "Florence's dream about us being in a luxurious hotel suite, and mine about becoming a horse with Florence riding me really turned us both on," Lou said. "So we decided to have a special weekend when we could actually live those dreams."

First, in an effort to recreate the atmosphere of Lou's dream, they spent a Saturday afternoon at the race track. "There was no horse with the name 'Nightingale' that day," Florence said. "But I placed a small bet on one called 'Silver Dream' and won twenty dollars. And the whole afternoon was fun and exciting." Lou added, "I kept thinking about the end of that dream all the time we were watching these terrific jockeys riding those magnificent animals. I kept flashing on that dream scene when I became the horse and Flo was riding me."

Then the couple had dinner at the same hotel Florence had dreamed about, and retired to a beautiful suite. "It wasn't really like the one in my dream," Florence reported, "but simply the idea that we were 'making our dreams come true' was so romantic. And," she said with a giggle, "Lou even carried out my dream wish, by initiating sex." Lou commented, "That part was easy! I was so turned on by the whole day, I could hardly wait!"

Starting a New Sex Life

As your relationship matures, so do your bodies. Once-thrilling sexual activities may become physically uncomfortable for one or both partners. Further, the lover is rare who is able to maintain a confident body image in the face of the changes aging brings. Gray hair or balding, weight gain or loss of muscle tone, wrinkles or varicose veins—all these may contribute to less self-esteem and the onset of sexual inhibitions in even the most confident of lovers.

However, it is possible to accept the effects of aging and continue to keep your romance strong. In fact, a number of couples have told me this acceptance has resulted in more deeply fulfilling intimacy than they ever had before. Some even call it a new sex life.

Accepting Your Body

Dr. Paul Pearsall says that how we think we look is an important key to the way we make love. Moreover, we tend to choose partners whom we think look a little better than ourselves. Pearsall says that most men believe their penises are too small, and most women believe their breasts are either too large or too small. In other words, most people have a distorted body image. When even tiny signs of aging appear, those who already believe they're unattractive may become irrationally upset, states which inhibit their sexual activities.

When these uncomfortable, self-conscious attitudes arise, there are several directions one or both partners may choose. These include:

- The path of least resistance
- Physical change
- Psychological change

GIVING UP. Unfortunately, many middle-aged people take the path of least resistance by postponing sexual intimacy or avoiding it entirely. While this attitude may provide a temporary, surface calm, it inhibits the release of normal tensions which sexual activity provides.

Further, and probably even more important, such denial or repression stunts emotional growth and limits the special bonded closeness which is uniquely sexual. Study after study establishes the fact that healthy men and women *continue to enjoy and desire sex well into their eighties*.

Even those with physical handicaps can find ways to be intimate which continue to provide sexual fulfillment to keep their romance alive. For instance, when Carl and Maureen were faced with her long recovery after major surgery for colon cancer, their dreams guided them to ways they could find sexual release. A month after Maureen's surgery, Carl, a forty-five-year-old auto mechanic, had this dream:

> I was test-driving a Corvette, a real beaut. Took it out onto some country roads and really opened it up, went up to about 125. It was a great feeling, really free. Then the engine began knocking so I slowed to a stop. Suddenly noticed all the land around me was bare and dried up. Looked like those pictures of the moon— dust and craters, everything gray. I felt really lonely, more than I've ever felt in my life. It wasn't fear. Just a deep, achy loneliness that it's hard to put in words. Felt like it went all the way into my bones. Woke up feeling like crying.

When Carl described this dream to Maureen, she said she herself was moved to tears. "I knew right away that Carl was feeling deprived," she told me. "He's always been so physical, so sexy. Our sex life was so great before I got sick." Both Carl and Maureen thought the beginning of his dream, and his feelings of elation and freedom, reflected their life together before she became ill. The change in his dream setting to barren, lonely grayness mirrored Carl's feelings now that the crisis of Maureen's surgery was behind them.

Maureen continued, "After we cried together awhile, we decided to talk to my doctor about just what we could expect." Maureen's physician assured her she could soon resume normal sexual activity, despite her colostomy. Meanwhile, she and Carl began making love by stimulating each other manually and orally. "I discovered a sensitivity and gentleness in my husband which I never knew he had," Maureen confided, "and it was like falling in love all over again for both of us."

CHANGING PHYSICALLY. When faced with the alarming onset of aging symptoms many people attempt to change themselves physically. For decades, our society has placed a premium on youthful appearance, so that millions of dollars pour into the coffers of health clubs, diet and fitness programs, the cosmetics industry, and plastic surgeons.

This situation is a mixed blessing. Certainly everyone can benefit from regular exercise and proper nutrition. Although many of the anti-aging claims of cosmetics companies are exaggerated, care of skin and hair does improve health and appearance. Plastic surgery, although it's usually quite expensive, can temporarily erase or remove wrinkles and sagging tissues. However, none of these measures will make anyone become a twenty-year-old again. The danger here is that many people become caught up in an unending cycle of hope, disillusionment, and budget-wrecking expenses.

CHANGING PSYCHOLOGICALLY. Recognizing that your body is changing irrevocably, and attempting to "grow old gracefully," may be a more realistic way of coping. A few of my students have sought help from sex therapists in their efforts to accept changing body image. Again, these methods have their limitations.

Some sex therapists show their patients pictures of nudes of all shapes and sizes, asking them to choose the ones they think they're most like. Not surprisingly, partners usually select more attractive images for each other than they do for themselves. Simply becoming aware of this disparity in their attitudes is sometimes enough to help couples improve their body image.

Another frequently effective process is for a couple to stand naked together in front of a mirror. (This may take courage, so if you try this, keep in mind that your partner is probably having the same misgivings you are experiencing.) Next, tell your partner what you think of each of your own body parts, beginning with your head. Pause after commenting on each part, giving your partner a turn. When this exercise is completed, take turns listening to each other's opinions.

Since this acceptance exercise is personal and private, when Rose-marie and Jim tried this method, she refused to share her reactions with our group. Instead, she and Jim turned on a tape recorder. Following are excerpts from a transcript of their experience with the mirror technique:

ROSEMARIE: Starting with my head. Okay, my hair is pretty even though I think it's getting a little thin. My eyes are all right, but I hate those crow's feet around them. My nose has always seemed a little silly to me—it's too turned up. My complexion is good, no wrinkles yet around my mouth. Oh— my mouth is not right. My lips are too full. Neck is okay, but there's a little sagging just starting around the jaw line. Ugh! Now it's your turn.

JIM: Well. My own hair is definitely getting thin. I hate it! Guess I've been out in the sun too much, cause I have enough wrinkles around my eyes and mouth for a man twice my age. Eyes are all right—at least I don't wear glasses yet. Nose is too long but my mouth is okay. Good teeth, thank God. My beard is too heavy—looks like I need a shave even after I just did.

ROSEMARIE: My breasts are definitely too large. I know men like that, but it's just a nuisance to me. Makes me look top-heavy, fat, dumpy. Ugh! And I worry that my upper arms are getting flabby although they look okay right now. Well, getting to the hard part, my stomach and pubic hair. Oh, I don't think I can do this anymore. (sobs)

JIM: Okay, I'll take over. Don't cry, Rosie, please. We're almost finished. Now, just look at that chest. That's one thing about me I like. All that working out at the gym, my biceps and chest are developed. But I have too much black hair on my chest and it even grows onto my back. Don't know how you stand it! Looks like I'm starting to get a pot belly, too. And the truth is, I've always wanted a bigger penis.

(After Jim and Rosemarie complete their "body survey," they next give each other feedback.)

ROSEMARIE: I couldn't believe it when you said your hair is thinning. I never noticed! And, I always loved your weather-beaten look. It's so rugged and masculine. That goes for your beard and body hair, too. Oh, Jim. How could you be so down on yourself? The parts you complain about are the very ones I love. And, if you're small, well I never noticed. When we make love, you feel just the right size for me! Any bigger might hurt.

JIM: You mean that? Guess I've been worried for nothing. Rosie, honey, talk about being down on yourself! First, your brown hair is beautiful, so soft and natural, I love to touch it. In fact, I love to touch all of you, from your cute little nose right down to your toes. Those breasts can send me into wet dreams just by thinking of them. And, that mouth! It's just made for kissing.

(Silence on the tape)

ROSEMARIE: You never did tell me about *this*, darling . . .

JIM: Let me show you what I really think. See?

Although they encountered some emotionally painful moments, Rosemarie and Jim's mirror survey was successful in that it helped them begin to accept what they considered their less-than-perfect bodies. It's also obvious that the exercise itself became erotically stimulating. Not only were they able to reassure each other about the pleasures they took in each other's appearance—merely doing so aroused them both.

However, this technique is not advisable for many couples. For instance, Carl and Maureen, whose sexual problems after her surgery were described earlier in this chapter, voiced these objections: Maureen declared, "I've had a colostomy, have to wear this rather disgusting bag, and no amount of reassurances will make me feel good about it." Carl said, "The way I deal with Maureen's feelings about her appearance is to just ignore her protests and show her I still love her and still think she's sexy." Concerning himself, Carl commented, "I know I'm overweight and have a pot belly. Okay, so I'm working on getting rid of it. But right now, if Maureen told me she just loves fat men, I'd think she was lying. If she said it doesn't matter, I probably wouldn't believe that, either. So, what's the point in bringing all this to her attention? I say, let's just turn out the lights and forget about how we look!"

Improving Your Sexual Techniques

Carl's commonsense approach may have more merit than any amount of confrontation processes, fad diets, or expensive cosmetic changes. Nevertheless, Carl and Maureen both endured some needlessly anxious weeks before admitting to each other that any problem existed.

If you or your partner are experiencing decreased sexual desire, and a physical checkup shows there's nothing amiss, you may be able to resolve the problem on your own by following these suggestions:

- Find dream clues
- Communicate with your partner
- Practice deep relaxation
- Experiment

DREAM CLUES TO LOW SEXUAL DESIRE. Since your dreams nearly always reflect your waking emotional state, your Dream Notebook probably contains a wealth of information about your personal sexual needs and attitudes. It's also important to remember that gender plays a part in sexual desires and capacity for enjoyment, so that a woman's dreams will usually require different interpretations than a man's.

For instance, in Chapter 4, women's dreams during the menstrual cycle were described. Studies of such dreams show that women are usually more sexually aroused at midcycle during ovulation, so that it's important to take this into account when looking for clues to sexual dysfunction. If your dreams never appear to indicate sexual desire, and if your sexual history shows that you've rarely if ever felt sexually aroused, you may need psychological counseling. Such cases are quite rare; usually, there is some obvious cause for absence of sexual desire such as disease, depression, low hormone levels (especially after menopause), fatigue, certain medications, overuse of alcohol, or—most commonly—some emotional conflict with the partner or stress caused by a specific situation.

In the case of Carl and Maureen, her disease caused a temporary yet lengthy halt to their sexual activities. Then, they both privately assumed their sex life was finished. It took Carl's dream of intense loneliness to make them both aware they ought to seek advice and explore alternatives.

If either you or your partner are suffering from a decrease in desire, a review of your dreams—especially the most recent ones—may offer guidance. Sean's and Margo's dreams during such a period illustrate the way dreams can help you come up with the cause of decreased sexuality. (Sean, the Air Force pilot, and his wife Margo's dreams, are quoted in Chapters 2 and 4.)

When Sean returned from overseas and the couple settled down more or less permanently in California, Margo found that she simply was not interested in sex. "At first, I put it down to the stress of moving, getting into the routine of my new job at the base, making new friends, all that," she said. "But now, it's been several months and I still just couldn't care less. Had a physical and the doc says I'm in good health so I guess it's all in my head." On his part, Sean was beginning to lose patience. "For the first time in years," he said, "we're finally in a pretty stable situation. I'm an Instructor, no more dangerous missions. This is what we both always wanted, and now Margo—well, she seems like a different person."

When we reviewed Margo's recent dreams, the following one provided clues to her baffling change of heart:

Dreamed I was in the kitchen preparing canapés for a party we were having. Sean would come in and get a tray and tell me to hurry up and come out with the guests, but I had to stay there and keep spreading the cheese on the crackers and I kept wondering when I'd finally have enough made. It seemed like an endless task. It seemed this went on for hours. Took off my high heels and tried to work faster but was getting so tired and bored with the whole thing. Then Sean came and said I must come out now as the party was almost over. So I went with him. When we got to the living room a woman pointed at my feet and laughed. I'd forgotten to put my shoes back on and my panty hose had a big run. I was so embarrassed! Woke up feeling mad with Sean for no real reason.

As we discussed her dream, Margo came to the realization that her waking life these days was "just like that party. I'm still behind the scenes doing all the work while everybody else is having fun!" She could also see that, when she does make an effort to join Sean with their new friends, she feels awkward and unattractive—symbolized in the dream by her shoeless state and torn stockings. "But I still don't see how this relates to our sex life," she said.

"Well, I do," Sean put in. "If you've been feeling like everything in our new life is a chore, and that you don't measure up to the other women we've met, that's bound to affect our relationship." As our discussion continued, this couple also became aware that their sexual activity up to now had been sporadic. Before, they rarely knew when Sean might be called away. "Every moment counted," Margo said, "and that somehow kept me excited. Now, it's all so predictable."

Obviously, Margo's disinterest in sex stemmed from more than her growing lack of self-esteem. While she didn't think she "measured up" to the other wives in their new circle of friends, Margo also longed for more variety in lovemaking. Once they understood the roots of Margo's decreased sexual desire, this couple was able to find solutions.

POSITIVE COMMUNICATION. Fortunately, Sean did not take personally Margo's comments about their sex life being boring and predictable. Many people would be so offended by such remarks that they'd be unlikely to be willing to search for solutions. A kinder and probably more effective way to communicate honest feelings about sexual matters is to tell your partner what he or she does which you do find pleasurable, before mentioning the activities you'd like to try.

Bear in mind that any discussion of sex between partners, no matter how close and loving you may be, is likely to evoke strong emotional responses. Criticism may be taken as an assault on your partner's very being, his or her sexual identity. To retain the trust and affection you still have for each other, avoid blaming or insulting words. Ask your partner what he or she wants sexually, and suggest that you both make renewed efforts to please each other.

LOWERING YOUR STRESS LEVEL. Even though Margo was aware that stress is an important factor in the sexual aspects of any relationship, she assumed that time alone would bring relief from the tensions of moving. She was surprised to learn that, although she and her husband had "settled in" at the new Air Force base, her body and her mind still suffered from the effects of the move.

This residue of stress became quite evident when I persuaded Margo to stretch out on the floor and relax, practicing one of the techniques outlined in this book's Appendix. After hearing a few minutes of my instructions to relax her upper body, Margo's arms and hands were still almost rigid. When Sean lifted one of her hands, it should have been as limp as a dishrag—yet it was obviously still very tense. We began again, this time with Margo taking extra time to relax each set of muscles and to breathe deeply and evenly, until the tension seemed to be literally draining into the carpet beneath her. Once Sean learned the method, he helped his wife continue the relaxation practice at home. They reported that this exercise alone caused Margo to become aroused. Perhaps all she needed was her lover's attention to her needs and feelings.

The relaxation techniques in the Appendix are not the only ways you can "limber up" before sexual activity. Regular exercise, Hatha Yoga, a long soak in a warm bath, listening to soothing music, and getting your partner to give you a massage are a few other suggestions which may help relieve any tension which blocks sexual desire.

SEXUAL EXPERIMENTATION. Once you have reviewed your Dream Notebook to find the possible causes of loss of sexual appetite, and have communicated honestly and positively with your partner about what pleases you both, it's time to start your new sex life by experimenting. Try lovemaking in a different setting and in different positions. Be daring: buy a vibrator with various attachments you can both enjoy; wear sexy lingerie; rent an erotic video and watch it together before bedtime; and use the suggestions provided in this book for exploring each other's fantasies.

Summary

In this final chapter, we have looked at some of the ways couples use their dreams and the powers of their imagination to keep their romance alive. Although a steadily rising divorce rate is one of the tragedies of modern life, recent surveys show that the longer a marriage lasts, the longer it is likely to survive. So, if you've been with your partner for a number of years, there's no need to despair even though life together is not as thrilling as it once was.

To revive those old fires and keep them aflame, make a habit of practicing this book's Dream Dyad techniques. By sticking to the ground rules, you can use the Dream Dyad to strengthen your abilities to compromise and be committed. The Dream Dyad also builds a climate of trust and enhances communication skills. Further, by discussing your dreams together, you and your mate can discover and confront those Hidden Agendas, the "secrets" which may be erecting barriers to fulfilling intimacy.

Review your Dream Notebooks together, noticing which dreams were sexually stimulating in the past. Then, act out these dream fantasies with your partner.

Reaching mid-life need not put a damper on your sex life. In fact, with years of getting to know each other behind you, the security this brings can help you start a brand new sex life, more satisfying than ever before. If worries about your appearance or diminishing sexual desire arise, there are many solutions available.

If you are healthy and have enjoyed sex in previous years, there's usually no reason you cannot continue to do so well into your eighties. (However, women—and sometimes men—who rarely or never experience sexual desire should consult a physician or sex therapist.) Should you find that you or your partner's sexual appetite has dramatically decreased, it's important to consider several factors.

The first of these is your image of your own body. When faced with the onset of wrinkles and other signs of aging, some people simply give up, resigning themselves to little or no lovemaking, erroneously believing that their mates will find them unappealing. Such defeatists postpone intimacy, making excuses, or actually believing that they no longer need or want sex. This denial or repression can make a wasteland of what could be a paradise.

Others seek relief through cosmetics, surgery, more exercise, and rigorous dieting. While all these pursuits are commendable in moderation, those who hope for miracles are inevitably disappointed. Still others try to compensate by changing their mental pictures of themselves. Sex therapists and counselors have had some success with such techniques as the "mirror process" in helping couples overcome pessimistic body image.

However, these methods may "backfire," causing some couples needless emotional stress. A wiser course to attempt by yourself is to work together to improve your sexual techniques. When one or both partners are experiencing decreased arousal, the first step is to find the cause.

Loss of desire may be due to disease, medication, too much alcohol, stress, fatigue, or depression. If none of these apply to you or your mate, it's likely the cause is related to some unexpressed emotional conflict or a specific situation. Your dreams are valuable clues to the discovery of these negative issues.

Once you've determined the apparent cause of your decreased interest in sex, communicate positively with your partner. This means "treading lightly" to avoid humiliating or causing emotional pain. Begin by mentioning the special qualities he or she has which stimulate you, moving then into a discussion of what you both can do to give each other more pleasure.

In addition to regular practice of the relaxation techniques described in the Appendix, explore various ways you can both release stress.

Undue tension often contributes to low sexual desire. Soak in a warm bath or a hot tub—together, if possible. Listen to soothing music, give each other a relaxing massage.

Lastly, and probably most important, *experiment*. Make love in a different place, change your usual positions, buy some sexual aids, and act out your fantasies. Let *Romantic Dreams* be your guide as you are transported into a waking dream of ecstatic intimacy.

In closing, it is my hope that those who read this book will find in these pages the strength and encouragement available to them in their dreams. In the words of Sir Walter Scott:

> *To all, to each, a fair goodnight,*
> *And pleasing dreams and slumber light.*

Bibliography

Anonymous (1989, November). Marriage: Get past the first years and you're golden. *Your Personal Best, 1,* No.7. p. 6.

Ansbacher, H. L., & Ansbacher, R. R. (1956). *The individual psychology of Alfred Adler.* New York: Basic Books.

Antrobus, J., & Singer, J. (1964). Eye movements during daydreaming, visual imagery, and other internally produced cognitive processes. *Journal of Abnormal Social Psychology, 79,* 244–252.

Avery, C. S. (1989, May). How do you build intimacy in an age of divorce? *Psychology Today,* pp. 27–31.

Bergland, R. (1986). *The fabric of mind: A radical new understanding of how the brain works.* New York: Viking.

Blakeslee, T. R. (1980). *The right brain: A new understanding of our unconscious mind.* New York: Anchor.

Bonime, W. (1989). *Collaborative psychoanalysis: Anxiety, depression, dreams, and personality change*. Cranbury, NJ: Fairleigh Dickinson University Press.

Boss, M. (1958). *The analysis of dreams*. New York: Philosophical Library.

Brauer, A. (1990). *The ESO Ecstasy Program*. New York: Warner Books.

Burns, D. D. (1989). *The feeling good handbook*. New York: Wm. Morrow & Co.

Cartwright, R. D. (1978). Affect and dream work from an information processing point of view. *The Journal of Mind & Behavior, 7*, 411–427.

Cartwright, R. D. (1978). *A primer on sleep and dreaming*. Menlo Park, CA: Addison-Wesley.

Crick, F., & Mitchison, G. (1983). The function of dream sleep. *Nature, 304*, 11–14.

Delaney, G. (1979). *Living your dreams*. New York: Harper & Row.

Delaszlo, V. S. (Ed.) (1959). *The basic writings of C. G. Jung*. New York: Modern Library.

Doress, P. B. & Siegal, D. L. (1987). *Ourselves growing older*. New York: Simon & Schuster/Touchstone.

Ennis, M., & Fonagy, P. (1989, May/June). Influence of monaural and dichotic stimuli on dreams. *Association for the Study of Dreams Newsletter*, p. 4.

Erikson, E. The dream specimen of psychoanalysis. In R. Knight & C. Freidman, (Eds.), *Psychoanalytic psychiatry and psychology*, (pp. 131–170). New York: International Universities Press.

Faraday, A. (1972). *Dream power*. New York: Coward, McCann, & Geoghegan.

Faraday, A. (1974). *The dream game*. New York: Harper & Row.

Farrell, W. (1986). *Why men are the way they are*. New York: Berkley Books.

Feinstein, A. D., & Krippner, S. (1988). *Personal mythology*. Los Angeles: Tarcher.

Foulkes, D. (1978). *A grammar of dreams*. New York: Basic Books.

French, T. M., & Fromm, E. (1964). *Dream interpretation*. New York: Basic Books.

Freud, S. (1965). *The interpretation of dreams* (2nd ed.). (J. Strachey, Ed. & Trans.). New York: Avon. (Original work published 1900.)

Friday, N. (1973). *My secret garden.* New York: Pocket Books.

Gackenbach, J., & Bosveld, J. (1989). *Control your dreams.* New York: Harper & Row.

Galin, D. (1979). The two modes of consciousness and the two halves of the brain. In D. Coleman & R. J. Davidson (Eds.), *Consciousness: Brain, states of awareness, and mysticism* (pp. 19–23). New York: Harper & Row.

Garfield, P. L. (1974). *Creative dreaming.* New York: Simon & Schuster.

Garfield, P. L. (1979). *Pathway to ecstasy.* New York: Holt, Rinehart & Winston.

Garfield, P. L. (1984). *Your child's dreams.* New York: Ballantine.

Garfield, P. L. (1988). *Women's bodies, women's dreams.* New York: Ballantine.

Garfield, P. (1988). Women's dreams. Paper presented at the annual meeting of The Association for the Study of Dreams, Santa Cruz, CA.

Goldberg, M. (1974). The use of dreams in conjunct marital therapy. *Journal of Sex and Marital Therapy, 1,* 75–81.

Greene, W. (1989, November). Boston University study cited in *Your Personal Best, 1,* 6.

Hall, C., & Van de Castle, R. (1966). *The content analysis of dreams.* New York: Appleton-Century-Crofts.

Hartmann, E. (1967). *The biology of dreaming.* Springfield, IL: Charles C. Thomas.

Hartmann, E. (1984). *The nightmare.* New York: Basic Books.

Hendrix, H. (1990). *Getting the love you want: A guide for couples.* New York: Harper & Row.

Jones, R. M. (1978). *The new psychology of dreaming.* New York: Penguin Books.

Jung, C. G. (1953). The relations between the ego and the unconscious. In *Collected Works, Vol. 7.* Translated by R. F. C. Hull. New York: Bollingen Foundation.

Keirsey, D., & Bates, M. (1984). *Please understand me: Character &*

temperament types. New York: Prometheus. (Original work published 1978.)

Keyes, K., Jr, & Keyes, P. (1979). *A conscious person's guide to relationships.* Coos Bay, OR: Living Love Publications.

Kramer, M., Whitman, R., Baldridge, B. & Ornstein, P. (1968). Drugs and dreams. *American Journal of Psychiatry, 124,* 1385–1392.

Krippner, S. (1980a). Access to hidden reserves of the unconscious through dreams in creative problem solving. *Journal of Creative Behavior, 15,* 11–23.

Krippner, S. (1980b). *Human possibilities: Mind research in the USSR and Eastern Europe.* Garden City, NY: Anchor Books.

Krippner, S. (1986). Dreams and the development of a personal mythology. *Journal of Mind and Behavior, 7,* 449–462.

Krippner, S., & Dillard, J. (1988). *Dreamworking.* Buffalo, NY: Bearly.

LaBerge, S. (1985). *Lucid dreaming.* Los Angeles: Tarcher.

Laqueur, H. P., LaBurt, H. A., & Morong, E. (1971). Multiple family therapy: Further developments. In J. Haley (Ed.), *Changing families.* New York: Grune & Stratton.

Lowy, S. (1942). *Foundations of dream interpretation.* London: Kegan, Paul, Trench, & Trubner.

Masters, W., & Johnson, V. (1986). *On sex & human loving.* Boston: Little, Brown.

Maybruck, P. (1986). An exploratory study of the dreams of pregnant women. Doctoral dissertation, Saybrook Institute, San Francisco, CA.

Maybruck, P. (1988). Symbiotic dreams. Paper presented at the annual meeting of The Association for the Study of Dreams, Santa Cruz, CA.

Maybruck, P. (1989). *Pregnancy and dreams.* Los Angeles: Tarcher.

McCarley, R. W., & Hobson, J. A. (1979). The form of dreams and the biology of sleep. In B. B. Wolman (Ed.), *Handbook of dreams: Research, theories and applications* (pp. 76–130). New York: Van Nostrand Reinhold.

Nicholson, J. (1984). *Men and women: How different are they?* Oxford: Oxford University Press.

Ornstein, R. (1986). *Multimind: A new way of looking at human behavior.* Boston: Houghton Mifflin.

Papp, P. (1976). Brief therapy with couples groups. In P. Guerin (Ed.), *Family therapy, theory and practice.* New York: Gardner Press.

Pearsall, P. (1987). *Super marital sex: Loving for life.* New York: Ballantine. (Original work published by Doubleday, a division of Bantam, Doubleday, Dell Publishing Group, Inc.)

Penney, A. (1982). *How to make love to a man.* New York: Dell.

Penney, A. (1983). *How to make love to each other.* New York: G. P. Putnam.

Perlmutter, R. A., & Babineau, R. (1983). The use of dreams in couples therapy. *Psychiatry, 46,* 66–72.

Perls, F. S. (1969). *Gestalt therapy verbatim.* Lafayette, CA: Real People Press.

Tennov, D. (1979). *Love & limerence—The experience of being in love.* New York: Stein & Day.

Tholey, P. (1988). Psychotherapeutic application of lucid dreaming. In J. I. Gackenbach & S. LaBerge (Eds.), *Conscious mind, sleeping brain: Perspectives on lucid dreaming.* New York: Plenum.

Trower, P. (1988). Making conversation. In P. Marsh (Ed.), *Eye to eye: How people interact* (p. 111). Topsfield, MA: Salem House.

Ullman, M., Krippner, S., & Vaughan, A. (1973). *Dream telepathy* (2nd ed.). Jefferson, NC: McFarland.

Ullman, M., & Zimmerman, N. (1985). *Working with dreams.* Los Angeles: Tarcher. (Original work published in 1979.)

Van de Castle, R. L. (1971). *The psychology of dreaming.* Morristown, N.J.: General Learning Press.

Whitehead, E. D., & Zussman, S. (Eds.) (1989, November). When a man loses his desire for sex. In *Sex Over Forty.* Newsletter, P.O. Box 1600, Chapel Hill, N. C.

Zilbergeld, B. (1968). *Male sexuality.* New York: Bantam Books.

Appendix
Relaxation Techniques for Dream Control

When normal tensions or concerns about daily events fill your mind, you may find it difficult to relax sufficiently to summon the powers of your unconscious. This deep relaxation is an essential prerequisite for the accomplishment of the dream control methods described in Chapter 8. Further, the effectiveness of the creative daydreams and visualizations suggested throughout this book will be enhanced if you learn to relax totally before attempting integration of such fantasies into your unconscious.

My clients and students who have learned either or both of two easy relaxation methods report the most success with efforts to incubate dreams and to program lucidity. These simple methods are Progressive Relaxation and Autogenic Training.

Although both methods appear similar at first glance, the effects are quite different. Most people who practice Progressive Relaxation find that they are able to reach a deeply relaxed state, similar to a light trance, while still remaining awake and conscious of their surroundings. In contrast, Autogenic Training usually causes people to fall into a deep, restful sleep.

If you wish to intregate a creative daydream or fantasy, Progressive Relaxation may be the method of choice, so that you remain awake and able to converse with your partner about your feelings. If you feel tense at the end of a hectic day, Autogenic Training may be the ideal way to unwind and prepare yourself for dreams of your choice. Try both methods to decide which one you prefer.

Preparation

To practice either Progressive Relaxation or Autogenic Training, choose a comfortably warm, private setting such as your bedroom or living room. Since cold air or drafts may prevent muscle relaxation, make sure the room temperature is mild. Choose a time and place without distractions or interruptions, and disconnect your telephone.

If you plan to fall asleep, or to make love with your partner, lie down on your bed before you begin. A sofa, or pillows on a floor mat or carpet are also acceptable. Stretch, take several deep, cleansing breaths, and settle down into your favorite position. Let go of all distracting thoughts. There's no place to go, nothing to do, nothing to worry about. If thoughts of daily concerns do arise, simply observe them, continue to breathe deeply, and dismiss them.

Now you are ready to practice one of the two methods described below. If possible, your partner should read the instructions aloud in a soft, gentle voice. If this is inconvenient, at an earlier time have your partner read the directions into a tape recorder—or record it yourself, and then play back the directions.

Progressive Relaxation

This method emphasizes control of each set of muscles in your body, progressing from your head to your toes. By effectively interrupting the tense-mind-tense-body cycle, Progressive Relaxation eliminates stress and allows your inner self to emerge. After preparing yourself in a comfortable environment, listen to these instructions:

1. Take three long, cleansing breaths by inhaling through your nose and slowly exhaling through your mouth. One, two, three. This is your special time to relax, with nothing to do, nothing to worry about. Just *relax . . . relax . . . relax . . .*

2. Now, think about your face. *Tighten* all the muscles of your face, squinting your eyes, tightening your jaw, clenching your teeth. Hold the tension for a count of three: one, two, three. Now, take a deep breath and as you slowly let it out, *let go* of all that tension. Breathe normally, and notice the difference. Close your eyes and feel how relaxed they are.

3. With your eyes still closed, bring your attention to your neck and shoulders. Try to *tighten* those muscles even more than they are already, and hold the tightness—one, two, three. Now, take a quick deep breath and exhale *very slowly*, releasing all that tension. Notice the difference. Now your head, neck, and shoulders are relaxed. Keep your eyes closed as you continue to relax the rest of your body.

4. Think about your chest and upper back. Take another breath and arch your back, making your chest expand until it feels *tight*. Hold the breath for three: one, two, three. Exhale slowly, letting your body sink down into deeper relaxation. Check your face, neck, and shoulders again. If they're beginning to tense up, take another breath, let it out slowly, and *relax* the entire top half of your body.

5. Concentrate now on your abdomen and lower back. Take a breath and tighten your stomach muscles, *tight, tight, tighter*. Hold for three: one, two, three. Now exhale very very slowly, letting go of that tightness. Stretch your arm over your head and *release* all the tension in your abdomen and lower back.

6. Now, bring your arms back by your sides, hands palm down. Concentrate on your arms. Take a breath and tense both arms *as tightly as you can*. Make a fist and contract every

muscle to its peak from shoulder to fingertips. Make it *really tight*. Hold the tension for three: one, two, three. Exhale *very slowly*, letting all the tension go. Feel that tightness draining out of your arms, wrists, hands, and fingers. If someone picked up your hand now, it would flop like a limp dishrag. If there is any tightness left in your arms, hands, or fingers, tighten them again, hold the tension, and then *slowly release* as you exhale. Now, your entire body from your head to your hips is relaxed. Enjoy the floating, light feeling of being relaxed with only your hips and legs holding you in place.

7. Next, concentrate on your pelvis and buttocks. Tighten the muscles of your buttocks. Make them *so tight* that your waist lifts up with the tension. Inhale, and hold the tightness for three: one, two, three. *Exhale slowly*. Feel your body sinking down once again as all the tension seeps into the surface beneath you.

8. Focus your attention on your thighs. Inhale and tighten your thigh muscles. *Hold the tightness* for three: one, two, three. Now exhale slowly, letting your thighs *relax . . . relax . . . relax . . .*

9. Now, tense the muscles of your calves. Make them *as tight as you can*. Take a breath and hold for three: one, two, three. Exhaling *slowly*, feel the relaxation spread down your legs all the way to your feet.

10. Think about your feet. Curl your toes or flex your feet in any way that makes them feel *cramped, tight, tense*. Breathe and count to three: one, two, three. Now release your breath, letting the last bits of tension flow out through your toes and heels all the way down into the floor. Imagine *all* your tension *draining out* of your body, into the surface beneath you, being pulled down by gravity into deeper and deeper levels until it spreads into the earth, leaving your body up above, *relaxed* and *floating*. Once more, check your body from your head through your neck and shoulders, your torso, legs, and feet.

If you notice even the slightest tightness, tense that set of muscles, exhale slowly, and *let go*.

11. Now that you are deeply relaxed, repeat your dream incubation sentence or your creative daydream. Before opening your eyes, stretch, yawn, and imagine the room. Notice that you feel relaxed and refreshed.

12. Allow your attention to return to the present and slowly open your eyes. If you wish to stand up, do so slowly, giving your circulation time to adjust so that you don't feel dizzy. To speed the circulation process, shake your hands, letting them flop from the wrists.

Autogenic Training

This technique is especially beneficial for people who suffer from insomnia. Unlike Progressive Relaxation, this method usually puts you to sleep, so that it may be difficult for you to repeat to yourself the topic you wish to dream about. However, you can add your incubation or lucidity sentences to the end of your tape. Or, if your partner is reading the instructions for you, have him or her include the special sentence where indicated.

Prepare yourself as before, making sure the lights are out or dimmed, and that you are as comfortable as possible. Take several deep, cleansing breaths, and listen to the following:

1. As you breathe deeply, allow your eyelids to close. Keeping your eyes closed helps you avoid visual distractions. Your eyelids feel *heavy and warm. Heavy and warm.* Don't try to *make* them feel heavy and warm. Just notice how they feel. There's nothing to do, nothing to worry about. Your eyelids feel heavy and warm. *Relax . . . relax . . . relax.*

2. Imagine a white billboard. Now, imagine that black paint spreads over the entire sign so that your field of vision is *totally black*. Let the darkness soothe and caress your closed

eyes. Now your eyelids feel pleasantly *heavy and warm, heavy and warm.*

3. Continue to breathe deeply, inhaling through your nose and slowly exhaling through your parted lips. Repeat to yourself, "My scalp and face and jaws feel *heavy and warm, heavy and warm."* Let the warmth and heaviness spread down to your throat and shoulders.

4. Your shoulders feel *heavy and warm, heavy and warm.* Give in. Let the heaviness and warmth pull you down, down, down, into restful relaxation.

5. The warmth and heaviness spread down your chest and into your pelvis. Your entire upper body feels *heavy and warm, heavy and warm.* Let yourself sink into the surface beneath you. *Relax . . . relax . . . relax.*

6. Continue to breathe deeply, in and out, in and out, letting your exhalations be longer each time. Return your attention to your head, repeating to yourself, "My whole head feels *heavy and warm, heavy and warm.* My neck, shoulders, chest, and stomach all feel *heavy and warm.* My back feels *heavy and warm."* Now, the feeling of "heavy and warm" flows down into your groin and thighs. Let the tension melt away under this feeling of being *heavy and warm, heavy and warm.*

7. Both your legs feel *heavy and warm.* Repeat to yourself, "Both my legs feel *heavy and warm, heavy and warm."*

8. Focus on your ankles and feet. Notice how they feel heavy and warm, heavy and warm. Your whole body feels *heavy and warm, heavy and warm.* If any part of your body does not feel heavy and warm, now is the time to relax that area. Think about that part of your body and let the heaviness and warmth engulf it. Imagine that a soft blanket wraps you from neck to toes, enveloping you with warmth, and soothing, warm relaxation.

9. Repeat to yourself, "When I wake up, *I will remember my dreams. I will remember my dreams."* Now is the time to repeat your incubation sentence or your creative daydream.

Say it silently, over and over, as you relax ever more deeply.

10. When you awaken, you will feel refreshed and alert. You will lie still a few moments, eyes closed, remembering your dreams. Then you will sit up slowly, opening your eyes and stretching, feeling refreshed and alert.

After you have practiced Autogenic Training several times, notice the point at which you usually fall asleep. Then, to create your own "internal alarm clock," add this sentence: "Tomorrow I will wake up at exactly (time)." Most people are able to awaken naturally in this manner and thereby can avoid the intrusion of a ringing alarm, which often seems to make us forget our dreams.

Index

Adler, Albert, 132
Aging
  dreams related to, 72–75, 119
  sex life and, 73–74, 233–43, 243–44
  sexual problems and, 213–15, 220,
    243–44
Antrobus, John, 12–13, 19, 207
Associations
  in Dream Dyad, 161, 177
  in dream interpretation, 128, 146–48,
    155
  to dreams, 39–40, 57
  to waking life, 40–43, 57
Autogenic Training, 185, 251–52, 255–
    57
Avery, Carol S., 60

Babineau, Raymond, 6
Bates, Marilyn, 111
Bonime, Walter, 132, 134
Boss, Medard, 132, 134
Bosveld, Jane, 189, 190, 193

Brauer, Alan, xvi
Briggs, Kathryn, 111
Burns, David D., 225

Cartwright, Rosalind, 75, 135–36
Communication skills, 5–6, 7–8, 15
Conflict resolution, 7–8
  dream incubation for, 186–87, 195–
    97
  as dream type, 45–47, 57
  as function of dreaming, 10
Crick, Sir Francis, 17

Daily reviews, 44–45, 57
Daydreams, 207–13, 219–20
Delaney, Gayle, 34, 136, 144
Delaney-Flowers method, 144–46, 154–
    55
Dillard, Joseph, 44, 55
Divorce/former spouses, 75–77, 119,
    136

Dream Dyad
 accepting emotions and offending attitudes in, 161–62, 177
 building trust with, 226–27, 242
 continuing, 222–30, 242
 described, 7
 encouraging associations in, 161, 177
 erotic/sexual dreams in, 167–77, 178–
  79
 forming, 156–59, 177
 ground rules of, 159–62, 177–78
 Hidden Agendas and, 163–67, 178
 improving communication with, 227–
  28, 242
 listening without interrupting in, 159–
  60, 177
 revealing secrets in, 228–30, 242
 strengthening compromise and commitment with, 223–26, 242
 suggesting alternate interpretations in,
  162, 177–78
 using Krippner-Feinstein Personal
  Mythology process in, 143
 withholding opinions in, 160–61, 177
Dream hieroglyphics/symbols, 9
 archetypal, 126, 130, 136, 137
 creating, 41
 methods for translating, 37–44, 56–
  57
Dream incubation, 9, 11, 124–25, 185–
  88, 200
 benefits of, 193–200
 for conflict/problem resolution, 186–
  87, 195–97
 dangers in, 198–200
 described, 10
 for erotic dreams, 187–88
 experience of, 194–95
 healing effects of, 197–99
 steps, 185–86
 for symbiotic dreams, 152
Dreaming
 ancient wisdom of, 124–25, 136
 effect of physiological/psychological
  states on, 74–75
 fluency in, 181–82
 frequency of, 22
 functions of, 8–9, 10
 history of, 123–37, 136
 making fantasies come true while,
  201–20
 reasons for, 16–32

 role of lower and upper brain in, 16,
  17–18, 207
 role of outside stimuli on, 20, 31
 role of physical body in, 16–17, 19–
  20, 31
 role of right and left brain in, 16, 17,
  18–20
 role of upper and lower brain in, 29–
  30, 31
 theories of, 16–17
Dreaming, lucid, 9, 15, 188–93, 200
 caused by electronic sleep mask, 135
 for conflict/problem resolution, 191–
  92, 195–97
 dangers in, 198–200
 described, 10
 effects of, 189
 gender differences in. *See* Gender
  differences
 healing effects of, 197–99
 research, 136
 sexuality in, 192–93
 using mnemonic induction, 189
 using waking thinking process, 190
Dream interpretation, 9, 15, 31, 121–22
 by individuals, 128
 by psychoanalysts, 128
 contributions of women researchers
  to, 135–36, 137
 defining dream elements in, 144–46,
  147, 154–55
 with Delaney-Flowers method, 144–
  46, 147, 154–55
 dependent on individual meaning,
  20–22
 eclectic approaches of, 132–35, 137
 Freudian theory of, 126–28, 136–37
 Gestalt theory of, 131–32, 137
 group interpretation processes, 138–
  55
 Jungian theory of, 128–30, 137, 149
 with Krippner-Feinstein Personal
  Mythology process, 143–44, 154
 levels of symbolic, 149–54, 155
 with Maybruck method, 146–54, 155
 parsing for, 146–48, 155
 role-playing for, 131–32, 137
 sexual elements of, 127, 137
 sharing dreams for, 128, 131–32, 137,
  147
 techniques, 136
 theories of, 125–37

with Ullman Group method, 139–43, 154

of unrealized parts of selves, 128–30

using archetypal symbols/images in, 126, 130, 136, 137

using collective unconscious in, 130, 137

using dream element analysis in, 126–27, 134

using free association in, 128, 146–48, 155

using patterns in dreams, 149, 154, 155

as wish fulfillment, 127

Dream Language of Love
  basics of, 1–2
  conversations in, 3–15
  fluency, 181–82
  history of, 9, 123–27, 136
  interpreting, 121–22
  learning, 8–12
  translating, 33–57

Dream Notebook, 56, 159
  creating new dreams from old ones with, 230–32
  directions for using, 34–36
  in dream incubation, 185
  making dreams and waking fantasies with, 232–33
  recording in, 146, 149, 155
  reviewing, 230–33, 242

Dream Power, 36–37, 56

Dreams
  as affirmations and inspirations, 47–50, 57
  altered states of consciousness during, 134
  associations from, 39–43, 57
  creating/controlling, 183–200
    benefits of, 193–200
    dangers in, 198–200
    relaxation techniques for, 251–57.
      See also Relaxation
    using methods of primitive peoples, 136
  as daily reviews, 44–45, 57
  as divine messages, 123–25, 136, 189
  effect of medication/drugs on. *See* Medication/drugs
  emotions and, 23–24, 31, 40, 57, 75
  erotic/sexual, 8, 12–13, 15, 53–54, 57, 167–77, 178–79

as dream type, 53–54, 57
  during ovulation, 169–71, 178
  of females reflecting conflict resolution, 173, 178
  frequency of, 12–13
  interpretations of, 96–97
  invoking, 13
  male nocturnal erections and wet dreams, 168–69, 178
  of males reflecting waking life concerns, 171–72, 178
  of physiological origin, 168–71, 178
  of psychological origin, 171–73, 178
  symbolic, 173–77, 178
  symbolic, of males, 174–75, 178
  through visualizations, 12
  values and standards and, 13
  voyeuristic, 175–77, 178–79

flying, 193, 200, 232

focal conflict in, 133

functions of, 22–32
  for conflict resolution, 27–29
  for diagnosing physical problems, 29–31, 32
  dreamers' theories of, 26–32
  for inspiration/creativity, 31–32
  for problem resolution, 25–26, 27–29, 31
  psychologists' theories of, 22–26
  theories of, 133, 134
  for unconscious help, 25, 32
  for understanding emotions, 23–24, 31

loving with, 156–79

manifest, 133–34

negative/recurring, 50–53, 57. *See also* Nightmares

as paranormal/anomalous, 55–56, 57

parsing, 38–39, 57

personality differences detected in, 61–62

as problem and conflict solvers, 45–47, 57

prophetic, 163–65, 196–97

for psychic or emotional balance, 133

recalling, 9, 33–37, 56

related to aging, 72–75, 119

related to background and value systems, 77–81, 119

related to divorce/former spouses, 75–77, 119, 136

related to physical state, 163–65

Dreams (*continued*)
  related to reproductive cycle/pregnancy, 64–66, 119, 130, 135, 136
  related to stress, 68–72, 119, 135, 163–65
  related to waking lifestyle, 40–43, 57, 132, 135
  REM sleep and. *See* REM
  sharing, 4–6, 14, 15
  sharing
    benefits of, 9
    as couples therapy, 6–8
    for interpretation, 128, 131–32, 137, 147
  sightseeing in, 202–06, 219
  of special groups, 134–35
  stories in, 9
  symbiotic, 151–52, 206–07, 219
  telepathic, 134, 135
  types of, 44–56
    See also Nightmares

Eclectic approaches, 132–35, 137
Emotions
  accepting, in Dream Dyad, 161–62, 177
  evoked, 23–24, 31, 40, 57
  importance of, 23–24, 31
  unexpressed, 75
Ennis, Maeva, 20
Erikson, Erik, 132, 133

Fantasies, 207–13, 219–20, 232–33
Faraday, Ann, 36, 136
Farrell, Warren, 97–98
Feinstein, David, 132, 163
Feinstein-Krippner method, 163
Flower, Loma, 144–45
Fonagy, Peter, 20
Foulkes, David, 132, 135
French, Thomas, 132, 133
Freud, Sigmund, xvi, 22, 23, 83
Freudian theory, 126–28, 136–37
  sexual images by males in, 173–75
Friday, Nancy, 171

Gackenbach, Jayne, 136, 189, 190, 193
Galin, David, 18
Garfield, Patricia, 16–17, 35, 62, 64, 72, 76, 135–36
Gender differences

  as help to men, 66–67
  as help to relationship, 63–64
  as help to women, 67–68
  not implying superiority, 63
  research indicating, 62–63
  to promote understanding, 64–66
Gestalt theory, 131–32, 137
Goldberg, M., 6
Greene, Wendy, 223

Haley, J., 6
Hall, Calvin, 132, 134
Hartmann, Ernest, 25, 72, 95, 132, 135, 168
Hendrix, Harville, 81
Hidden Agendas, 7, 163–67, 178
Hobson, Allan J., 17

Inspirations, 47–50, 57

Jones, Richard M., 130, 134
Jung, Carl, 23, 84–86, 111, 120
Jungian theory, 126, 128–30, 137
  of archetypal images, 130, 137
  of collective unconscious, 124, 130, 137
  of dream series, 149
  personality types, 84–85, 120

Keirsey, David, 111
Keyes, Ken and Penny, 60
Kiersey Temperament Sorter, 111
Kramer, Milton, 132, 135
Krippner, Stanley, 44, 55, 132, 134, 135, 138–39, 140, 143–44, 163
Krippner-Feinstein Personal Mythology process, 143–44, 154

LaBerge, Stephen, 132, 135, 189, 190
Love, true
  expectations of, 59–61, 119
  resemblance of mate to parents and, 81–82
Lowy, Samuel, 132, 133
Lucid dreaming. *See* Dreaming, lucid

McCarley, Robert W., 17
Masters (W.) and Johnson (V.), 14, 73–74, 213, 214
Mate
  finding ideal, 8, 15
  dream clues for, 58–120

resemblance to parents and, 81–82
Maybruck method, 146–54, 155
Medications/drugs
  dreaming and, 135
  nightmares and, 25–26, 72
  sexual problems and, 74, 215, 243
MILD (Mnemonic Induction of Lucid
    Dreams), 189
Myers, Isabella, 111
Myers-Briggs Type Indicator, 111

Nicholson, John, xvi
Nightmares
  as dream type, 50–53, 57
  effect of medications on, 72
  purposes of, 25–26
  related to aging, 72

Papp, P., 6
Paranormal/anomalous dream type, 55–
    56, 57
Parsing, 38–39, 57, 146–48, 155
Passion. *See* Romance
Pearsall, Paul, 14, 59–60, 233
Penney, Alexandra, 60, 98, 172
Perlmutter, Richard, 6
Perls, Frederick S., 131–32
Personality types, 82–84
  anima and animus as expression of,
    128–30, 137
  differences based on background, 119
  differences based on similarity to par-
    ents, 119–20
  differences based on transitions, 68–
    77, 119
  differences based on value systems,
    119
  differences on basis of gender, 62–68,
    119
  differences in, 61–62
  extraversion-introversion, 84, 120
  extraverted, bilateral men, 90–93
  extraverted, bilateral women, 97–101
  extraverted, left-brain men, 85–88
  extraverted, left-brain women, 93–94
  extraverted, right-brain men, 88–90
  extraverted, right-brain women, 95–
    97
  frequency of nightmares and, 26
  hemispheric brain, classifications of,
    84–85, 120
  introverted, bilateral men, 106–07

introverted, bilateral women, 109–11
  introverted, left-brain men, 101–03
  introverted, left-brain women, 107–08
  introverted, right-brain men, 104–06
  introverted, right-brain women,
    108–09
  Jungian, 84–85, 120
  practicing understanding of, 117–18
  profiles of, 9
  quiz for identifying, 112–17
  tests and measurements for, 111–12
Progressive Relaxation, 185, 251–55

Quiz to Identify Personality Types, 112–
    17

Relaxation
  Autogenic Training for, 251–52, 255–
    57
  Progressive, 251–55
  techniques, 184–85, 190, 200, 241,
    243
  for dream control, 251–57
REMS (rapid eye movement), 207
  altered states during, 134
  cause of, 31
  effect of awakening during, 22, 34
  electronic sleep mask for, 135
  as indication of dreaming, 8, 17
  outside stimuli recorded during, 20
Romance
  enhancing, 13–14, 15
  history of, 59
  keeping alive, 221–44

Sex life
  accepting the body and, 233–38, 243
  aging and, 73–74, 233–43, 243–44
  improving sexual techniques for, 238–
    42, 243
  physical changes and, 235, 243
  positive communication in, 240–41,
    243
  psychological changes and, 235–38,
    243
  sexual experimentation in, 241–42,
    244
  starting new, 233–43
Sexual problems
  acting out erotic dreams for, 217–19
  aging and, 213–15, 220, 243–44
  dream clues to, 216–17, 220

Sexual problems (*continued*)
  low sexual desire, 238–40, 243
  lowering stress level for, 241, 243–44
Singer, Jerome, 12–13, 207
Stress
  dreams and, 68–72, 119, 135, 163–
    65
  lowering, 241, 243–44
Symbols. *See* Dream hieroglyphics/
    symbols

Tennov, Dorothy, 60
Tholey, Paul, 190
Trower, Peter, 228

Ullman, Montague, 22, 23, 127–28, 132,
    134, 139
Ullman Group method, 139–43, 154,
    162

Value systems, 77–81, 119
Van de Castle, Robert, 62, 64, 132, 134,
    135
Visualizations, 207–13, 219–20

Westheimer, Ruth, 168

Zilbergeld, Bernie, 168, 214–15
Zimmerman, N., 127–28